CO2 PISTOLS & RIFLES

JAMES E. HOUSE

©2003 by
James E. House

Published by

700 East State Street • Iola, WI 54990-0001
715-445-2214 • 888-457-2873
www.krause.com

Our toll-free number to place an order or obtain a free catalog is 800-258-0929.

Library of Congress Catalog Number: 2003108884

ISBN: 0-87349-678-7

Designed by Ethel Thulien
Edited by Joel Marvin

Printed in the United States of America

About the Author

JAMES E. HOUSE shot airguns and firearms as a young lad growing up in southern Illinois. During his first two years at Southern Illinois University in Carbondale—where he earned bachelor and master's degrees—he was a member of the Air Force ROTC rifle team. He later earned his doctorate at the University of Illinois.

House has been a faculty member and administrator at Illinois State University in Normal for the past 32 years, and currently serves there as professor emeritus of chemistry.

He has written three textbooks on chemistry and quantum mechanics, including one that he co-authored with his wife, Kathleen A. House.

Since his retirement, he and his wife have traveled extensively in the mountain states, where they enjoy time afield with airguns. House has applied his long-held interest in ballistics to airgunning, with many of his results found in this book. He has published several articles on airguns in such periodicals as *Fur-Fish-Game*, *Predator Extreme*, and *U.S. Airgun*. He is also a contributing editor for *Airgun Illustrated* magazine and a staff editor for *The Backwoodsman*.

CO_2 PISTOLS AND RIFLES

TABLE OF CONTENTS

ACKNOWLEDGMENTS

Many individuals have provided information and materials that made the writing of this book easier and more pleasant. Some of these individuals have given unselfishly of their time during my repeated telephone calls. I would especially like to acknowledge the help provided by Sara DeMuzio, John Goff, and Kirby Kaiser of Crosman Corporation. It is also a pleasure to acknowledge the cooperation of Joe Murfin, Denise Johnson, Susan Gardner, and Teresa Wrazel of Daisy Outdoor Products. Brett Daniels of Wal-Mart has gone well beyond the required level of dedication in printing the photographs that are an integral and significant part of this book. I would also like to express my appreciation to Don Gulbrandsen and Joel Marvin of Krause Publications for their support and confidence in this project from its inception. As usual, this book could not have been produced without the assistance and understanding of my wife, Kathy. Her help with data collection and photography has been second only to her encouragement during the work. To all who have helped, I send my thanks.

PREFACE

For many years, pellet and BB guns powered by carbon dioxide, CO_2, have held a fascination for many shooters. While airguns also have a great deal of appeal, many shooters do not like to pump them up. The spring piston air rifles are heavy, long, and require a considerable force to cock them. The fact that a small cylinder of liquefied CO_2 can be inserted in a pistol or rifle and many shots fired without having to do manual labor to supply power must appeal to many shooters. As a result, the demand for CO_2-powered guns is at an all-time high. To meet the demand, manufacturers have produced some of the most innovative tools in the shooting sports. New models appear frequently with a degree of realism that has to be seen to be believed.

Although air and CO_2 guns are often considered together, there are significant differences between them. Because the CO_2 guns contain enough propellant to fire numerous shots, the emphasis is on making repeating guns that hold several pellets in readiness for subsequent shots. By holding the pellets or BBs in a magazine (cylinder or in-line), the shooter can fire a series of shots simply by pulling the trigger. Modern manufacturing methods allow the external shell of the handguns to resemble almost any firearm. The result is that CO_2 handguns are virtually indistinguishable from the firearms they mimic. This is undoubtedly one of the primary reasons for their popularity.

While the fascination that comes with shooting a CO_2-powered pistol or rifle that looks and functions almost like a firearm is considerable, many of the guns powered by CO_2 are very capable instruments. Some are capable of outstanding accuracy and some have enough power to make them useful to the small game hunter and pest shooter. Many of the CO_2 guns have features that make them logical choices for training persons new to the shooting sports. However, the most compelling aspect of CO_2 guns is that they are fun to shoot. Even when the cost of the CO_2 cylinders is included, shooting a CO_2 gun is an inexpensive sport.

In spite of the immense interest in CO_2 guns, there does not exist a book devoted solely to these guns. My intent in writing this book is to provide a user's guide to CO_2 guns that gives their specifications, instructions for their use, and the performance characteristics for almost all of the available models. Along with this information, also presented are a brief history of the development of CO_2 guns, an elementary discussion of the basic principles of CO_2 power, and a simplified treatment of ballistics as related to pellets. A major portion of the book is devoted to detailed discussions of specific models of CO_2 pistols and rifles. In addition to almost all of the currently produced models, many of the vintage CO_2 pistols and rifles are also discussed in detail. Much of the information found here has not previously been collected in a single volume. It is hoped that this book will be widely viewed as the textbook of CO_2 guns.

CHAPTER 1

THE HISTORY OF AIR AND CO$_2$ GUNS

THROUGHOUT HISTORY, MAN has sought for ways to launch projectiles that would eliminate the necessity for being close to a target, whether food or foe. David did not engage in hand-to-hand combat with Goliath but let fly a stone at his opponent. In that case, the swirling sling generated a force on the stone that when released sent it outward with considerable force. Archery has been employed for perhaps 4000 years. Pulling the bowstring to the rear causes the limbs of the bow to be flexed due to the stored energy. The work done by the archer pulling back on the string appears as stored energy in the bow. Upon release, the arrow is driven forward with considerable velocity. The use of a solid propellant that burns rapidly to generate a large volume of gas behind a projectile and thus drive it down a bore has been known for perhaps 1000 years. Work to develop new projectile systems is not a recent thing.

Probably the first use of a compressed gas to force a projectile down a tube involved the use of air compressed in the lungs and mouth of some fellow using a wooden tube as a blowgun. However, when and where we do not know. Blowguns shooting poisoned darts are lethal to both humans and game and they are still employed in some parts of the world. Even when used with nonpoisonous darts, blowguns are used to take small game and pests. Airguns that have some type of reservoir for holding compressed air and then releasing it behind a projectile have been used for over 400 years. Since the invention of the airgun sometime in the late 1500s, many designs have come into being. While there is an impressive array of makes and models of airguns available today, the basic power plant designs can be placed in a small number of categories. Interestingly, the power plants that we will describe are used in both rifles and handguns.

Airgun Power Plants

Some airguns surviving from the 1600s have hollow buttstocks that can be pumped up to hold compressed air. The stock is then

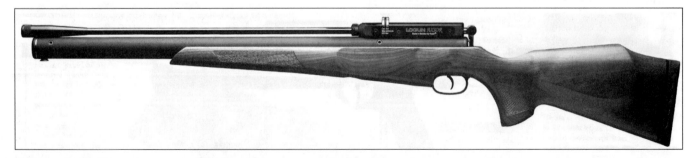

Precharged pneumatic rifles such as the Logun Axsor are powerful and accurate and hold enough compressed air for several shots. Photo courtesy of Crosman Corporation.

screwed onto the receiver and the compressed gas is sufficient to fire 20 or more shots before the stock must be recharged. One air rifle from the 1700s, the Girandoni, had a bar that ran across the action at the breech. That bar had cavities which held 10-12 lead balls and simply moving a lever caused the bar to move laterally to line up a ball with the breech for quick reloading. Other types of rifles had a hollow metal sphere, which could be pumped up to a high pressure, attached to the bottom of the action to provide sufficient compressed air for several shots. These types of rifles are known today as pre-charged pneumatic (PCP) rifles.

Most PCP rifles today have a large hollow tube or reservoir that lies below the barrel. That reservoir can be charged to high pressure (2,000-3,000 psi) by means of a special pump or by attaching a scuba tank. Precharged rifles are very powerful and because only air moves at the instant of firing, the rifles do not have the undesirable feature of a heavy piston flying forward then coming to a stop while the pellet is being moved down the bore. As a result, PCP rifles offer the ultimate in power and accuracy. Keep in mind that many blackpowder percussion rifles operate

at only 6000-8000 psi, so a PCP rifle can be powerful indeed. Some models have the advantage of variable power via a power regulator that controls the amount of air released. Some PCP rifles also have mechanisms that hold more than one projectile so they can function as repeaters. Today, PCP rifles are made in a variety of calibers with the 22 and 25 being popular. Rifles in calibers up to 50 are available and they are very powerful.

A second type of power plant that is very popular today is the spring piston or break-barrel action. Rifles of this type have a cylinder inside the receiver that is backed by a strong spring. The barrel is hinged at the rear and it has a lever attached that forces the piston back against the spring as the barrel is forced downward at the muzzle. When the piston is engaged by the sear mechanism, a pellet is inserted directly into the breech and the barrel is elevated until it locks into place. With most break-action rifles of recent manufacture, the safety is placed "on" automatically during the cocking action. A variation of the break-action rifle is one with a stationary barrel that has a lever alongside the action (side lever) or below the barrel (under barrel) that is used to cock the piece. It is believed

Spring piston rifles like the Winchester 1000X have been popular for many years.

the fixed-barrel models are capable of slightly better accuracy than the break-barrel guns because there is always some question as to whether the hinged barrel returns to exactly the same place each time it is locked shut.

Although break-action rifles are made with all levels of power, it is the more powerful models that have received the most attention. An air rifle that generates at least 12 ft-lbs of energy is called a "magnum" and some of the break-action rifles are capable of generating 20-25 ft-lbs of energy at the muzzle. These are the air rifles often selected by small game and varmint hunters. The reason some of these rifles are so powerful is that as the piston moves forward at the time of firing, air is compressed as the piston moves. By the time the piston reaches its forward position, the pressure in the chamber may be as high as 1200-1500 psi. The most powerful break action rifles can fire 177-caliber pellets at velocities in the 1100-1200 fps range or 22-caliber pellets at 850-900 fps.

We have already mentioned that at the time of firing, the piston and spring lurch forward, which forces the rifle backward. When the piston reaches the forward end of the cylinder, it comes to a sudden stop with the compressed air functioning as a shock absorber. This action drags the rifle forward. Therefore, firing a break-action rifle involves a backward motion of the rifle, which is followed by a forward motion. All this motion is not conducive to accuracy by an inexperienced shooter. Having said that, it must be mentioned that many of the excellent break-action rifles are capable of a high level of accuracy, but achieving it in a real world environment is not easily accomplished.

Break-action rifles are available in 177, 20, 22, and 25 calibers. However, this type of rifle is more efficient in smaller calibers unless they have enormous cylinder/piston assemblies that are motivated by very powerful springs. Some of them have exactly that combination of design elements and as a result, are very powerful. The Webley Patriot, which is 46 inches long and weighs 9 pounds, is just such a rifle, and it performs well even in 25 caliber. Many of the popular models of intermediate power are available in 177, 20, and 22 calibers. It is generally true that the smaller calibers produce energies just about

as high as those produced by the 22 caliber. Unless a break action with a very robust power plant is selected, there is little to be gained by selecting the larger calibers.

A third type of power plant for airguns is the multi-pump pneumatic or "pump up" models. This type of rifle has a very small reservoir that is charged with air to a high pressure (up to 800-1000 psi) by means of several pump strokes. The pump handle and lever lie below the barrel in this type of rifle that is primarily an American phenomenon. If everything is working properly and the rifle has not been over-pumped, all of the air is discharged

Multi-pump pneumatic rifles are a classic design. The Sheridan Silver Streak (left) and the Daisy PowerLine 880 (right) are typical multi-pump rifles.

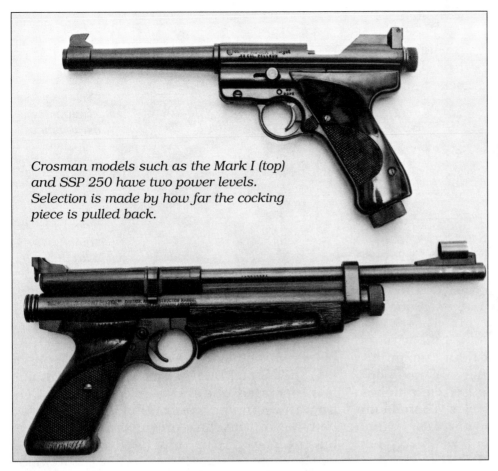

Crosman models such as the Mark I (top) and SSP 250 have two power levels. Selection is made by how far the cocking piece is pulled back.

in one shot. Because only air moves when the pressure is released, there is virtually no recoil to make accurate shooting difficult. The multi-pump pneumatic has a lot in common with the PCP except that the reservoir must be filled for each shot. This has not always been the case, however, as some long-discontinued models were set up to fire a few shots before the pumping had to be repeated.

There are some popular misconceptions regarding multi-pump pneumatics. The first one is that the velocities produced by multi-pump rifles are not very uniform. I have tested a couple dozen such rifles and shot-to-shot velocities are so uniform that standard deviations of only 3 or 4 fps are the norm regardless of whether the rifles were new or well-used. I have tested perhaps a dozen break-action rifles as well and none gave smaller standard deviations in measured velocities. Until well broken in, most break actions were far more erratic in the velocity produced.

Second, there is a misconception that the rate of pumping causes considerable variation in the pressure achieved and thus in the veloc-ity of the pellet. I have conducted extensive testing of many multi-pump rifles and so have other experimenters. It simply is not true. The velocity produced by most multi-pump rifles varies only a few feet per second even when the pumping rate varies widely.

The third misconception is that if a multi-pump rifle is pumped up and allowed to stand for a while, the velocity will be lower. The reasoning is that when air is compressed, it gets warmer, and on standing, this heat is lost. Shooting immediately after pumping involves hot air (higher pressure) while shooting at some later time involves cool air (lower pressure). The fact is that the small amount of heat generated as the very small amount of air is compressed in the reservoir dissipates as the pumping is taking place. As a result, there is very little difference in the pressure in the reservoir at the time of the shot. To test this, I have pumped a multi-pump eight strokes and fired it immediately to determine the velocity. The test was repeated with eight strokes and the same type of pellet but with the rifle allowed to sit for 30 minutes or an hour. In no case (except for one rifle that had a leaking valve) has there been more than 5-7 fps difference.

A final misconception is that multi-pump rifles are not accurate. This simply is not so. I have some multi-pump rifles that are more accurate than others, but the same is true of my break-action rifles. Several of my multi-pump rifles will produce 1/2-inch groups at 25 yards and so will two or three of my break-action rifles. My best break-action and multi-pump rifles are about equal in accuracy. However, my best multi-pump rifles cost about half as much as my best break actions and the multi-pumps are much easier to shoot accurately. Admittedly, the break

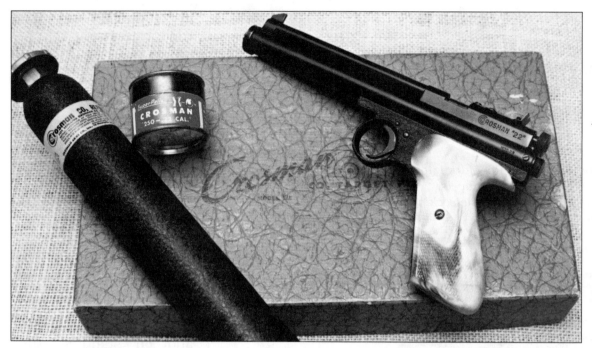

Crosman firmly established CO_2 as a power source with models such as the 22-caliber Model 116 shown here with the original box, papers, and 10-ounce cylinder.

actions are more powerful than the multi-pumps, but multi-pump rifles are not pop-guns. The break actions are also a few inches longer and a few pounds heavier. There is no such thing as a free lunch.

CO_2 Guns in the Beginning

This brief introduction to airguns brings us to the subject of this book, CO_2-powered guns. Paul Giffard in France seems to have been the inventor of the first rifles that successfully used compressed CO_2 as the propellant although his first rifles were actually airguns. A spring piston rifle (I will use the term "rifle" since it was fired from the shoulder although the piece had a smooth bore), which was made in 6 mm (about 24 caliber) and 8 mm (about 32 caliber), was patented by Giffard in 1862. Later, Giffard produced prototype rifles that used pre-charged cartridges containing compressed air. This was, in effect, a pre-charged pneumatic where the pressurized cylinder gave power for a single shot. It is interesting to note that revolvers are currently available in which the pellet and compressed air are contained in a case that functions in the same way as the bullet and powder do in a metallic cartridge. These pre-loaded air/pellet cartridges are loaded into a revolver for firing.

After his work with airguns, Giffard turned his attention to the use of "liquefied carbonic acid gas," which we call carbon dioxide and for which the chemical formula is CO_2. He patented the devices using this power source in 1889. Since the blow of an external hammer operated the valve releasing the CO_2 from the container, regulating the blow of the hammer on the valve provided a way of varying the power. This principle has been used by Crosman in the Mark I and SSP 250 models (see Chapter 10). Giffard founded the Giffard Gun Company in London where gas-powered guns (smooth bore) and rifles were made. Giffard's early rifles were made in 295 caliber. Let me reiterate that some writers, especially those who are British, choose to distinguish a smooth bore piece as a "gun" while a shoulder fired piece with a rifled barrel is a "rifle." In this book, the term "gun" means a device that fires projectiles (as the term is used in the phrase "gun control"). A gun that is fired from the shoulder is a rifle and a gun that is fired with one hand is a handgun or a pistol. The term pistol includes revolvers, single shots, and semi-automatic or autoloaders. Purists may disagree, but I believe that the historic use of the terms is justified. Furthermore, it is quite common for guns that use either compressed air or CO_2 as the power source to be referred to as "airguns." In fact, the box for one of my rifles states that it is a "CO_2 air rifle."

CO_2 Guns in the United States

In the United States, Crosman pioneered the use of CO_2 as the propellant in

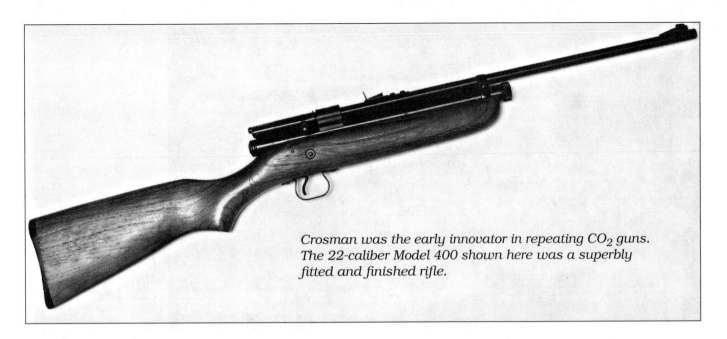

Crosman was the early innovator in repeating CO_2 guns. The 22-caliber Model 400 shown here was a superbly fitted and finished rifle.

pellet guns in 1931. The rifles were similar to the Model 102 multi-pump of that time period except they were attached by a tube to a large CO_2 tank that serviced several rifles at the same time. They were set up for use as a shooting gallery. Other early Crosman models were intended for use by commercial shooting galleries and they used 21-caliber pellets, which were available only from Crosman. By 1947 Crosman had introduced the Model 101CG (the CG on early Crosman models indicated "compressed gas" to distinguish them from air-powered guns). This model had a cylinder of CO_2 measuring approximately 2 inches by 6 inches attached to the bottom of the action just in front of the trigger. The cylinder held enough CO_2 for approximately 200 shots.

By 1950, Crosman had introduced the Models 111 and 112 single-shot pistols and Models 113 and 114 rifles that had full length gas tubes below the barrels. The Models 111 and 113 were 177 caliber while the 112 and 114 were 22 caliber. The large CO_2 reservoirs of these guns were filled by means of an external tank that held enough gas (about 10 ounces) to recharge the gas tubes of the guns several times. In other words, the external tank held enough CO_2 for hundreds of shots. The pistols had long barrels that measured 8-1/8 inches in length so the gas tubes that extended below the barrel were also long. In 1951, the Models 115 (177 cali-

ber) and 116 (22 caliber) pistols having 6-inch barrels were introduced. Crosman introduced new models frequently during this time period and the Model 118 repeating 22-caliber rifle was one of those introduced. Shooting kits that contained a pistol, external gas cylinder, pellets, and other ancillaries were available during the early 1950s. Some of the models were also produced for sale by mass merchandisers like Sears, a practice that continued for many years.

In 1954, the CO_2-powered guns took a quantum leap forward with the introduction of the now standard power source, the 12-gram CO_2 cylinder. Guns are made with one of these small cylinders enclosed, which provides power for a large number of shots. The first pistol so designed was the Crosman Model 150. In 1955, Crosman introduced what has come to be considered the finest CO_2-powered sporting rifle ever made, the 22-caliber Model 160 and the companion 177-caliber Model 167, which was never as popular as the 160. This rifle was a well-finished metal and wood piece that was powered by two 12-gram CO_2 cylinders. They were contained in a tube below the barrel with the first being inserted neck first and the second inserted butt first. After a year or so, the Model 160 was available with a peep sight and sling in shooting kits for more serious target practice and club use. The Crosman Model 160 is the standard by which all other CO_2 rifles will be judged. So highly is the 160

The 22-caliber Benjamin Franklin Model 252 is a compact CO₂ pistol.

The Benjamin Model 30-30 was powered by an 8-gram CO₂ cylinder and fired BBs as a repeater.

regarded that a virtually identical model made in China by Shanghai Airgun Company is currently available. Also offered were the Models 180 and 187, which were scaled down versions of Models 160 and 167. In 1957, Crosman introduced the Model 400, a 22-caliber repeater that held 10 pellets by making use of an in-line magazine. Many of the early Crosman models had provision for varying the power by changing the amount of CO_2 released. In most models this was accomplished by turning a screw although other models utilized a rotating cocking knob to make the adjustment. There are many other Crosman models that could be discussed, but this history brings us to the content of Chapter 10, which deals with vintage CO_2 rifles and pistols. In that chapter, many of the other fine Crosman CO_2 rifles and pistols will be discussed.

While Crosman has certainly been the dominant force in CO_2 guns in the U.S., it is by no means the only one. Benjamin has manufactured many models that use CO_2 for power. Some of the early models made use of a shorter

CO_2 cylinder that held 8 grams of propellant. At one time, these small gas cylinders were popular for use in machines that made carbonated water at home. For many years, the Benjamin guns have made use of the now-standard 12-gram cylinders. Benjamin's 177-caliber Model 250 appeared in 1952 as its first CO_2 pistol and soon after that the 22-caliber Model 262 appeared. By 1956, the original Model 250 had updated to the Model 267. After the early models, other CO_2 rifles that had two power settings were produced. CO_2 guns carrying the Benjamin name are still produced.

Although Sheridan began to produce airguns in Racine, Wisconsin, in 1948, it was 1974 before the first CO_2-powered Sheridan rifle appeared. The air rifles had been designated as the "C" series since the earliest days, but the CO_2 rifles were designated as the "F" series. Sheridan produced the "E" series CO_2 pistols beginning in 1977. Like Sheridan guns of today, the CO_2 rifles and pistols were produced in 20 caliber.

Having mentioned the Crosman, Benjamin, and Sheridan companies, it is worth giving a very brief summary of their history. Benjamin Air Rifle Company came into being in 1902 when Walter Benjamin, originally from Bloomington, Illinois, obtained the rights to the St. Louis Air Rifle Company. Except for a 2-year span from 1904 to 1906, Benjamin produced airguns in St. Louis, Missouri, until 1986. The Sheridan Company of Racine, Wisconsin, was acquired by Benjamin in 1977 and the companies were combined at the Wisconsin location in 1984. The Crosman Corporation acquired the combined Benjamin-Sheridan Company in 1992. By 1994, operations at Racine were phased out and Crosman, Benjamin, and Sheridan guns were produced at the Crosman factory in East Bloomfield, New York. Today, Benjamin and Sheridan guns are virtually identical. However, in keeping with the Benjamin and Sheridan traditions, 20-caliber guns carry the Sheridan name while those in 177 and 22 have the Benjamin label.

America's oldest airgun maker, Daisy Outdoor Products (known for many years as Daisy Manufacturing Company), has not been absent from the manufacture of CO_2 guns. Keep in mind that Daisy is best known for the production of BB guns and entered the pellet gun field only in 1972 with the introduction of the PowerLine 880, which has been in continuous production ever since. Since Daisy's first CO_2 gun was introduced in 1962, it fired BBs. It was the semi-automatic pistol known as the Model 100, but it lasted only a year before being followed by the Model 200, which was produced from 1963 to 1976. The Model 200, which in my

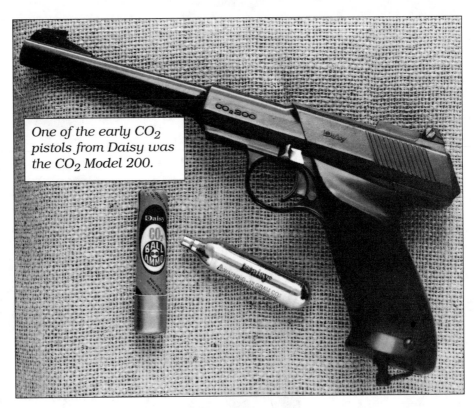

One of the early CO_2 pistols from Daisy was the CO_2 Model 200.

opinion is probably the finest CO_2 BB pistol ever produced, is discussed in detail in Chapter 10. Daisy's first CO_2-powered rifle was the Model 300, produced from 1968 to 1975. This rifle was also produced with a gold colored receiver for sale by Sears. As you will see from the evaluations presented in later chapters of this book, Daisy has become a major producer of CO_2 guns.

In addition to the familiar names of American airgun makers, the Healthways Company marketed CO_2 pistols in the 1960s and 1970s. One of the models, the Healthways Plainsman, will be described in detail in Chapter 10.

CO_2 as a Power Source

The key behind the use of CO_2 as the propellant gas is that a small cylinder can hold the CO_2, which has been compressed in order to liquefy it. When the gun is fired, a valve opens and a small amount of liquid CO_2 escapes due to the pressure within the cylinder. Because the boiling point of liquid CO_2 is very low, the liquid is converted to a gas almost instantly, generating a high pressure behind the projectile. As we shall see later, the pressure generated has an upper limit that is determined by the amount of liquid that escapes and its temperature. In short-barreled

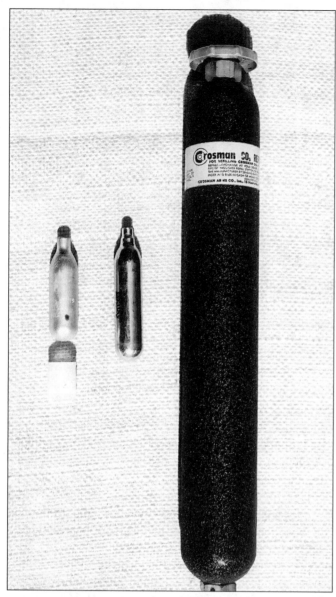

For a few years, at least three types of CO_2 cylinders were in use. The large cylinder holds 10 ounces of CO_2 while the small ones hold 12 and 8 grams. Using an adaptor, the 8-gram cylinder could be used in a gun that was designed for using the 12-gram cylinder.

The 12-gram CO_2 cylinder introduced by Crosman in 1954 has become the standard power source for most CO_2 guns. Older cylinders have the "bottle cap" seal shown on the right.

handguns, even if a larger amount of liquid CO_2 is metered into the chamber behind the pellet, the velocity will not be increased much because the pellet will exit the muzzle before the additional liquid CO_2 can evaporate. In other words, it takes only a small amount of CO_2 being converted to a gas to get the pellet out of the barrel before the rest of the CO_2 evaporates. In rifles with long barrels, valves that meter out a larger amount of CO_2 will result in higher pellet velocity because the pellet will be in the bore longer and the greater amount of CO_2 will keep the pressure higher throughout the pellet's travel along the bore.

The standard CO_2 source in most rifles and pistols today are the cylinders that hold 12 grams. This has not always been so and some of the early CO_2-powered guns utilized smaller cylinders that hold 8 grams of CO_2. A shorter cylinder could be used with an adapter on its base to make it fit in spaces designed to hold the longer 12-gram cylinders. Other CO_2 guns have large built in cylinders (usually below the barrel) that are filled from an external bulk tank. The external tank has a fitting that can be screwed into the end of the reservoir and a valve opened to fill the reservoir in the gun. After such a filling, the gun can be fired numerous times before refilling is required. The biggest drawback to this type of gun is that if you are going to be out shooting for some time, you must also take along a large tank that is bulky and heavy. A few high quality target rifles use large, built-in CO_2 cylinders.

There are some disadvantages to shooting CO_2-powered guns. First, CO_2 cylinders increase the cost of shooting such guns compared to those powered by air. At the time of

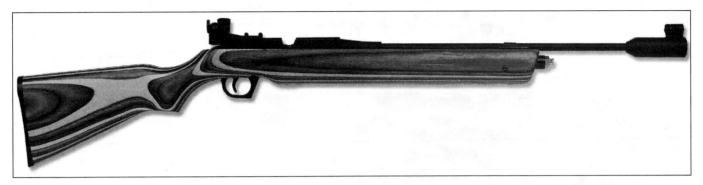

Daisy's Avanti Medalist 888 is a CO_2 rifle that is intended for competition. It has a built-in cylinder that holds 2.5 ounces of CO_2, enough for up to 300 shots. Photo courtesy of Daisy Outdoor Products.

A CO_2-powered target rifle such as the Crosman Challenger is very accurate and convenient to use. Photo courtesy of Crosman Corporation.

this writing, a package of five 12-gram cylinders costs approximately $3.00. Each cylinder will provide power for perhaps 40-60 shots depending on the type of gun in which it is used. If you take an average number of shots per cylinder to be 50, this means the cost of CO_2 is approximately 1 cent per shot. The cost of some of the inexpensive types of pellets is also in this range, which means that half of the cost of shooting is represented by the cost of the CO_2. As a rough estimate, shooting a CO_2 gun can be about twice as expensive as shooting one that utilizes air as the propellant.

Another disadvantage of CO_2-powered guns is that the tendency of the liquid to vaporize depends on the temperature. On a warm day, the pressure inside the CO_2 cylinder is higher (they come with a warning to store them at a temperature below 120°F because they might rupture). Therefore, the velocity produced will be higher than it is on a cool day. We will explore this in greater detail in Chapter 4. When the temperature is cooler than approximately 55-60°F, the velocity will be significantly lower which means that the point of impact will change.

Because an internal CO_2 cylinder provides enough propellant for numerous shots, it is easy to design a mechanism that holds several pellets so the gun can fire several times as a repeater. The only action required is some means of bringing another pellet into battery while cocking the piece. One pistol even used CO_2 power to recock the pistol and bring a pellet from the magazine into position. In other words, it was a true semi-automatic. That pistol was the legendary Crosman Model 600, still one of the most highly prized CO_2 pistols ever made (see Chapter 10). This speed of fire with a minimum of effort means that many CO_2 guns resemble firearms in both form and function. For some shooters, this adds to the fun even if it does not necessarily add to the accuracy with which such guns can be fired.

Collecting

As I visit antique malls and stores, I see a bewildering array of items that encompass almost every area of human endeavor. There are slide rules that were once used by engineers to solve problems. There are fishing lures that once provided hours of recreation.

The Crosman 600 is the standard by which all other semi-automatic CO₂ handguns are judged.

older Crosman models are highly prized. The production runs of some of the early models were not large, which means they may be hard to find. The law of supply and demand works in collecting in any area, including CO_2 guns.

I am often asked by some non-collector how much a particular model is worth. There are two answers to that question. First, the *Blue Book of Airguns* is a "must-have" reference. In addition to containing a wealth of data, this book gives a range of values for specimens depending on their condition. The published prices give a guide as to what you can expect to pay, but remember condition is everything. Second, the value of a particular CO_2 gun depends on how much you want it. If you have a collection that is missing one model out of a series and you happen to run across a good one, disregard the suggested prices and add the piece to your collection. In my case, my collectibles are also shooters. I picture almost every air or CO_2 gun in my possession as a potential starling gun. Therefore, I am more concerned with shooting condition than I am with the cosmetic features. Different "collectors" pursue their activities with different objectives.

Other collecting themes might include CO_2 guns from a particular time period or of a particular type (those that shoot BBs, revolvers, etc.). It is up to the individual to decide what type of collectible items are worthy of his or her time and resources. It is unlikely that a collector would go to the trouble and expense of assembling a collection of material without first having a serious interest in the area, which means such a collector already knows the types of items he/she wishes to collect. Few collectors enter the arena as complete novices.

If you search long enough in enough places, some bargains will turn up. Among my most prized CO_2-powered Crosman pistols are a

There are cooking utensils that once rattled in someone's kitchen as they were used to prepare meals. And, sometimes, I find an old air or CO_2 gun or some of its accessories. Many a young lad received a CO_2 gun, which was used until something else became more important. After many years, the CO_2 gun came out of the attic to be passed on at an estate or yard sale. From there, it may have been transported along with other collectibles to an antique mall. These items have become highly collectible. As will be discussed in later chapters, some of the older CO_2 guns are highly prized as shooting pieces. Some are even highly sought to provide the basic platform on which to build custom guns with enhanced performance.

Without specifically considering the pieces that are desired for continued use, the collector of CO_2 guns has a wide range of material to collect. Probably most serious collectors (which does not include me—I am strictly a small-time collector) specialize. The most obvious area of specialization is by manufacturer. Because of the preeminence of Crosman in the development of CO_2 guns in this country,

The Crosman 262 is one of the vintage CO_2 rifles that performed well in the tests.

Reference material in any field is indispensable.

The Daisy 200 and the Crosman 116 were found in antique malls and the Crosman Mark I was found in a pawnshop. A year later the Mark I was still there and by that time I knew I really needed it. I routinely shop antique malls, flea markets, and pawnshops in search of additional material to add to my collection. Today, one can search the Internet and find almost anything and this includes collectible CO_2 guns and accessories.

In my opinion, the person who is serious enough about air and CO_2 guns to be reading this book and who has even a slight interest in building a collection of guns and accessories should begin by assembling a set of resources. I hesitate to call it a library, but I believe you should begin by building a knowledge base by acquiring and studying the following books. In that way, you will have a better idea how the guns work, whether all the parts are there and "what does this button do?"

Suggested Reading

Beeman, Robert D. (1977). *Air Gun Digest*, DBI Books, Northfield, IL.

Beeman, Robert D. and Allen, John B. (2003). *Blue Book of Airguns*, 3rd ed., Blue Book Publications, Inc., Minneapolis.

Elbe, Ronald E. (1992). *Know Your Sheridan Rifles & Pistols*, Blacksmith Publications.

Fletcher, D. T. (1998). *75 Years of Crosman Airguns*, Portland, OR.

Fletcher, D. T. (1999). *The St. Louis & Benjamin Air Rifle Companies*, Portland, OR.

Galan, J. I. (1988). *Air Gun Digest*, 2nd ed., DBI Books, Northfield, IL.

Galan, J. I. (1995). *Airgun Digest*, 3rd ed., DBI Books, Northfield, IL.

House, James E. (2001). *American Air Rifles*, Krause Publications, Iola, WI.

Wesley, L. and Cardew, G. V. (1979). *Air-Guns & Air-Pistols*, Cassell Ltd., London.

near-mint Mark I and a like-new bulk-fill Model 116 complete with 10-ounce cylinder in the original box. I also have a mint Daisy CO_2 200 semi-automatic BB pistol that was found in its original box. These three pistols were obtained at prices that were below or far below the prices listed in the price guide for guns in their condition. Alas, I have also passed up some pieces that in retrospect I wish I had bought. Such is the nature of collecting.

CHAPTER 2

TESTING AND USING CO₂ GUNS

ALTHOUGH GUNS POWERED by CO₂ have not been produced nearly as long as airguns, there is a great deal of overlap in use, function, and production of the two types. While a brief history of the two types of guns was given in Chapter 1, this chapter will present an overview of the characteristics of CO₂ guns as well as describe the testing procedures that were used in evaluating the many CO₂ guns described in this book. We will also provide a short course on safety and describe some of the procedures related to shooting

CO₂ guns. It is appropriate to cover this material before describing the characteristics of the various models and their performance.

Surveying the Field

There are many types of CO₂ pistols and rifles available. While we are on the subject of types of "guns," let me state some basic premises on the subject. First, when applied to the subject of gun control, all types of firearms are referred to as guns. I am fully aware that in the classic sense, it was appropriate

Almost all of the CO₂ handguns that outwardly resemble semiautomatics are actually revolvers.

to refer to shooting a rifle or gun, especially in British writing. The term "gun" was applied to a piece that had a smooth bore (shotgun) and the term "rifle" was used to refer to a piece that had a rifled barrel. However, the generic term "long gun" applies to either, and if we drop the adjective "long," the term "gun" could apply to either. Accordingly, we will refer to a CO_2 gun without regard to whether it has a rifled barrel or not. It should also be mentioned that even some manufacturers refer to "CO_2 air guns" because guns using CO_2 and air as the power source serve the same purposes and are used similarly. Technically, a gun that makes use of CO_2 as the power source should probably be called a compressed gas gun. Some early Crosman pieces had model numbers that were followed by "CG" to give such a designation. They are not firearms, and they are manufactured by the same companies that produce airguns, so they are often lumped together.

In the case of handguns, we also have pieces that have smooth bores and rifled tubes. There are handguns that are single

shots and those that hold several rounds, the repeaters. The repeaters have the general configuration of a revolver or a semi-automatic arm. The term "pistol" has been employed historically to mean any hand-held firearm. It is clear that it was intended to apply to both those arms with revolving cylinders ("revolvers") as well as those without (single shots and semi-automatics). The issue is even more clouded in the case of CO_2 pellet pistols because even those that outwardly look like semi-automatics hold the pellets in a cylinder that rotates. This is true even of those 177-caliber pistols that resemble Colt, Beretta, Walther, and other famous semi-automatic firearms. In the case of CO_2 pistols that fire BBs, the magazine is usually a tube with a spring-loaded plunger (the magazine follower) that causes the BBs to move under pressure into firing position. In this book, the term "pistol" will be used to refer to any CO_2 handgun regardless of what type of mechanism is used to move the next projectile into firing position.

Although many CO_2 pistols are shaped like semi-automatic pistols, most make use of cyl-

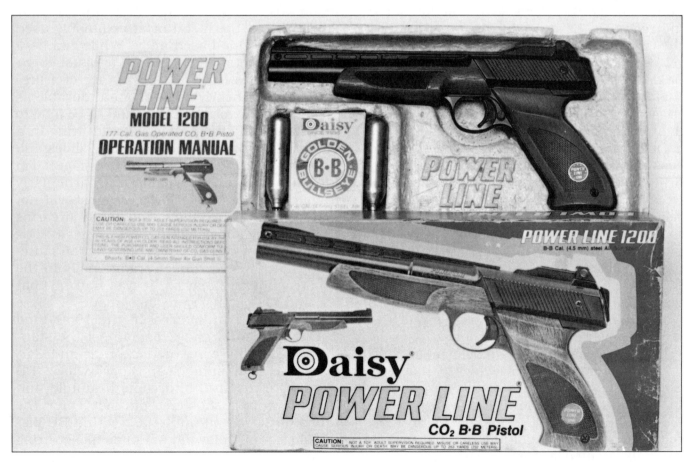

The Daisy PowerLine 1200 is a classic BB repeater that is cocked manually for each shot.

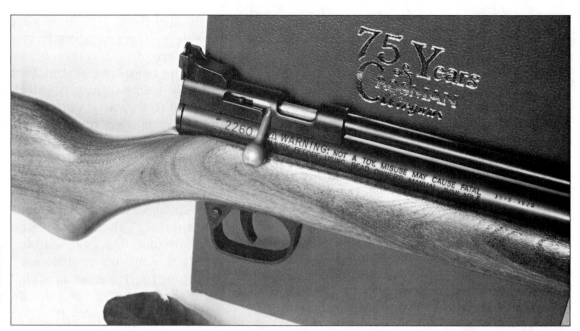

The Crosman 2260 is crafted of wood and metal in the classic style.

inders to hold the pellets. Unlike the case of revolvers with exposed cylinders, the cylinders used in so-called semi-automatics are completely enclosed. Whether the cylinder is exposed or hidden, both types are actually revolvers in terms of function.

Firing a CO_2 revolver or semi-auto can be done in one of two ways. Single-action shooting refers to the procedure in which pulling the trigger performs only one action, the release of the hammer or sear. Cocking must be done manually in a separate operation. In this firing mode, very little movement of the trigger is required so trigger action is usually light and crisp.

Double-action shooting refers to the process in which pulling the trigger tensions the firing mechanism of the piece and releases it. Because a spring must be tensioned before release occurs, the trigger pull tends to be rather long and heavy. Moreover, because many CO_2 pistols do not have parts made of highly polished and hardened metal, moving parts are sometimes rough. As they move across each other, there is some roughness, which manifests itself in a trigger pull that requires a variable or uneven force.

I prefer always to shoot single action since greater accuracy can be achieved that way. Some of the inexpensive pistols can be fired in only one or the other firing modes. A double-action-only pistol is usually going to be regarded as a plinking, fun gun because of its generally limited accuracy. To me, a single-action-only (not to be confused with single-shot) pistol is not a handicap because in my shooting I am perfectly willing to trade speed of fire for the better trigger pull of the single-action-only pistol.

There is another fact of life in regard to CO_2 pistols. Even the most expensive models are made of metal that is not high quality alloy steel. In fact, the metal most commonly used is zinc or a zinc-based alloy. While zinc is a wonderful metal that permits a pistol to be made with the feel and appearance of a firearm, it is not nearly as strong and durable as steel. Do not expect a CO_2 pistol to be able to withstand too much abuse. Rapid firing in a double-action mode and slamming slides and cylinders around can lead to breakages. I'm not saying that CO_2 pistols are particularly fragile. They are not. However, most will not endure the torture tests that many firearms are routinely subjected to.

Metal and wood are the construction materials that have been used traditionally in the construction of firearms. It was natural that air and CO_2 guns were also made of these materials for many years. In the 1950s and 1960s, Benjamin and Crosman set the standard for quality construction of air and CO_2 guns. Keep in mind that Daisy, whose BB guns were the stuff of dreams of untold millions of young shooters, did not enter the arena of CO_2 guns until 1962 with a BB pistol. Moreover, Daisy did not make pellet-firing guns until 1972. Therefore, it is not slighting

These 22-caliber Crosman pistols show the plastic and the classic. On the left is the plastic Model 2210 while on the right is the classic metal Mark I.

Daisy to accord due recognition of Crosman and Benjamin for their products.

The Crosman Model 160 rifle and the Model 600 pistol are widely recognized as the epitome of CO_2 guns. Those models were made of the best materials and feature excellence of design. In terms of quality, some of the early Benjamin guns were similar, having been made of finely finished brass and wood. These were guns from the "golden era" of airgun manufacture in this country and they are classic guns. As manufacturing techniques developed so did the materials available. Plastics were improved to the point that they were strong, corrosion resistant, and easily shaped (especially by molding). Air and CO_2 guns came to have more plastic parts, including receivers, stocks, barrel shrouds, sights, etc. "Classic" had become "plastic" in terms of construction.

Over the years, air and CO_2 guns became much more sophisticated in some respects. Realism became the objective as pistols were made to resemble some firearm and the rate of fire came to be an advertising point. There is nothing operationally wrong with these changes, but I have to question the wisdom of marketing BB and pellet guns that resemble submachine guns. I am not sure guns so popular with young shooters should be made to resemble military assault rifles, but that is a personal opinion.

As break-action air rifles made of fine steel and wood became more common and more shooters discovered how wonderful the air and CO_2 guns from the classic period were, the market changed. While the inexpensive plastic guns will probably always be with us (hopefully), there is a growing demand for high quality CO_2 guns. Although it is doubtful we will see anything equivalent to a Crosman 600 or 160 or a Daisy CO_2 200 in the near future, we are seeing more and more fine CO_2 guns become available. Notable developments include the Crosman C40, a metal CO_2 pistol that resembles a large-caliber Smith & Wesson semiautomatic. Umarex, the parent company of Walther in Germany, has produced several outstanding CO_2 pistols that carry names like Beretta, Colt, Walther, and Smith & Wesson. The named companies market some of these but others are marketed by American companies. Crosman markets the Walther, Smith & Wesson, Colt, and Beretta CO_2 guns. Most of these pistols are of very high quality in fit and finish.

In the area of CO_2 rifles, Crosman produces the excellent Model 2260, which has a very nice wood stock and steel-sleeved barrel although the receiver is made of a composite material. It is not equivalent to a Model 160, but it is nonetheless a fine rifle. Daisy produces an outright target rifle, the Medalist 888, that is powered

These elegant Smith & Wesson revolvers are typical of the high quality CO_2 handguns available today. They represent a return to classic design and construction.

by a large internal CO_2 cylinder that holds 2.5 ounces of propellant. It is equipped with high quality target sights and a beautiful laminated stock. Crosman markets the Model CH2000, which is also a target rifle designed for three-position match shooting.

With these recent developments in CO_2 pistols and rifles, there are now more choices of high quality CO_2 guns than ever before. Some of the current models will undoubtedly hold the title of "classic," now held by some of the vintage models. In some ways, it seems we have seen an evolution of CO_2 guns from classic to plastic back to classic. The makers of such guns now offer something for everyone.

There are so many different models and variations of the pistols available that it is not practical to test them all. The range of models tested is quite large and it includes the majority of CO_2 pistols available. In some cases, more than one specimen was tested.

Safety

In perhaps no other sport is safety more important than in the shooting sports. The shooting sports are currently under unprecedented attack by legislatures, consumer groups, and the media. There is a large segment of the population that has no interest in guns and does not understand why many of us do. I grew up in a remote area with shooting as a way of life that began when I was quite young. I later competed as a member of a very successful ROTC rifle team while a college student. Shooting sports have been a part of my life for approximately 60 years. To me, there is no difference between trying to put a little white ball in a hole in the ground and trying to put a projectile in a black dot on a piece of paper.

Airgun competition has been an Olympic sport since 1984, and the first gold medal won by the United States in the 2000 Olympics was won by Nancy Johnson in women's airgun shooting. From the perspective of one who has been shooting for three score years, I believe that the interest in air and CO_2 guns is at an all time high and the choice of equipment has never been better. Having said that, I believe it is absolutely essential those of us who enjoy the shooting sports do everything we can to spread the word in a positive way. While other companies are involved, Daisy Outdoor Products and the Crosman Corporation have done much to promote airgun shooting. For many years, Daisy has sponsored the Jaycees BB gun competition and has recently outfitted a long trailer as a mobile airgun range. This facility has been taken to locations in many parts of the country to give youngsters the opportunity to learn shooting skills and safety. In 1987, Crosman developed a biathlon shooting program combined with bicycling. Crosman also cooperates with the National Rifle Association and numerous clubs and organizations in fostering marksmanship programs. Another Crosman program is known as Education in Airgun Shooting for Youth (EASY). These fine companies deserve our support in taking a proactive approach to the shooting sports.

I believe that interest in shooting is perfectly natural, but many people do not. At a book signing recently, a young lad of perhaps 10 years of age expressed a keen interest in my book on air rifles. His parents were completely bewildered and the mother exclaimed, "I don't know where he gets this from! We hate guns!" It was as if the lad's interest was some sort of disease. After some discussion, we learned the boy's father participated in archery, which was acceptable since no gun was involved. After spending some time with my wife and me, the lad's parents pronounced, "You don't seem like fanatics at all!" It was as if somehow my wife and I should have come across as wild-eyed, babbling gun nuts. Unfortunately, this scenario is typical in dealing with many uninformed, anti-gun people. Their rabid anti-gun stance is based on media "information."

Safety is not a sometime thing. Safety must be stressed to the point that safe gun handling is second nature. Gun etiquette is an acquired skill. Any accident, even a minor one, gives fuel to the fire that is trying to consume the shooting sports. A few accidents that are well publicized by the biased media (ever note how there is virtually no coverage of the shooting sports in the Olympics?) do irreparable harm to shooting.

In several chapters of this book, instructions are given for loading a CO_2 cylinder and ammunition. Although is it not stated explicitly in the discussion of each model, the safety should always be in the "on" position. Unless the safety is on, there is danger in piercing a CO_2 cylinder in a gun already having BBs or pellets in it or in placing projectiles in a gun pressurized with a pierced CO_2 cylinder.

The following rules of safe gun handling are very simple, but they need to be reinforced at every opportunity.

1. Treat every gun as if it were loaded.

2. Always keep the muzzle pointed in a safe direction.

3. Load and make ready to fire only when you are in the shooting area.

4. Know your target and what is behind it.

5. Always wear adequate eye protection and, if needed, ear protection.

6. Never cross a fence, stream, or other barrier with a loaded gun.

7. Check your gun to see that the bore and muzzle are clear before loading.

8. Always store your unloaded gun in a secure place.

9. Never shoot at a hard surface, water, or other surface that might cause a ricochet.

10. Always respect the property and rights of others.

These rules should also be taught to beginning shooters before any use of a gun is undertaken. Beginners should be instructed in the handling characteristics of their particular guns to learn how the controls operate before any shooting occurs.

Special consideration should be given to securing a safe shooting area. Because they have low power and are quiet, CO_2 guns are appropriate for shooting indoors. I have routinely done this in testing these guns by firing into a suitable backstop. One of the most effective and inexpensive backstops for either BBs or pellets consists of a large paper bag filled with newspapers. Place several thick newspapers in the back of the bag

Crosman includes a trigger lock with each of their CO_2 pistols.

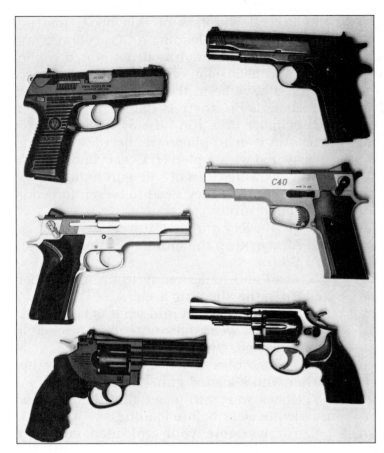

This photo shows firearms and CO$_2$ pistols. Can you identify them?

The way this 22-caliber Crosman pointed pellet penetrated this board shows that CO$_2$ guns are not toys.

then crumple several papers loosely to fill the front of the bag. In this way, the pellets or BBs enter the bag and are slowed by the loose papers before being stopped by the thicker papers at the back. Also, there is very little likelihood that projectiles striking the folded papers will bounce back through the loose papers. Never fire BBs or pellets at any firm backstop! They will bounce back even from a stack of tightly packed newspapers or magazines, and from a board, plywood, or particleboard, they can bounce back at high velocity. I once made the mistake of placing a paper target on a piece of particleboard and at the first shot, the pellet came back and actually went through my hair! The glue and resin in the particleboard provided a resilient surface from which the pellet was launched backward. ALWAYS wear shooting glasses and shoot into a suitable backstop.

Another aspect of safety with CO$_2$ guns deals with the fact that many of them closely resemble firearms. To some extent, air and CO$_2$ guns have always resembled firearms,

but the realism has increased dramatically in recent years as more of the fine CO$_2$ guns are made of metal and to the exact dimensions of a Beretta, Colt, or Smith & Wesson firearm. I once showed a photograph of eight handguns arranged in a circle to three Department of Natural Resources employees at a state park. The photograph included five CO$_2$ handguns and three firearms. The DNR employees studied the photograph for several minutes, but they never did identify correctly each of the handguns as firearm or CO$_2$ gun. Of course CO$_2$ guns are actually guns; they are simply low-powered ones.

There is a danger in having an air or CO$_2$ gun that is so easily mistaken for a firearm. You cannot expect a police officer who encounters a situation in which someone is holding one of the wonderful CO_2 guns to be able to read "for 177-caliber pellets only" on the barrel. An officer in that situation may believe that he/she has encountered a person armed with a firearm. Such accidents have occurred with disastrous results. Never use an air or CO_2 gun anywhere or in any way where the use of a firearm would be inappropriate. Some jurisdictions are passing or attempting to pass stringent regulations on purchasing and possessing even toy guns, and in some places the possession of air and CO_2 guns is highly regulated already. Along with the realism of air and CO_2 guns comes the responsibility of using them just as you would a firearm. To not do so is to invite many problems.

Sights

I grew up shooting airguns and 22 rimfire rifles equipped with open metallic sights. Later, my rifles occasionally wore a scope. While a college student shooting on an ROTC rifle team, I used a Winchester Model 52D equipped with the outstanding micrometer sights employed in target shooting. I now have several air rifles that have peep sights, some that wear scopes, and many that have open sights.

The majority of CO_2 guns described in this book are pistols. Handguns for use in formal target shooting have traditionally been equipped with a front sight having a square-topped post (usually on a ramp) and a rear sight with a square notch that can be adjusted for windage and elevation. Even in a day when all sorts of optical devices are available, this constitutes my preferred sighting equipment on handguns. Sights on the current models of CO_2-powered handguns range from lousy to lovely. Some have front sights with round tops, many have rear sights that are not adjustable, and others have a fiber optic element in the front sight. As you will see when you read the descriptions of the guns, sights on each gun are described in detail since this feature has much to do with accurate shooting. Most of the guns have provision for attaching optical sights, especially the red dot and laser types. Some can even accommodate scope sights.

Some of the inexpensive pistols like the Crosman AutoAir II shown here have excellent sights.

In my opinion, it is difficult to equip a handgun with better sights for target and sport shooting than is afforded by a front sight consisting of a square-topped post and a rear sight that has a well-shaped square notch that is fully adjustable. That arrangement is the favored or required one for formal target shooting in which the sights and target are aligned in what is known as the six o'clock hold. This arrangement has the front sight aligned even with the top of the notch of the rear sight with a sliver of space on either side and the gun held so the black bullseye is sitting on top of the post. Very precise shooting can be done with such sights so aligned.

A few of the CO_2 pistols in this work have outstanding sights of the type just described. However, several have sights that enable such an arrangement of sights and target to be made, but have rear sights that are not adjustable. If you are shooting such a CO_2 handgun, you may find that the pellets do not strike the center of the target when you apply the six o'clock hold. Even though your pistol may not have adjustable sights, there are a few things that you can do to change the point of impact on the target so that hits are near the center. First, if the point of impact is satisfactory horizontally but is higher or lower than you wish it to be, change pellets. In Chapter 3, weights are given for a large

The front sight on a Crosman 2210 (top) shows the trendy design while that on the Crosman 454 (bottom) shows a much more functional design.

made by changing the width of the notch in the rear sight by removing material on one side only. This changes the midpoint of the sight so that the front sight blade will appear to be in a different position when it is centered in the notch. Remove a small amount of material with a jeweler's file. If the point of impact needs to be moved to the right, remove material from the right hand side of the notch. I actually do not recommend this procedure except in extreme cases because once the material is removed it can't be put back. If you try this method of making small windage adjustments, do so very carefully.

In recent years, the number of air and CO_2 guns made with a fiber optic insert in the front sight has increased dramatically. In fact, this has become the standard for almost all models produced by Crosman and Daisy. The idea behind this type of sight is that the fiber optic insert absorbs light from the sides and the end pointing toward the shooter appears to glow. In almost all cases, the bright spot is somewhere about the mid-point of the front sight. While it shows up brightly even in dim light, it is impossible to use the midpoint of the front sight in a six o'clock hold. The main advantage of having a bright front sight is to pick it up quickly against a target. This type of shooting has some merit as combat training.

Another phenomenon in sighting equipment of CO_2 pistols is the red dot sight. With this type of sight, a red dot powered by a battery is projected on a clear plastic lens with either circles or cross hairs on which to locate the dot as it simultaneously rests on the target. This red dot sight covers part of the target so it does not permit highly precise sight placement. However, it does permit rapid shooting in the general vicinity of the target. Several models of CO_2 pistols come as kits with this type of sight or they can be added as after-market accessories that sell for $12-15. In most cases, red dot sights are mounted on the dovetail grooves now present on the top of most CO_2 pistols.

Laser sights have become enormously popular for combat-style shooting with firearms, and they have become commonplace with shooters of air and CO_2 guns. The laser projects a red beam onto the target. When the sight is properly adjusted so that the gun

number of pellets. From a CO_2 pistol, a heavier pellet will usually strike lower on the target than a lighter one. Select a heavy pellet if you want a lower point of impact or a lighter one if you want a higher point of impact. I have used this procedure with one of my Colt 1911 pistols that shot too high with a 7.9-grain pellet by selecting a pellet that weighs 9.4 grains. With the heavier pellet, the point of impact was almost perfect.

While some of the CO_2 handguns have rear sights that are not adjustable for elevation, they are adjustable for windage. Several models require a locking screw to be loosened before the sight can slide left or right. Remember, move the rear sight in the direction you want the point of impact to move on the target. If the rear sight is not movable, small variations in point of impact can be

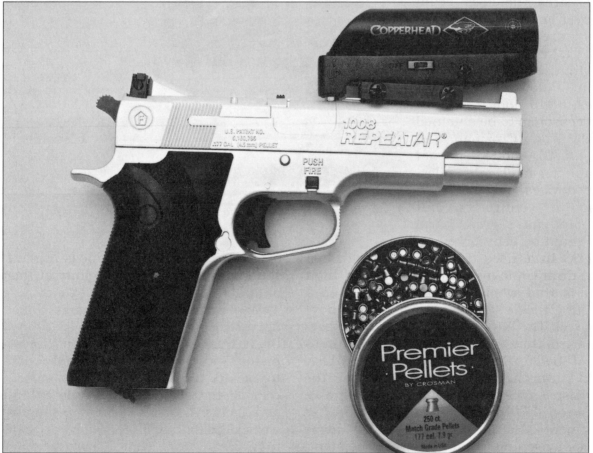

Red dot sights like those from Daisy (top) and Crosman (bottom) offer additional sighting options.

shoots to the point of aim of the laser, target acquisition requires only placing the laser beam on the target and firing. There is nothing to line up with something else since where the beam points, is where the pellet will hit. In fact, the gun can be held in any position as opposed to being held with an out-stretched arm to acquire a correct sight picture. This appeals to some shooters although it is not without its problems. First, the laser beam covers part of the target so it does not lend itself to high precision. Second, the laser beam may be hard to see in some lighting conditions or may have limited range. The longer the distance to the target, the greater area the laser beam will cover on the target. Third, lasers are dangerous! It doesn't take much direct contact with the eye to cause permanent damage. It is interesting to note that of all the accessories to be obtained directly from Crosman, the laser is the one item not available for mail order sales. These devices may be fascinating to youngsters, but they can cause great harm and should be kept locked up when not in use.

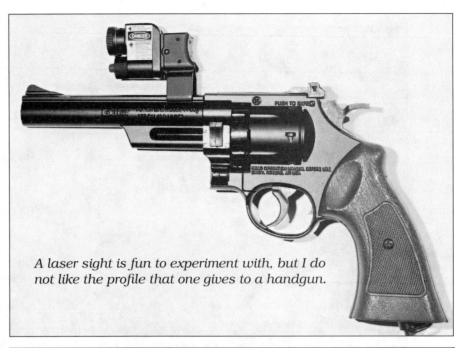

A laser sight is fun to experiment with, but I do not like the profile that one gives to a handgun.

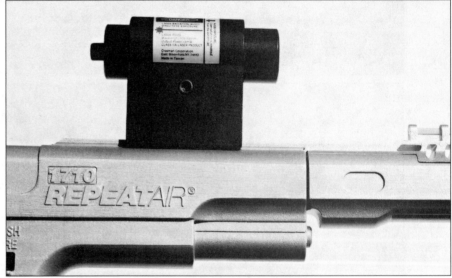

Crosman's laser sight can be easily attached to many CO_2 pistols.

One disadvantage of both red dot and laser sights is that when they are clamped on a handgun, they extend some distance above the barrel. The lumpy sight on top of the barrel does nothing good for the looks or handling of the gun, and they are not particularly durable. Another disadvantage is that the inexpensive types, which would be suitable for use on CO_2 pistols, do not have precise adjustments. Setting elevation and windage involves loosening a screw, moving the sight, and tightening it. There are no precise click stops or reference marks. You may wish to try a red dot or laser sight on your CO_2 pistol, but I believe that for most shooting a good set of target type sights will be preferable.

Sights on CO_2 rifles generally consist of an open rear sight with a notch and some sort of blade front sight. As in the case of sights on pistols, probably the most convenient sights to use are the square-topped post front and a rear sight with a square notch. Such an arrangement makes it easy to obtain the six o'clock hold that is conducive to high accuracy. Bead front sights have a rounded top that makes it difficult to tell exactly how high the sight is on the target. Such sights are not

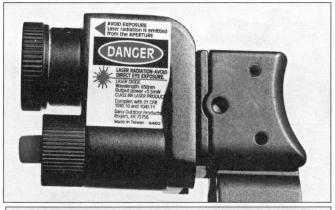

Laser sights are potentially hazardous as clearly indicated on these models from Daisy (top) and Crosman (bottom).

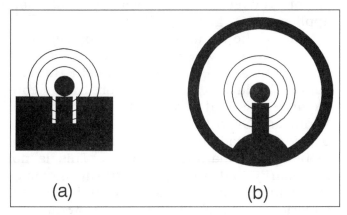

The correct sight picture for a six o'clock hold with open sights is shown in (a) and with a peep sight in (b).

common on CO_2 rifles. What has become common is the post front sight with a fiber optic insert, which gives a glowing dot at or near the top of the sight. It is more difficult to get a repeatable six o'clock sight picture with such a sight. If the red dot is placed on the target, it covers too much unless the target is very close. I suspect the fiber optic sights are intended for exactly that type of shooting. If the dot covers half of the pop can at 10 yards, who cares? Well, the person who is trying to

A peep sight like the Williams model shown on a Benjamin G397 permits greater accuracy than is possible by using open sights.

do fine shooting and dot the "i" in the name of the type of soda.

A type of sight that provides great accuracy without changing the dimensions or weight of a rifle is the peep or aperture sight. That such sights lend themselves to highly accurate shooting is obvious from the fact that aperture sights are used on some of the finest target rifles. The peep sight has a small opening or aperture through which the shooter looks at the front sight. In target shooting, the front sight is usually placed on the bull as in the six o'clock hold. No attempt is made to focus the eye on the aperture. The shooter merely looks through it because the eye naturally selects the brightest spot, which is the center. With open sights, the shooter must try to focus on both the rear and front sights and the target simultaneously. Because of only looking through the peep sight—not at it—there is one less object to try to keep in focus. Very accurate aiming is therefore possible.

When using a peep sight on a rifle used to shoot targets of irregular shapes at varying distances, I prefer to adjust the sight so the point of impact coincides with the top of the post. In that way, I simply put the top of the post where I want the shot to hit, center the top of the post in the aperture, and squeeze off the shot. It doesn't matter whether the target is a pop can, a starling, or a black circle; I

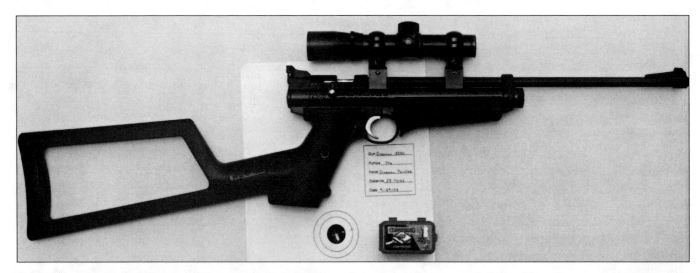

Accuracy like that shown in this target shot at 25 yards using a Crosman 2250 with a Simmons 2.5X scope illustrates what is possible when a scope is used.

know the pellet will strike where I hold the top of the post. This procedure works best for air or CO_2 guns used in hunting or pest control.

For use on rifles, the ultimate sight is the scope. With a scope, there is no need to align two or more sighting features with the target. A scope is constructed so that as you look through it and align the cross hairs on the target, both appear to be at the same distance from the eye. Additionally, the scope provides magnification, which makes it easier to see the target and where the cross hairs are placed on it. There are, however, some drawbacks to scopes on CO_2 rifles. First, they add bulk and weight, which makes the rifles less convenient to handle. Second, some CO_2 rifles are not constructed well enough to enable rigid mounting of a scope. These are minor, qualitative considerations, and there is no question the most accurate shooting of a rifle can be done with a properly mounted and sighted scope.

Testing Procedures

In testing the many guns involved in this work, several things became apparent. While there are features I like and some I dislike on most of the CO_2 guns, all of the guns work. That may sound a little trite, but occasionally I read some piece in which the author either states or implies that a certain model of CO_2 gun fires for a few shots then falls apart. The companies that make CO_2 guns do not make them only to have 90% of them returned. Some are made almost entirely of plastic and

feel flimsy. Some have poor trigger action and some have poor sights. These are generally the lower-priced models that, in spite of their shortcomings, are still able to provide a lot of recreation and fun. Even with some of the low-end models, I have been very impressed with how well they work. As you read through the evaluations, keep in mind that the principle of "you generally get what you pay for" applies to CO_2 guns.

Most of the air and CO_2 guns of a generation or two ago were made of metal. They had the weight and feel of a firearm. In the language of today, a gun that is more than a couple of decades old is referred to as "classic" or "vintage." Over the years, more and more parts were made of plastic as is true of automobiles and many other items. This is not necessarily bad because plastics (composites may sound more impressive) of today are far superior to many of those of yesterday. In fact, plastics may even be superior to metals for many uses. Do not underestimate the performance and durability of some of the guns made using plastic materials. However, there are available today many CO_2 handguns made of metal and whose fit and finish are comparable to those of firearms. They generally sell in the $100-$200 range, but they are exquisite pieces. Several such models have been evaluated as part of the data collection for this book. Also, some of the CO_2 rifles are made primarily of metal and have walnut stocks. These are rifles that represent a return to the classic equipment of yesteryear.

Testing the multitude of CO_2 handguns required many hours of shooting as my wife recorded data.

The majority of CO_2-powered guns are handguns. Models are available that fire BBs, or pellets of 177, 20, or 22 caliber. The handguns include single-shot and repeater models. There are models that are inexpensive while others cost as much as $200 or more. CO_2-powered pistols truly offer something for everyone.

As stated earlier, a major objective of this book is to give enough information on the performance of CO_2 guns to help the prospective buyer select the equipment suitable for his or her intended purposes. Additionally, this book is intended to serve as a user's guide to CO_2 guns. In order to be of maximum use, the details of the operation of the guns tested will be given. Several of my guns, especially the older ones, have been obtained as used items. In almost every case, an owner's manual did not accompany the gun. The evaluations of CO_2 guns presented in Chapters 5-10 will include complete descriptions of how they operate. The descriptions will be of use to owners of CO_2 guns of many types as well as provide a great deal of reference material on these guns.

In order to adequately document the performance of a plethora of CO_2 handguns, several parameters have been collected. First, the weight was determined with no CO_2 cylinder or ammunition in the gun and using a postal scale that determines weight to the nearest 0.1 ounce. This may sound trivial, but I have found the weights given in the manufacturer's literature may differ by anywhere from a tenth of an ounce to several ounces from the actual weight. The weights given in this book are the actual weights determined unless otherwise noted.

A characteristic that is important to many shooters of CO_2 guns is the weight of the trigger pull. However, not a single owner's manual for any of the CO_2 guns gives this information. Therefore, trigger pull was measured for each CO_2 gun tested using a Lyman digital trigger pull gauge. This instrument measures the trigger pull required to fire the gun to the nearest one-tenth of an ounce. If the gun being tested can be fired in both single- and double-action modes, the trigger pull was measured for firing both ways. Several trials were made with each gun and the trigger pull weights reported are the averages of several determinations. I do not know of any other source of data on trigger pull for such a large number of models of CO_2 guns.

A third type of test data obtained deals with the pellet or BB velocities. Several factors affect pellet velocity, some of which are determined by the construction of the gun. Barrel length, bar-

A chronograph is an indispensable tool for determining the performance of CO_2 guns. This photo shows a Crosman 2240 being tested.

rel to cylinder gap, barrel dimensions and smoothness, etc. are factors over which the average shooter has no control for a particular gun. Of the factors that influence pellet velocity, temperature and pellet weight are the most important. In the tests conducted, velocity was measured using a Competition Electronics ProChrono Chronograph. Several types of pellets were used with each pellet-firing gun and at least two types of BBs were used in each BB gun. The temperature was noted in most cases. In order to allow each gun to reach equilibrium temperature between shots, shots were fired at approximately two-minute intervals.

Firing a CO_2 handgun in the double-action mode may result in a slightly different velocity than obtained when the same gun is fired single action. The reason is that the hammer is not in exactly the same position at the instant of firing in both modes. Therefore, when the hammer falls, it strikes the release pin with a slightly different force, which alters slightly the amount of CO_2 released. For guns that can be fired either single or double action, pellet velocity was measured by firing in the single-action mode. If you are firing fast enough to need to shoot double action, you are probably not interested in velocity because the rate of firing a CO_2 gun has a pronounced influence on velocity due to the cooling effect of the expanding gas (see Chapter 4).

Testing implies measuring something, which means you need a device to measure the property or characteristic being studied. Ideally, the measurement is not dependent on the skill of the person making the measurement. This is the case when you place a CO_2 pistol on a postal scale and the digits on the dial read 27.3 ounces. This is not the case when accuracy of a gun is measured because someone has to fire the piece (unless you have an elaborate set up). Not all people shoot equally well.

Most CO_2 guns are inherently accurate. As a practical matter, sights, trigger pull, weight distribution, and other factors come into play when the piece is fired. Obtainable accuracy may be quite different from intrinsic accuracy. The accuracy obtained depends on the shooter, so the accuracy you achieve with a particular CO_2 gun may be somewhat different from what I get. I lay no claim to being a great marksman. Having said that, I should mention that my involvement in the shooting sports spans well over half a century and it includes almost all types of sporting firearms and airguns. Someone else might fire the guns used in these evaluations and get better results. However, I doubt the results would be very much better. In view of the variability of accuracy as determined by different shooters, I have chosen to include limited accuracy

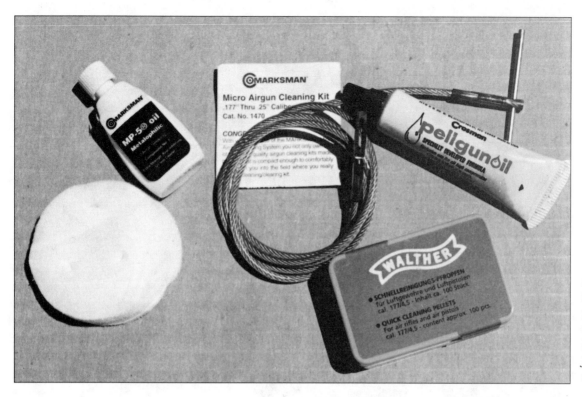

Proper maintenance of your CO_2 gun is easy and will keep it functioning for many years.

data especially with the handguns. I believe the results I have obtained provide useful reference and comparative data showing the capabilities of the guns.

Tips for Using CO_2 Guns

Like most other mechanical objects, CO_2 guns respond to proper care and maintenance. A few basic ideas have come to be accepted practice with regard to long life and trouble free service. One critical component in a CO_2 gun is the seal around the piercing pin, which keeps gas from escaping. The CO_2 cylinder fits against the seal when it is installed in the gun and tightened into place. Because CO_2 under high pressure is in contact with the seal, the gas can become absorbed in the plastic seal. I have read of cases where the seals have ruptured when the CO_2 cylinder was removed due to the tendency of the CO_2 trapped in the seal to escape. I have not had this experience, but others have. To help minimize the amount of CO_2 that gets absorbed in the plastic seal, most owners' manuals recommend that a pressurized CO_2 cylinder not be left in the gun for long periods of time. In fact, I have been told this very same thing by service technicians at some of the factories. How long is too long? There seems to be no agreement

on this, but I know that some older guns (including my own) have been left pressurized for weeks. Seals in recently manufactured guns do not seem to be made of the same material, and I am told that even a few days will cause damage even to some of the expensive models. The best advice seems to be to empty the cylinder during a shooting session and remove it. For example, the owner's manual for the Walther Lever Action states, "Do not store your air rifle with CO_2 cylinders in it. This ... will prolong the longevity of your air rifle seals."

Another concern related to the plastic seals is that if the piercing mechanism is too tight it will force the neck of the CO_2 cylinder against the plastic seal so hard the plastic will be squeezed and compressed enough that it may permanently change the shape and thickness of the seal. Do not turn a piercing screw too tightly and be sure that pistols having a lever piercing mechanism are set for the proper amount of travel to pierce the cylinder but not put undue pressure on the seal and piercing pin.

Seals that are treated with a proper lubricant such Crosman Pellgun Oil® or other lubricant specified in the owner's manual will maintain the desired flexibility and resiliency longer. Some owner's manuals indicate that a

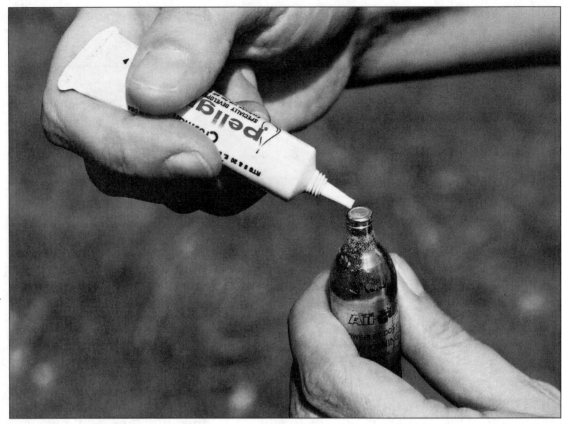

A drop of Crosman Pellgun Oil applied to the CO_2 cylinder is the accepted procedure for lubricating seals and valves.

drop of lubricant should be placed on the end of each CO_2 cylinder before it is inserted and pierced. In my opinion, this is sound advice. In fact, Crosman Copperhead Powerlets® contain a small amount of lubricant in the CO_2 to maintain proper lubrication of the valve. However, owners' manuals caution against over lubrication.

Finally, there are slight differences in neck dimensions for the various brands of CO_2 cylinders. Make sure the neck diameter of the cylinder is correct for your gun. The "small neck" cylinder, which measures approximately 0.290 inch, is now standard.

A common complaint about air and CO_2 guns is that the trigger pull is heavy and rough. In many cases this assessment is correct. However, I have found the trigger action on some guns improves markedly as the guns

are used over a period of time. Parts of a CO_2 gun are not made of the same materials and the fit and finish are not as good as on a firearm that costs several hundred dollars. With use, burrs and rough spots can smooth off so that the trigger action improves. It is not uncommon for the overall function of the gun to improve with use. If you buy a new CO_2 gun that does not seem to function smoothly, use it for a period of time before you assume that you got a bad specimen.

With a small amount of care and maintenance, a CO_2 gun will give many years of trouble free service. I have bought some vintage CO_2 guns in antique malls and pawn shops that still function perfectly. How much attention their former owners gave them I cannot say. All I know is that many of these fine guns are very durable.

CHAPTER 3

AMMUNITION

THE DEVELOPMENT OF guns using CO_2 for power—beginning with the work of Paul Giffard a century ago through the developments of the manufacturers of today—has led to highly sophisticated and capable guns. However, the developments in the design and manufacture of pellets have been equally impressive. The availability of uniform pellets in a variety of types adds immeasurably to the performance of any air or CO_2 gun.

Pellets come in several general types although almost all of them have one design feature in common. That characteristic is that they are larger in diameter in the head

and skirt areas than they are in the middle. They have a "waist" in the middle that results in a design known as the *diabolo* shape. There are several reasons for pellets having this general design. First, the head area is solid and that keeps the pellet flying head first since the skirt is hollow. The behavior is sort of like the shuttlecock used in badminton. Second, the diabolo shape minimizes the area of the pellet that is in contact with the bore, which reduces friction as the pellet moves down the barrel. Third, the diabolo shape results in a favorable weight distribution, which helps to stabilize the pellet in

Shooters of CO_2 guns have dozens of types of pellets to choose from.

The Crosman Premier pellets are available in 177, 20, and 22 calibers and have a diabolo shape.

The original 20-caliber Sheridan cylindrical pellet (left) did not have a smaller midsection as does the newer version.

flight. The hollow skirt of most pellets is quite thin which allows the skirt to expand to fit the bore better. While there are several types of specialized pellets available in other shapes and designs, the diabolo shape is by far the most common.

One pellet of note that deviated from the diabolo shape was the famous Sheridan 20-caliber pellet that was popular for many years. That pellet was cylindrical in shape and it had a rounded nose. The base had a very shallow hollow skirt and a small flange around the base provided the gas seal. The Sheridan pellet was very solid in construction, which accounted for the phenomenal penetration attributed to it. However, a few years ago the pellet was redesigned and even though it now has a waist, it is still a very solid, sturdy pellet.

Air and CO_2 guns frequently show marked preferences for certain types or brands of pellets. You should try several types of pellets in your gun to see how it performs with them. In your testing, you should try to keep all the other variables the same except for the variation in pellet type. Shoot from a rest, keep a consistent sight picture, and squeeze off the shots carefully. Try to see what the effect of

the pellet is, not what happens when several things are not kept constant.

Pellet Types

Although there are some exceptions, pellets generally are of four basic types. These types are the flat-nose (wadcutter), round-nose (domed), pointed, and hollow-point types. The wadcutter design includes some inexpensive general-purpose pellets as well as some of the expensive target types. In general, wadcutter pellets of high quality will give accuracy that is unexcelled by any other type. If your CO_2 gun is specified for use only with wadcutter pellets, do not dismay because that is not a severe limitation, especially for a CO_2 pistol. Pistols that hold the pellets in a head-to-tail arrangement in an in-line magazine must be used with wadcutter pellets. These pistols function by pulling one pellet laterally out of the line, so the pellets will hang up if the head of one does not slide easily across the base of another.

While there are many good wadcutter pellets available, let me give some of my thoughts on certain ones. The Crosman Copperhead wadcutter pellet is one of my favorites because it has a very solidly constructed

Pellets are available with several point shapes. Shown here (left to right) are the flat-point, domed, pointed, and hollow-point styles.

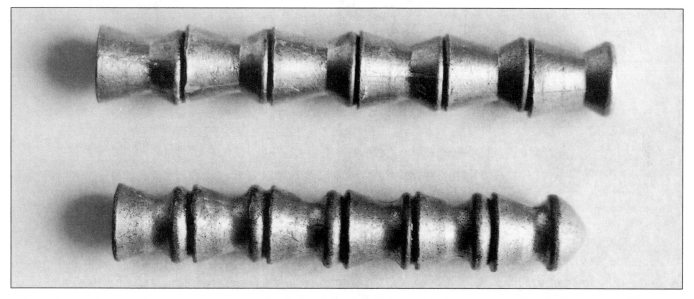

If a CO_2 gun has an in-line magazine, only flat-pointed pellets will feed properly. Pointed pellets will not slide laterally across each other.

forward section and shallow skirt area. As a result, this pellet gives very good penetration. The Dynamit Nobel (D. N.) Meisterkugeln flat-nosed pellet has an excellent reputation for accuracy in a wide variety of air and CO_2 guns. I have tested literally dozens of air and CO_2 guns and have never found one that did not perform acceptably well with the Meisterkugeln. It may not have given the very best accuracy, but it always has performed very near the top. Another wadcutter pellet that I favor is the D. N. Supermag. In 177 caliber, this is a heavy pellet (9.356 grains) and it is also very sturdy. This pellet has solved some sighting problems for me that occurred with guns having fixed sights. If such a gun shoots high when the sights are correctly aligned, a lower point of impact can sometimes be achieved by using a heavier pellet. I have found the Supermag has done just that in a couple of my pistols. Switching to a lighter

pellet will often raise the point of impact for guns with fixed sights that shoot low.

In addition to the wadcutter pellets described above, there are a great many others available. The Gamo Match is a rather light pellet (7.51 grains) so it generally gives slightly higher velocities than some of the others.

Domed pellets are quite popular for many uses, and in general, they hold their velocity well. Outstanding among pellets of this type is the Crosman Premier, one of the most widely used pellets in field target competition. The Premier is available in 177, 20, and 22 calibers. In 177 caliber, there are two versions, the heavy 10.5-grain and light 7.9-grain pellets. In both 20 and 22 calibers, the Premier weighs 14.3 grains. While the Premier pellets are often used in field target shooting, I have several air and CO_2 guns that do not give best accuracy with them. This is not a negative reflection on the Pre-

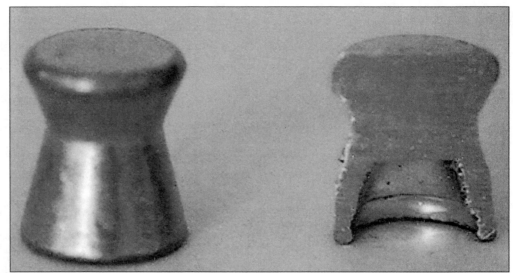

Of the classic wadcutter pellets, the Crosman Copperhead has the sturdiest construction.

Note the difference in the internal cavities of the Crosman pointed (left), Beeman Silver Jet (center), and Beeman Kodiak (right) pellets. Solid pellets penetrate better.

mier pellet. It simply shows that some airguns (like some firearms) have strong preferences in ammunition.

Another domed pellet that has given good performance in some of my guns is the D. N. Superdome. This pellet weighs 8.346 grains in 177 caliber and 14.5 grains in 22 caliber. Keep in mind that some round-nosed pellets may be too long for use in a CO_2 gun that has a rather short, thin cylinder.

Pointed pellets have been popular for many years. They hold their velocity well and they generally give good penetration. Within this general pellet type, there is a great deal of difference in the construction. The Crosman Copperhead pointed pellet is among the most solid nosed and sturdiest in design. It gives outstanding penetration. On the other hand, some of the pointed pellets (e.g., the Beeman Silver Jet and the Daisy Pointed) have very deep internal cavities and even the nose area is hollow. Such pellets tend to flatten or rivet

on impact so that penetration may not be very impressive. For some targets, not much penetration is required, so this may not be a major disadvantage. The overall length of pointed pellets is generally greater than that of either flat-nosed or domed pellets. As a result, they may not be suitable for use in CO_2 guns that hold the pellets in cylinders. One notable exception is the 22-caliber Daisy PowerLine 622X, which has a cylinder specifically designed to handle pellets of the pointed and domed types (see Chapter 8).

Another type of pellet that performs well in certain uses is the hollow point. This type has become very popular in recent years for shooting small pests and vermin. The two hollow pointed pellets I have used most extensively are the Beeman Crow Magnum and the D. N. Super-H-Point. The Crow Magnum is a rather heavy pellet in 177 and 22 calibers, weighing 8.3 grains and 18.47 grains respectively. However, in 20 caliber,

Two popular hollow pointed pellets are the Beeman Crow Magnum (left) and the Dynamit Nobel Super-H-Point (right).

Many of the CO$_2$ handguns use cylinders to hold the pellets. In some cases, the cylinders are thin so that pointed pellets are too long to allow the cylinder to rotate.

the Crow Magnum weighs 12.99 grains, which means it is rather light for that caliber. On the other hand, the D. N. Super-H-Point weighs 7.277 grains in 177 caliber and 14.32 grains in 22 caliber, which is rather light compared to the Crow Magnum.

The Beeman Crow Magnum has a generous hollow cavity that causes it to expand rapidly even at relatively low velocity. This is important where CO$_2$ guns are concerned because none of them give velocities that are very high. The Crow Magnum is one of the best pellets to use for pest shooting because it gives rapid energy deposit on the target. However, even though the Crow Magnum shoots well in almost all of my air and CO$_2$ guns, it does not give accuracy quite equal to that of several other types of pellets. In fact, it does not give the best accuracy in any gun I have tested. In spite of this, the accuracy is more than adequate for the intended uses of this pellet.

I have done less testing with the RWS Super-H-Point pellet than I have with the Crow Magnum. There seems to be no great difference in accuracy between the two types but your particular gun may perform differently. In general, velocities are higher with the Super-H-Point because it is a lighter pellet than the Crow Magnum. Keep in mind that neither of these hollow pointed pellets can be used in many of the CO$_2$ guns having cylindrical magazines.

Pellet Weights

One of the most significant characteristics of the ammunition used in CO$_2$ guns (or any type of gun for that matter) is the projectile weight. While pellet velocity is related to pellet weight, so is the trajectory. Several of the CO$_2$ pistols tested in this work do not have sights that are adjustable for elevation. This includes some of the lower-priced models but also expensive models such as the Colt 1911 and the Beretta 92 FS. I have found that a few of my pistols that do not have provision for elevation adjustment may shoot either high or low with a particular type of pellet. It is often possible to move the point of impact by selecting a heavier or lighter pellet without the sights being adjusted in any way. For centerfire handguns, a lighter bullet normally strikes lower on the target than does a heavier one when the same sight picture and setting is used. The reason is that the recoil moves the muzzle up slightly before the bullet exits and the heavier the bullet, the greater the rise of the muzzle. Since recoil is almost nonexistent for CO$_2$ pistols, a heavier pellet usually strikes lower on the target because it has lower velocity. Muzzle jump is not a factor. In some instances, I have been able to tailor the point of impact to the sight setting by selecting a pellet of a different weight.

Because pellet weight is so important, a table of weights is provided on the next page for reference. Such data is often provided by the manufacturers, but I have found that measurements published often differ from those I

Weight Determinations for 20-Pellet Samples of Various Types

Pellet	Average	Weight in Grains High	Low	Std. Dev.
177-Caliber Pellets				
Beeman Crow Magnum	8.280	8.347	8.228	0.036
Beeman Copper Point	7.409	7.451	7.361	0.023
Beeman Flathead	8.341	8.509	8.197	0.089
Beeman Hollow Point	7.191	7.306	7.111	0.060
Beeman Silver Bear	7.230	7.349	7.137	0.060
Beeman Silver Sting	8.383	8.457	8.285	0.046
Crosman Domed	7.864	7.963	7.761	0.066
Crosman Pointed	7.968	8.083	7.852	0.066
Crosman Premier (L)	7.941	8.034	7.725	0.076
Crosman Premier (H)	10.50	10.60	10.44	0.04
Crosman Premier Match	7.909	8.000	7.818	0.047
Crosman Wadcutter	7.930	8.032	7.843	0.061
Daisy Lead Free	4.980	5.103	4.912	0.047
Daisy Power Pellet	9.304	9.829	8.718	0.306
Daisy Pointed	7.143	7.318	6.981	0.079
Daisy Wadcutter	7.756	7.881	7.583	0.100
D. N. Club	6.979	7.210	6.806	0.118
D. N. FTS (Field Target)	10.47	10.70	10.31	0.096
D. N. Hobby	6.994	7.113	6.738	0.080
D.N. Meisterkugeln	8.225	8.312	8.060	0.054
D.N. Superdome	8.346	8.503	8.248	0.068
D.N. Supermag	9.356	9.460	9.268	0.082
D.N. Super-H-Point	7.277	7.350	7.219	0.046
D.N. Superpoint	7.924	8.117	7.647	0.145
Eley Target	7.504	7.548	7.455	0.027
Eley Wasp	7.521	7.562	7.469	0.022
Gamo Master Point	7.839	7.907	7.779	0.037
Gamo Hunter	7.378	7.412	7.301	0.028
Gamo Magnum	8.287	8.376	8.190	0.059
Gamo Match	7.510	7.532	7.464	0.021
Marksman Laserhawk	3.187	3.233	3.113	0.038
Predator	9.005	9.403	8.675	0.192
Winchester Hunting	7.502	7.549	7.463	0.025
20-Caliber Pellets				
Beeman Crow Magnum	12.99	13.16	12.76	0.10
Beeman H & N Match	10.32	10.39	10.20	0.05
Beeman Ram Jet	11.46	11.79	11.06	0.19
Beeman Silver Ace	12.58	12.87	12.41	0.12
Beeman Silver Arrow	15.32	15.50	15.09	0.10
Beeman Silver Bear	9.995	10.07	9.907	0.042
Beeman Silver Sting	11.17	11.40	11.06	0.09
Benjamin Diabolo	14.26	14.39	14.11	0.09
Benjamin Cylindrical	14.28	14.41	14.10	0.09
Crosman Domed	14.28	14.40	14.09	0.07
Crosman Premier	14.32	14.44	14.18	0.09
Sheridan Cyl. (new)	14.31	14.44	14.16	0.09
22-Caliber Pellets				
Beeman Crow Magnum	18.47	18.68	18.25	0.10
Beeman Kodiak	21.41	21.74	21.21	0.16
Beeman Silver Jet	14.24	14.40	14.04	0.10
Beeman Silver Sting	15.74	15.85	15.52	0.10
Benjamin Diabolo	14.24	14.37	14.13	0.07
Crosman Pointed	14.35	14.42	14.26	0.04
Crosman Premier	14.34	14.44	14.26	0.06
Crosman Wadcutter	14.32	14.46	14.20	0.07
Daisy Pointed	15.68	15.78	15.54	0.08
D. N. Hobby	12.00	12.12	11.89	0.08
D.N. Meisterkugeln	14.26	14.50	14.10	0.09
D.N. Superdome	14.49	14.57	14.38	0.05
D.N. Superpoint	14.69	14.86	14.60	0.07
D.N. Super-H-Point	14.32	14.56	14.20	0.10
Eley Wasp	14.43	14.52	14.39	0.03
Gamo Hunter	15.33	15.44	15.22	0.07
Gamo Magnum	15.41	15.51	15.25	0.07
Gamo Master Point	16.32	16.44	16.15	0.07
Gamo Match	13.88	13.95	13.78	0.05
Predator	17.02	17.41	16.53	0.26
Ruko Magnum II	15.54	15.65	15.46	0.06
Ruko Match	13.86	13.97	13.77	0.05
Winchester Hunting	15.20	15.29	15.14	0.04

D.N. is used as an abbreviation for RWS-Dynamit Nobel.

Pellet length is an important consideration.

Compare the cylinder thickness of your CO_2 gun to the lengths of pellets given in the table.

have measured on a laboratory balance (that weighs objects to four decimal places) by a significant amount. Therefore, I have listed the actual weights as they were determined for a sample of 20 pellets chosen at random. In the table, I have given the average weight as well as the highest and lowest weights for pellets in the sample. Also listed is the standard deviation, which gives a measure of the reproducibility of the weights. The smaller the standard deviation, the more uniform the pellets.

Pellet Dimensions

If you look at catalogs from companies that sell airguns and supplies, you will see there are dozens of types of pellets available. You do not need to try all types in your guns but you should try perhaps five or six. One thing to be kept in mind is that many of the CO_2 guns use cylinders that hold six, eight, or ten pellets in individual chambers. For some of the guns, the cylinders are thin enough that some pellets may be too long to chamber in the cylinder and still allow it to turn in the gun. As a result, some of the CO_2 guns can be used only with rather short pellets. Of course, the short pellets are those that have the flat nose or wadcutter design. In the chapters that give the results of testing the various CO_2 guns, the cylinder thickness is given so you can consult the table below to see which pellets have lengths greater than the thickness of the cylinders. Some guns have cylinders that will accommodate almost any type of pellet while the cylinders of others are much more restrictive.

Some pellet manufacturers list dimensions for their pellets but many do not. Moreover, I have found significant differences between what I see in print and what I obtain from my dial caliper. Accordingly, I have included on page 45 the results of my measurements on many types of 177-, 20-, and 22-caliber pellets. In each case, five pellets were selected out of the can and the measurements were taken using a dial caliper. Pellet length, head diameter, and skirt diameter were determined. The values shown in the table are the average values for the measurements on the five-pellet sample of each type.

As can be seen from the table, there are significant differences in the measurements of pellets within a given caliber. Part of the difference, especially in length, is attributable to the shape of the head. However, even for several pellets of the same general type, there can be a pronounced difference in dimensions. This fact suggests that if your particular CO_2 gun does not perform particularly well with one brand and type of pellet, you should try several others. I have noted that some of my air rifles perform much better when pellets having the larger skirt diameters are used in them. Shooting air and CO_2 guns is an experimental science so do not hesitate to try different combinations.

Specialty Pellets

If you have an interest in centerfire rifles and ammunition, you are undoubtedly aware of some of the recent developments in bullet

The Daisy Power Pellet is a 177-caliber offering that has a 0.125 inch steel ball in the nose.

This pellet is the plastic tipped 177-caliber Predator. It is also available in 22 caliber.

design and construction. There are bullets with polycarbonate tips, bonded cores, partitions, and special coatings to reduce friction. Engineering innovation has also been directed toward the development of pellets having unusual designs. One of the designs that has been around for a long time has an outer plastic sleeve or sabot and an inner core of some metal harder than lead. The idea behind this development is that lead airgun pellets tend to flatten or "rivet" when they strike a hard object. The sabot construction enables a plastic sleeve to be in contact with the barrel while the hard inner core gives good penetration. Several metals including zinc, copper, and iron have been used as cores. One such pellet that has been available for several years is known as the Prometheus. With these pellets, penetration of sheet metal or bone is significantly better than with a lead pellet.

Daisy has taken a somewhat different approach with the 177-caliber pellet known as the Daisy Power Pellet. This design has a 0.125-inch steel ball embedded in the nose of a lead body that resembles a spool. The Power Pellet is rather heavy with an average weight of 9.30 grains and it is expensive. If your rifle shoots this pellet accurately, it should be very effective on pests and small game.

The Marksman Laserhawk is an ultra-light pellet in 177 caliber. It consists of a plastic body that has a small steel ball in the nose. Because it weighs only 3.19 grains, it gives very high velocities, but it also loses velocity very rapidly.

A recent innovation in pellet design features a polycarbonate tip in a lead body. This pellet is known as the Predator, and it is available in 177 and 22 calibers. Basically, the Predator resembles a hollow-point design with a sharp pointed plastic cone in the cavity. The plastic nose cone extends into the hollow body of the pellet and is visible when the pellet is viewed from the base. My testing has showed the Predator to be sufficiently accurate for hunting applications. Predator pellets are very long due to the plastic tips. They are not suitable for use in pistols except the single-shot models.

Although it is not unique, the 177-caliber Daisy Lead Free pellet has the advantage of being just that—lead free. I don't think much lead comes off pellets into the atmosphere but some does get on hands while handling them. The Daisy Lead Free pellet is made primarily of tin so it enables a shooter to avoid contact with lead. Because it is made of a metal that is less dense than lead, the Lead Free pellet weighs only 4.98 grains. This

A Summary of the Average Dimensions of 67 Types of Pellets

Pellet	Head Diameter	Skirt Diameter	Length
		Average Dimension in Inches	
177-Caliber Pellets			
Beeman Crow Magnum	0.178	0.185	0.238
Beeman Copper Point	0.175	0.184	0.260
Beeman Flathead	0.176	0.184	0.222
Beeman Hollow Point	0.176	0.186	0.215
Beeman Silver Bear	0.176	0.186	0.219
Beeman Silver Sting	0.177	0.186	0.268
Crosman Domed	0.176	0.180	0.223
Crosman Pointed	0.175	0.183	0.226
Crosman Premier (L)	0.177	0.180	0.223
Crosman Premier (H)	0.178	0.182	0.264
Crosman Premier Match	0.176	0.181	0.204
Crosman Wadcutter	0.175	0.181	0.213
Daisy Lead Free	0.178	0.182	0.251
Daisy Pointed	0.175	0.185	0.217
Daisy Power Pellet	0.176	0.180	0.256
Daisy Wadcutter	0.176	0.185	0.206
D.N. Club	0.176	0.186	0.214
D.N. FTS	0.177	0.189	0.267
D.N. Hobby	0.176	0.186	0.211
D.N. Meisterkugeln	0.176	0.186	0.216
D.N. Superdome	0.176	0.189	0.252
D.N. Supermag	0.177	0.186	0.228
D.N. Super-H-Point	0.176	0.184	0.220
D.N. Superpoint	0.176	0.187	0.270
Eley Target	0.175	0.185	0.208
Eley Wasp	0.176	0.185	0.206
Gamo Master Point	0.178	0.185	0.275
Gamo Hunter	0.176	0.187	0.230
Gamo Magnum	0.175	0.187	0.270
Gamo Match	0.175	0.186	0.204
Predator	0.176	0.184	0.340
Winchester Hunting	0.177	0.185	0.230
20-Caliber Pellets			
Beeman Crow Magnum	0.199	0.204	0.284
Beeman H & N Match	0.199	0.204	0.230
Beeman Ram Jet	0.198	0.206	0.278
Beeman Silver Ace	0.195	0.201	0.250
Beeman Silver Arrow	0.200	0.208	0.302
Beeman Silver Bear	0.198	0.207	0.235
Beeman Silver Sting	0.195	0.209	0.298
Benjamin Diabolo	0.197	0.202	0.297
Benjamin Cylindrical	0.198	0.200	0.273
Crosman Domed	0.197	0.200	0.298
Crosman Premier	0.200	0.201	0.298
Sheridan Cyl. (new)	0.197	0.200	0.273
22-Caliber Pellets			
Beeman Crow Magnum	0.217	0.225	0.309
Beeman Kodiak	0.217	0.223	0.333
Beeman Silver Jet	0.216	0.224	0.311
Beeman Silver Sting	0.217	0.224	0.341
Benjamin Diabolo	0.215	0.222	0.269
Crosman Pointed	0.216	0.222	0.278
Crosman Premier	0.217	0.220	0.269
Crosman Wadcutter	0.215	0.222	0.251
Daisy Pointed	0.215	0.226	0.350
D. N. Hobby	0.215	0.227	0.252
D.N. Meisterkugeln	0.215	0.225	0.251
D.N. Superdome	0.216	0.225	0.298
D.N. Superpoint	0.216	0.225	0.341
D.N. Super-H-Point	0.215	0.226	0.272
Eley Wasp	0.217	0.230	0.246
Gamo Hunter	0.215	0.224	0.296
Gamo Magnum	0.214	0.225	0.349
Gamo Master Point	0.215	0.225	0.352
Gamo Match	0.214	0.226	0.258
Predator	0.217	0.219	0.444
Ruko Magnum II	0.215	0.224	0.348
Ruko Match	0.214	0.223	0.262
Winchester Hunting	0.219	0.225	0.296

D.N. is used as an abbreviation for RWS-Dynamit Nobel.

Weight Determinations for 20-BB Samples of Various Types.

Weight in Grains

	Average	Highest	Lowest	Std. Dev.
Crosman Copperhead	5.140	5.261	4.980	0.068
Crosman Premier	5.364	5.418	5.296	0.037
Crosman Premier (washed)	5.359	5.414	5.287	0.036
Daisy Max Speed	5.412	5.557	5.267	0.074
Gamo Lead	8.144	8.247	7.998	0.069

interesting pellet has a pointed shape, and it can be driven at high velocity.

While there are numerous other specialty pellets available, this brief discussion shows some of the approaches recently taken in pellet development. There are three factors to consider in regard to specialty pellets—accuracy, cost, and availability. Because of their having more complex construction, some pellets with inserts, sabots, etc. are not quite as accurate as conventional pellets. Only shooting them in your air or CO_2 gun will let you know with certainty how accurate they are in your gun. The complex structure and use of materials more expensive than lead adds to the costs. Some of the special pellets cost two or three times as much as high quality pellets of conventional construction. Some of the more exotic pellets are available only in specialty stores or by mail or Internet order.

While the pellets of special design have some obvious limitations, they are worth considering. After all, when it comes to air and CO_2 guns and accessories, my guiding principle can be stated as "so much to test, so little time."

BBs

In the early days of BB guns, getting uniform ammunition presented quite a problem. Not only has the development over the years led to excellence in pellet uniformity and design, but also the manufacture of BBs has improved enormously. While there is a seemingly endless variety of pellets available, the BB shooter has a much narrower range of ammunition. Crosman and Daisy are the largest producers of BBs and their products are outstanding. Since so much has been made of the weights and dimensions of pellets, it seemed logical to extend the data to include BBs although the number of types included is small. I do not use BBs in the quantity that I do pellets so only four types were studied. The nominal diameter of a BB is 0.175 inches and all are very close to that size. While pellets have three dimensions that need to be considered, the spherical BB has only one. Because of this, I did not measure diameters but restricted the measurements to the weights. The following table shows the data for weight determinations on a 20-BB sample of four popular types of BBs.

Crosman Premier BBs have a black coating that easily rubs off. In order to see how much difference there was in weight when the coating was removed, the same sample of 20 BBs was washed with acetone to remove the black slimy lubricant. The weights for the washed BBs are also shown in the table.

As can be seen from the above table, the various types of BBs are very uniform in weight. The data also show that removal of the black, slimy coating on Crosman Premier BBs makes a difference of only 0.005 grains in average weight. In my shooting of BB guns, I have not been able to discern that the type of BB chosen results in any significant difference in performance. This is decidedly different than the situation with guns firing pellets where there is often a considerable difference in accuracy depending on which pellet is used.

The information presented in this chapter on ammunition for use in air and CO_2 guns provides reference data to help you in the selection of ammunition for your guns. All of the data are from measurements that I carried out rather than on some manufacturer's specifications. Hopefully, you will see that not all ammunition is the same and that you have a wide selection to choose from.

CHAPTER 4

PRINCIPLES OF PROPULSION

THE BASIC PRINCIPLES of propulsion are actually quite simple. Launching a projectile makes use of a gas that has previously been compressed being allowed to expand and in the process move some object on which the gas is directed. In a firearm, solid propellant burns quickly to generate a considerable volume of gas. That gas expands to push the projectile down the bore. In a compressed air gun, the compressed air expands against the base of the pellet, forcing it down the barrel. It doesn't matter whether the air is compressed by several strokes of a pump lever or by a piston moving in a chamber behind the barrel. The multi-pump pneumatic rifles characterize the first compression technique while the latter is the procedure employed in a spring piston rifle.

There are certain other principles involved. First, there is an upper limit to the amount of work that can be done by a given amount of compressed gas. You cannot get more energy back than was used in the compression of the gas. This is one of the fundamental laws of thermodynamics. Moreover, if some of the energy stored in compressing the gas is lost due to friction of moving parts or the projectile moving down the barrel, you will actually get less energy back than was used in compression of the gas. Part of the stored energy is lost by overcoming friction. This is another of the principles of thermodynamics.

When a liquid is converted into a gas, the gas occupies a much greater volume than that occupied by the liquid. If a suitable liquid could be transferred from a reservoir to a chamber behind a pellet, the volatilization of the liquid and expansion of the gas could be used to push the projectile down the barrel. There are some requirements that the liquid must meet. First, it has to be non-toxic. It would be poor form to be squirting poisonous gas along with pellets out of your gas-powered gun. Second, the liquid has to be inexpensive. Some exotic compound that costs a week's wages for a couple shots just will not work. This requirement is somewhat relative, but shooting a pellet gun should be a rather inexpensive proposition. Third, the gas should be non-corrosive to metal parts of the gun. We want the pellet gun to last for some considerable time rather than being eaten up by a corrosive gas. Fourth, the propellant gas should be environmentally friendly. We do not want to destroy the ozone layer or cause mutations of plants and animals by shooting our gas guns.

Launching projectiles at high velocity requires high gas pressures. In fact, it is generally true that the higher the pressure, the higher the velocity a projectile can be launched. This will be discussed in greater detail later. Because of the high pressure required, the propellant must be a gas that generates a high pressure as it expands or evaporates.

A gas that meets the requirements for a propellant used for launching BBs and pellets is carbon dioxide, CO_2. The use of carbon dioxide was pioneered by Paul Giffard in France about 1889. One of the disadvantages of CO_2 is that its tendency to evaporate is

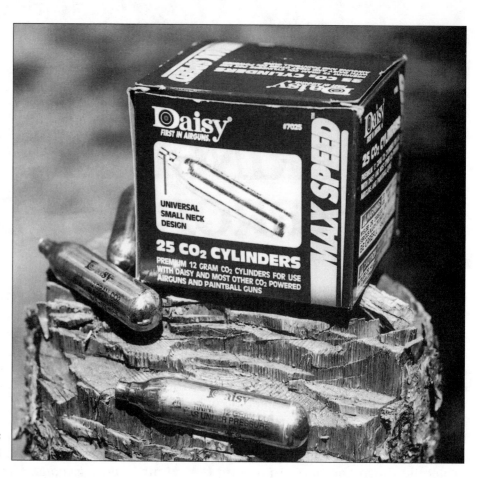

Power for a large number of shots is provided by each CO_2 cylinder.

determined by temperature. In fact, the tendency of any liquid to evaporate is determined by temperature. The higher the temperature, the greater the tendency of the liquid to evaporate. Although not a precise definition, we call the pressure generated by an enclosed evaporating liquid its vapor pressure. Because the individual particles of a liquid (molecules) differ in structure from those of a different liquid, the two liquids will have different vaporization tendencies at the same temperature. For example, the vaporization tendency of water is different from the vaporization tendency of alcohol. However, the tendency to vaporize (the vapor pressure) of all liquids increases as the temperature increases. This is a fundamental fact concerning the nature of liquids.

As a result of the vapor pressure depending on temperature, decreasing the temperature causes a decrease in the vapor pressure of a liquid. Therefore, on a cool day, a gun that makes use of the vaporization and expansion of CO_2 will not be as efficient as on a warm day. The result is the velocity given by that gun with a particular projectile will vary with the temperature of the gun. On a warm day, the velocity will be higher while the velocity will be lower on a cool day. That is a fact of life in regards to the behavior of CO_2 guns. Because the internal pressure of the liquid CO_2 guns depends on temperature, one of the basic ideas we need to understand is just how the vapor pressure of the liquid depends on temperature. Typically, the variation in vapor pressure of a liquid with temperature is shown as a graph known as a vapor pressure curve. Figure 4.1 shows this graph for CO_2.

As can be seen from the graph, the vapor pressure increases as the temperature increases. For example, the vapor pressure for CO_2 is about 850 lb/in^2 (read as pounds per square inch) when the temperature is 70° F but it is only 750 lb/in^2 at a temperature of 60° F. What this means is that with a given type of pellet and gun, the muzzle velocity will be considerably higher when the temperature is 70° F than when it is only 60° F. This will be explained and some actual examples given later in this chapter, but the bottom line is lower velocity results when CO_2 guns are used at lower temperatures.

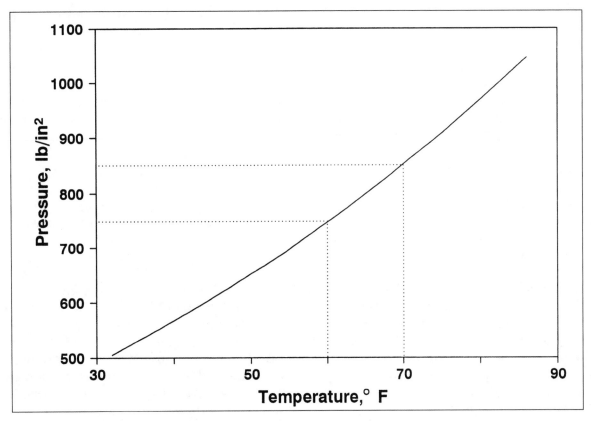

Fig. 4-1 The variation in vapor pressure of carbon dioxide with temperature.

Pressure, Work, and Energy

Any device that launches projectiles operates according to the laws of physics. You need not fear this relationship because the laws of physics are probably more familiar to you than you think. For example, you know that it takes more energy (work and energy are similar as we will explain later) to lift a 100-pound object to a height of 5 feet than it does to lift a 50-pound object to the same height. You also know that it takes more work to lift a 100-pound object to a height of 5 feet than it does to lift it to a height of 3 feet. The weight of an object is the result of the earth's gravitational field pulling on the object. An object that weighs 6 pounds on earth would weigh about 1 pound on the moon because the moon's gravitational field is only about one-sixth that of the earth's. Actually, the weight of an object on earth is just the force with which the earth is pulling on the object due to the force of gravity. For a 100-pound object, the force that the earth is exerting on the object is 100 pounds.

In this discussion, we are going to introduce a very limited amount of mathematics to describe some of the basic principles. Do not be dismayed by this because mathematics is nothing more than economy of expression where a symbol represents one or more words. A relationship between two or more quantities is most easily stated in the form of a mathematical expression. Since you are reading a book that deals with the shooting sports, it is quite likely that in your prior reading you encountered the expression for the kinetic energy (KE) of a moving projectile. That relationship is written as

$$KE = 1/2 \ mv^2$$

where KE is the kinetic energy, m is the mass of the object, and v is its velocity. We could state the principle in words as "the kinetic energy of a moving object is one-half times the mass of the object times the square of the velocity of the object." Note that the equation states the same thing more economically. Never be discouraged when you encounter a small amount of mathematical material because it is necessary to explain the basic principles that underlie our sport.

Because the shooting sports employ devices that use energy stored in some form to launch projectiles that have kinetic energy, shooting any type of gun involves converting energy from one form to another. The relationships that involve energy are central to understanding how a CO_2-powered gun operates. In this section, a brief discussion of the basic principles will be given. Of course, the guiding principle is that you cannot get more energy back than was stored initially. In fact, no mechanical device is 100% efficient, so you can never get back as much energy as was stored.

The field of study that deals with the principles of propulsion as applied to arms is known as interior ballistics. At an elementary level, we must deal with the forces involved. There is a very simple relationship that relates the amount of work done to the force that must be applied and the distance over which that force is exerted. It is stated as "the amount of work done is equal to the force exerted multiplied by the distance over which the force is applied." In the form of a mathematical equation, it is written as

$$\text{Work} = \text{Force} \times \text{Distance}$$
$$\text{or}$$
$$W = F \times D$$

where W is the work, F is the force, and D is the distance. Suppose we wish to determine the amount of work done in lifting a 100-pound object to a height of 5 feet. Using the relationship above,

$$W = 100 \text{ lbs} \times 5 \text{ ft} = 500 \text{ ft-lbs}$$

Accordingly, to lift a 100-pound object to a height of 5 feet requires 500 ft-lbs of work. Note that work in this case is expressed as foot-pounds, the units most familiar to shooters in this country. In many countries, work or energy is expressed in joules. There is no difference in the amount of milk in a jug even if in reading the label we find that 1 gallon of milk is 3.785 liters. The same amount of milk is contained in the jug but the units are different. A pellet that has a kinetic energy of 12 ft-lbs has a kinetic energy of 16.4 joules. In other words, 1 ft-lb = 1.3558 joules. If we are concerned with the kinetic energy of a pellet, why do we need to be concerned with work? The answer is because the pellet exiting the muzzle will have an energy (*kinetic* energy because it is energy due to its motion) that is precisely the same as the net amount of work done in pushing it down the barrel. The total amount of work would be greater because we have actually ignored the work lost because

of friction between the pellet and the bore but that is another matter to be dealt with later.

Where does the work (energy) come from that pushes the pellet out of the barrel? It comes from the expansion of a gas. In a firearm, the gas is generated by the burning powder. In an air rifle, the gas is the air that was previously compressed by pumping. In a CO_2-powered gun, the gas comes from the expansion of the gas and liquid in the CO_2 cylinder as it vaporizes. There is a very simple relationship between the pressure generated by the expanding gas and the amount of work done while pushing the pellet down the barrel.

Let me begin this explanation with describing what pressure is. Inside a tire the pressure may be 30 pounds per square inch (indicated as psi or lb/in²). What this means is that there is a force of 30 pounds on each square inch of area on the inside of the tire. We stated earlier that a pound is a measure of force. Therefore, pressure can be described as the force operating on something divided by the area on which the force is pushing. If the force is expressed in pounds and the area is expressed in square inches, we can write the relationship as

$$\text{Pressure} = \frac{\text{Force}}{\text{Area}} = \frac{\text{Pounds}}{\text{inches}^2} = \frac{\text{lb}}{\text{in}^2} = \text{lb/in}^2$$

Inside a CO_2 cylinder the pressure may be somewhere in the range of 800-1200 lb/in² and when the valve opens, gas having that pressure is exerted on the base of the projectile. While this is a relatively high pressure, the base of a pellet is a very small area. Also, as the pellet moves down the bore, the gas expands to fill the space behind it so the volume occupied by the gas increases. For a given quantity of gas, the larger the volume it occupies, the lower the pressure it will generate. This causes the pressure to drop rapidly as the pellet moves down the barrel and the force acting on the pellet decreases. The pressure is highest when the gas is first released from the valve and then it decreases as the pellet moves along the barrel.

If we take the base of a pellet to be a circle, it is easy to determine the area of the circle because it is given by

$$A = \pi r^2$$

Where A is the area, r is the radius of the circle, and π is 3.1416. For a pellet with a diameter of 0.177 inch, the radius is half that distance or 0.0885 inch. Thus, the area of the base of the pellet is

$$A = 3.1416 \times (0.0885 \text{ in})^2 = 0.0246 \text{ in}^2$$

If the pressure on the base of the pellet is 800 lb/in², the force acting on the pellet will be given by

$$F = 800 \text{ lb/in}^2 \times 0.0246 \text{ in}^2 = 19.7 \text{ lbs}$$

We have just calculated that a force of 19.7 lbs is exerted on the base of a 177-caliber pellet by a gas at 800 lb/in² pushing on it. If the same gas pressure were applied to the base of a 22-caliber pellet, the force on the pellet would be much greater because the area of the base is larger. In fact, the skirt diameter of most 22-caliber pellets is approximately 0.224 inch so the radius would be 0.112 inch. The area of the base of the pellet is calculated as

$$A = 3.1416 \times (0.112 \text{ in})^2 = 0.0394 \text{ in}^2$$

so the force on the base would be given by

$$F = 800 \text{ lb/in}^2 \times 0.0394 \text{ in}^2 = 31.5 \text{ lbs}$$

We see there is a much greater force pushing on the base of a 22-caliber pellet than on one of 177 caliber even though the gas pressure is 800 lb/in² in both cases. Now we need to describe how the force on the base of a pellet helps us understand how much velocity the pellet will be given as it moves down the barrel.

An exact analysis of the complex problem that deals with all the forces acting on a pellet as it is fired from an air or CO_2 gun is far beyond the level of this introductory book. What we will do is to make some crude approximations and simplifying assumptions that reduce the complex problem to a level that will allow us to use basic principles to formulate a solution. It is the standard technique of taking a complex problem you cannot solve and simplifying it to obtain one you can solve even though the new problem does not exactly describe the system.

Unfortunately, the force on the base of the pellet caused by the gas is not the only force acting on the pellet. In order for the pellet to move down the bore, it must overcome friction. The skirt of the pellet is large enough to engage the rifling, which means the pellet will become graved by the lands or ridges. Also, it requires some force to move the pellet along in contact with the barrel. While we know there is some force of friction, we do not know exactly how much it is. Furthermore, the fric-

tion would certainly depend on how fast the pellet is moving while it is in contact with the bore. We do not have a good way to determine this quantity in any simple procedure. For the sake of the simple approach being taken here, we will assume that it takes a force of 6 pounds to overcome the friction acting on the pellet as it moves through the barrel.

Now we have another problem. While the force generated by a gas at 800 lb/in² on the base of a 22-caliber pellet was calculated to be 31.5 lbs, that is only at the beginning of the movement of the pellet. As the pellet moves, the gas behind it expands to fill the available volume, which is increasing. So while the gas pressure is initially 800 lb/in², it rapidly decreases to a much lower value as the pellet approaches the muzzle. Let us suppose that the gas pressure has decreased to approximately zero by the time the pellet leaves the muzzle. Therefore, the force on the base of the pellet is initially 31.5 lb, but it has decreased to zero by the end of the motion of the pellet in the barrel. Now we have another sticky problem. How does the force vary in the interval between when the pellet starts moving and when it exits the muzzle? In this case, we can make a reasonable guess. The volume behind the pellet is a linear function of the distance the pellet travels. In other words, when the pellet has moved ten inches, there is twice as much volume available for the gas to occupy as when the pellet has moved only five inches. Because this is true, the pressure would vary linearly between the initial value of 31.5 lb/in² and zero, just before the pellet exits from the bore. Therefore, the average force acting on the pellet is the average of 31.5 and 0 which is $(31.5 + 0)/2 = 15.7$ lbs.

While this is the average force on the base of the pellet, there is a loss of 6 pounds because of friction. This leaves a net force on the pellet of 15.7 - 6 = 9.7 lbs. We showed earlier that the work done by a force is given by the force times distance. If we take the barrel length to be 20 inches or 1.667 feet, the work in this case is given by

$$\text{Work} = 9.7 \text{ lbs} \times 1.667 \text{ ft} = 16.2 \text{ ft-lbs}$$

Since this is the amount of work or energy given to the pellet, it should also be the kinetic energy the pellet has when it exits the muzzle, its muzzle energy. However, we know that a 22-caliber pellet gun such as the Cros-

Because the velocity produced by a CO_2 gun depends on temperature, I always record both temperature and velocity.

man 2260 will drive a 14.3-grain pellet at approximately 600 ft/sec (depending on the temperature), which corresponds to a muzzle energy of 11.4 ft-lbs. This value is considerably lower than the calculated value of 16.2 ft-lbs based on our several assumptions.

There are several factors not considered in our simplistic approach, all of which reduce the amount of work done on the pellet, which in turn decreases the muzzle energy. First, because of friction, the pellet becomes warmer as it moves down the bore. Therefore, some of the work done by the expanding gas is lost as heat in the pellet and bore. Second, most gases, and CO_2 is one of them, become cooler when they expand quickly. As a result of cooling, the pressure drops compared to what it would be if the gas stayed at the same temperature as it expands. Therefore, the cooling effect reduces the amount of work or energy available to the gas for moving the pellet. Third, as the pellet moves down the bore, the pressure drops. We assumed it dropped to zero at the muzzle when the barrel has a length of 20 inches. However, my Crosman 2250, which has a barrel slightly greater than 14 inches, gives velocities within 10-25 ft/sec of those given by my Crosman 2260, which has a 24-inch barrel. It appears the gas has done almost all of its useful work in the first 14-16 inches. Incidentally, this has been verified by other experimenters. If a 30-inch barrel were placed on a Crosman 2260 with no other modification, the muzzle velocity would probably be lower than with the standard 24-inch barrel. The pressure due to the gas released would drop to zero before the pellet traveled the 30 inches and friction would cause it to lose velocity.

The first two of the factors considered above probably have a very small effect on the velocity of the pellet. The third factor is likely to be much larger. Let us assume this is the factor we need to incorporate into our simple model. If the average force that we calculated (9.7 lbs) is acting on the pellet but for only 15 inches (which is 1.25 ft), the calculation of the work done on the pellet becomes

Work = 9.7 lbs x 1.25 ft = 12.1 ft-lbs

Keep in mind the net amount of work done on the pellet by the expanding gas should equal the kinetic energy with which the pellet leaves the muzzle. The amount of work calculated above is very close to the approximately 11.4 ft-lbs that a Crosman 2260 will actually produce. The significance of this approach is to show that we actually have a reasonably good understanding of the basic science involved in the principles of propulsion in regard to CO_2 guns. It is not a highly accurate model, but it is useful for predicting how changing variables will affect the performance of CO_2-powered rifles and pistols.

Effect of Temperature

We have already explained that the efficiency of a gun powered by CO_2 decreases as the temperature decreases. In order to show this is true, data were obtained by firing a 22-

caliber single-shot Crosman 2240 pistol at 68° F and 80° F. This pistol was selected because it gives excellent velocity uniformity, and being a single shot, there is no gas loss due to a gap between the magazine and the barrel breech. The two pellets used were the Crosman Copperhead pointed and the Gamo Match. Five-shot strings were fired with each pellet, and the average velocity and the standard deviation were determined.

The average velocity obtained at 68° F with the Crosman Copperhead pointed pellet was 443 ft/sec with a standard deviation of 7 ft/sec. At 80° F with the same pellet, the average velocity was 460 ft/sec with a standard deviation of 3 ft/sec. When the Gamo Match pellet was used, the average velocity at 68° F was 440 ft/sec and the standard deviation was 3 ft/sec. At 80° F, the average velocity was 470 ft/sec with a standard deviation of 1 ft/sec. The average velocities for each pellet at the two temperatures are clearly outside the range of shot-to-shot variation and indicate the velocity loss of approximately 20-30 ft/sec accompanies a temperature change from 80° F to 68° F. Certainly no claim is going to be made that this is an exhaustive study, but it does put some actual numbers to the well-known effect that the velocity produced by a CO_2-powered gun decreases as the temperature decreases.

Effect of Rate of Fire

Owner manuals frequently contain some statement that performance decreases when shots are fired rapidly due to the cooling effect of the expanding CO_2. This effect was not exhaustively studied because most shooting activities involve skill rather than firepower. One simple test that was conducted was to load a Crosman 2210 with a cylinder (seven shots) containing Crosman Copperhead wadcutter pellets. The seven shots were fired at 5-second intervals using a fresh CO_2 cylinder and the velocity measured with a chronograph. Measured velocities in ft/sec at an atmospheric temperature of 80-82° F were as follows:

Shot	1	2	3	4	5	6	7
	394	385	375	364	357	350	349

It is clear when shots are fired as fast as every 5 seconds, the velocity decreases substantially. The fact the velocity seems to stabilize at approximately 350 ft/sec may indicate

that with the air temperature being as high as it was the day of the test, the CO_2 cylinder does not fall below some specific temperature. If you fire a CO_2 pistol or rifle rapidly, the velocity decreases with each shot. This effect is not conducive to accurate shooting or to obtaining the best performance from a CO_2-powered gun. Keep in mind this test was conducted with a 22-caliber Crosman 2210, so the results obtained with a different pistol might be somewhat different. However, there is no question that cooling due to rapid firing takes a toll on the performance of any CO_2 gun.

If a CO_2-powered pistol or rifle is fired rapidly, expansion of the gas causes the cylinder to cool markedly. By shooting rapidly to empty a cylinder then quickly removing the grip panel, I have observed frost on the outside of the very cold CO_2 cylinder.

Shots Per Cylinder

Most CO_2 guns are designed so that the cylinder holding the gas must be small. In fact, the standard gas cylinder is the 12-gram CO_2 cylinder. When this quantity of liquid CO_2 is converted to a gas in small amounts with each shot, the 12-gram cylinder contains enough CO_2 for a relatively large number (25-50) of shots.

One of the most frequently asked questions regarding CO_2 guns is how many shots a cylinder of CO_2 will give. Owner manuals and manufacturer catalogs generally give a wide range such as 30-60 shots. In conducting the tests for this book, the number of shots per cylinder was determined for a Walther CP99 pistol. The tests were conducted at a temperature of 80° F with 2 minutes between shots to allow for temperature equilibration. The results for the Walther CP99 shooting Crosman Copperhead wadcutter pellets are shown in the following table.

How many shots can you get from a CO_2 cylinder? There is no easy answer, but I would say for the Walther CP99 the number is approximately 45 because the velocity is still approximately 300 ft/sec after that many shots. However, it depends on what you are attempting to do with the pistol. For plinking pop cans, 300 ft/sec is still a respectable velocity adequate for the job. If you are trying to get small groups by doing very accurate shooting, the number is smaller. To get a high level of accuracy, the shots must be of uniform

Velocity (ft/sec) Variation With Number of Shots
(Crosman Wadcutter pellets, 80° F).

Shot No.	Velocity	Shot	Velocity	Shot	Velocity
1	356	19	—	37	335
2	—	20	365	38	326
3	371	21	365	39	313
4	378	22	364	40	321
5	370	23	349	41	308
6	366	24	371	42	316
5	364	25	—	43	295
8	369	26	362	44	305
9	367	27	356	45	278
10	368	28	352	46	280
11	353	29	342	47	280
12	351	30	357	48	283
13	363	31	355	49	285
14	360	32	340	50	269
15	370	33	327	51	252
16	366	34	330	52	244
17	352	35	336	53	240
18	360	36	—	54	222

No velocity indicates chronograph malfunction.

velocity and the velocity has decreased substantially (about 10%) after only about 35 shots. In casual shooting for fun, you may squeeze out more shots per cylinder than you would if engaged in serious shooting. In the test, the velocity was recorded for only 54 shots because by that time the velocity had decreased to only about 60% of what it was for a full cylinder. Keep in mind this test involved only one pistol and one pellet type. Different combinations of gun and pellet will give somewhat different results.

Pellet Weight and Velocity

The concept that it takes more force to move a heavy object than it does to move a light one is not difficult to understand. When this concept is applied to CO_2 guns, it simply means that a heavy pellet will not be given a velocity as high as will a lighter one. Because the pressure of the gas determines the magnitude of the force on the base of the pellet, there is no way to increase it as long as the temperature does not change. There is only a certain force that can be applied by a gas at a fixed pressure. If a heavier pellet is used, the velocity will be lower as long as there is no major difference in the type of pellet used.

In order to show the effect of pellet weight on velocity, I used the 20-caliber Sheridan E9A pistol and selected seven types of pellets that had weights ranging from 10.00 to 14.32 grains. With each of these types of pellets, five shots were fired across the chronograph at 2-minute intervals to allow the pistol to reach temperature equilibrium. The temperature at the time of firing was 80-82° F. The average velocity was calculated for each type of pellet, and a graph was prepared showing pellet velocity versus pellet weight. Figure 4.2 shows the relationship. There is a reasonably good linear relationship between the muzzle velocity of a pellet and its weight. The relationship is an inverse one because as pellet weight increases, muzzle velocity decreases. Even though this type of relationship is expected, it is reassuring to see it demonstrated. When you consider that Newton's Second Law of Motion says that force equals mass times acceleration,

$$F = ma,$$

there is no other conclusion possible. Force and mass probably need no explanation, but the acceleration, a, is a measure of how fast the velocity is changing. For a given magnitude of force, if m increases, a must decrease because the two multiplied together must equal the same number, F. If the acceleration of the pellet in the barrel is lower, the velocity does not increase as rapidly, and the pellet will exit the muzzle with a lower velocity.

It is even more remarkable that the relationship between pellet weight and velocity is so nearly linear when you consider that sev-

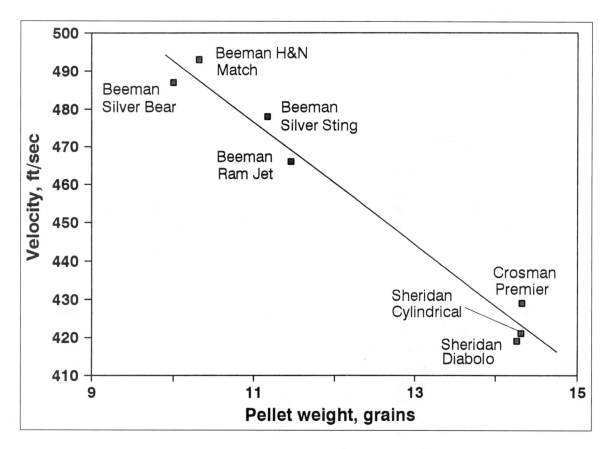

Fig. 4-2 Velocity variation with pellet weight for the Sheridan E9A.

eral types of pellets have considerably different construction characteristics. As was shown in Chapter 3, pellets of the same caliber have different head and skirt diameters. There is also a considerable difference in the shapes and sizes of the internal cavities. When these differences are considered, such a good linear fit to the data may be surprising. However, the major difference between how pellets are accelerated as they pass through the bore is in their masses. The other factors mentioned are not nearly as important as is the amount of mass that must be forced from a standing start to a considerable velocity. The two major factors that determine pellet velocity from a CO_2 gun are the mass of the pellet and the temperature.

The simple ideas here are not restricted to gas pressure generated by CO_2. In fact, we should expect this type of relationship for any type of air or CO_2 gun. The dependence of velocity on the weight of the pellet has been demonstrated for many types of air guns.

Firearms constitute a somewhat different situation because different propellants are normally used for light and heavy bullets. The propellants have different burning rates so the pressure does not vary in the same way as the bullet moves. Normally, faster burning propellants are used in loading a 30-06 with 125-grain bullets than would be chosen to load 200-grain bullets. We have no such choice to make with a CO_2 gun in which the pressure forcing the pellet down the barrel is the same regardless of the weight of pellet used, and the propellant gas generates a specific pressure at the temperature of use.

While only basic ideas dealing with internal ballistics of CO_2 guns have been considered, this chapter should enable you to understand how principles of propulsion apply to these fascinating guns. Probably most shooters will be content to insert a CO_2 cylinder and some pellets and go shooting. This chapter is for those shooters who want (or need) to know more about how their CO_2 guns propel pellets.

CHAPTER 5

EVALUATION OF BB PISTOLS

SOME OF THE CO_2 BB pistols function in a true semi-automatic mode rather than as revolvers because the BBs are not held in a cylinder. As was discussed earlier, the majority of pellet pistols are repeaters, but the pellets are held internally in a revolving cylinder. They actually function as revolvers regardless of whether firing is done single action or double action. However, the pistols that fire BBs hold the ammunition in linear magazine tubes with each BB forced into the chamber by a spring-loaded magazine follower. Pulling the trigger cocks the internal mechanism and releases it. Therefore, the BB pistols function exactly like double-action-only semi-auto firearms. This is true of all the current pistols tested that fire BB ammunition but not for the classic Daisy CO_2 200 and the manually cocked Daisy PowerLine 1200, 1270, and 1700 (see Chapter 10).

I grew up with a BB gun that was fired by cocking it with a lever and pulling the trigger. Those single-stroke guns, as well as their modern counterparts, give a muzzle velocity of only about 275-300 ft/sec. As a result of extensive handling of such BB guns, it is easy to get the notion that any gun that fires only BBs is a low powered device. Because carbon dioxide generates a pressure of around 800 lb/in^2 at typical temperatures of use, it is possible to launch a BB at a velocity as high as 500 ft/sec. Accordingly, the actual kinetic energy of a BB fired from a CO_2 pistol may be almost three times as great as that of a BB fired from a typical spring powered rifle. NEVER make the mistake of thinking that a CO_2-powered BB gun is a toy! I will make this point repeatedly, but I don't believe it can be stated too emphatically or too often. These pistols generate about the same energy as the 177-caliber pellet pistols discussed in the next two chapters. Moreover, steel BBs are notorious for ricochet because they do not expend energy by flattening out on impact.

The discussion of the 177-caliber pellet pistols will be presented in two chapters because there is such a wide range of models, with plastic pistols costing only a few dollars at one end and the metal guns that resemble firearms at the other. Some of the elegant upper-end models cost $200 or more. In Chapter 6 we will discuss the lower-priced models while Chapter 7 will be concerned with the higher-priced elite models. In contrast, only one chapter is needed for the BB pistols because there are only a few models of BB-only pistols and they are all modest in cost. That is not to say they don't perform well because they certainly do. It is just that the BB pistols are not made with the same level of excellence in choice of materials and fit and finish as the upper-end pellet pistols. They are comparable to some of the less expensive 177-caliber models discussed in Chapter 6.

While it was not possible for me to test every model of BB pistol marketed, the selection chosen includes the most popular models. Performance of models not tested should be comparable to that of the several models discussed in this chapter. In the descriptions that follow, instructions are given for installing a CO_2 cylinder and loading each of the models. Although is it not stated explicitly in the discussion of each model, the safety should always be in the "on" position when loading a CO_2 cylinder or BBs. There is danger in piercing a CO_2 cylinder in a gun that might already have BBs or pellets in it or in placing projectiles in a gun that is pressurized with a pierced CO_2 cylinder.

The Daisy PowerLine 15XT

Introduced in 2002, the Daisy PowerLine 15XT CO_2 BB pistol resembles a compact centerfire semi-auto. I think everything externally visible on the pistol is made of black plastic. The 15XT is one of the two smallest of the CO_2 pistols evaluated.

Daisy's PowerLine 15XT is a lightweight BB pistol that resembles a compact firearm.

The PowerLine 15XT has cosmetic features that make it look like a firearm. The large thumb safety and slide release on the left-hand side of the frame and the hammer are fakes. They are simply molded plastic lumps. The actual safety is of the cross bolt type, and it is located behind the trigger. Pushing it to the right places the safety on while pushing it to the left takes it off and exposes a red firing indicator.

Unlike the Daisy PowerLine 93, which has a removable magazine, the magazine of the 15XT, which holds 15 BBs, is built in. It is located on the top left-hand side of the fake slide. A small tab that protrudes slightly from a slot is attached to the spring-loaded magazine follower. Pushing the tab forward in the slot moves the magazine follower so that BBs can be dropped into a hole that is about two-thirds of the way toward the front end of the slot. There is no provision for locking the magazine follower in its forward position so it must be held there while BBs are loaded.

Sights on the PowerLine 15XT consist of a square-topped front and a square-notch rear. The sights are very similar in appearance to those found on fixed-sighted Colt 1911 pistols, and there is no provision for adjustment. There is also a dovetailed bar below the barrel where optical (laser) sights can be attached.

BBs are loaded in the PowerLine 15XT by pulling the magazine follower forward, holding it there, and dropping BBs in the opening.

Type of BB	Velocity, ft/sec			
	Ave.	High	Low	Std. Dev.
Daisy Max Speed	432	435	428	3
Crosman Copperhead	424	427	419	4
Crosman Premier	437	442	433	3

In this photo, the piercing pin can be seen at the top of the grip frame of the 15XT.

The PowerLine 15XT is a double-action-only pistol. As a result, trigger movement during firing is rather long, but my 15XT specimen probably has the best double-action pull of all the "auto" pistols I have tested. The pull averaged about 6.8 pounds and was smooth throughout trigger travel.

Loading a CO_2 cylinder in the PowerLine 15XT consists of removing the left-hand grip panel by pushing outward on the tab located at the bottom and placing the cylinder neck up in the grip. Piercing of the CO_2 cylinder is accomplished by turning the piercing screw, which has a large, comfortable, plastic head in the shape of a wing nut.

There are several subjective things that I like about the PowerLine 15XT. First, it is small, light, and portable. It measures only 7.25 inches in length and weighs only 13.3 ounces. Second, the black plastic grips have excellent feel and they are quite attractive. The

checkering on the grips and on the back strap gives a good purchase in the hand. Finally, even though the CO_2 cylinder is contained in the grip, it still has a very nice contour. It fits my hand much better than do the bulky grips on some other CO_2 pistols. My wife liked the weight and feel of the 15XT so much that she almost kept it. Like some other CO_2 pistols marketed by Daisy, the PowerLine 15XT carries the "made in Japan" statement.

Even though it is small, this attractive little pistol is no toy. It has an advertised muzzle velocity of 400 ft/sec. As shown by velocity the data in the accompanying table, this is actually a conservative value.

The PowerLine 15XT is a handy, light-weight pistol that fires BBs with high and uniform velocity. My 15XT easily exceeded the advertised maximum velocity. A few minor things came to light during the tests with this pistol. First, the tab on the magazine follower is very small and it hardly protrudes from the slot in which it moves. Because there is no notch for locking it in the forward position while loading BBs, it must be held with one thumb while BBs are inserted into the tiny loading port. This is not the easiest BB pistol to load. However, there is no removable magazine to drop or lose. Second, while the trigger action is not bad for the double action only firing, it will require some skill to shoot this pistol accurately.

For a pistol that measures only 7 inches in length and weighs only about 13 ounces, the PowerLine 15XT offers outstanding performance. Incidentally, the suggested retail price is about $36, although the actual price is usually below $30; so it offers a lot of fun for the money.

The Daisy PowerLine 93 and 693

Patterned after a Smith & Wesson center-fire autoloader, the Daisy PowerLine Model 93 is a 15-shot BB pistol. The external parts of the Model 93 are made largely of black

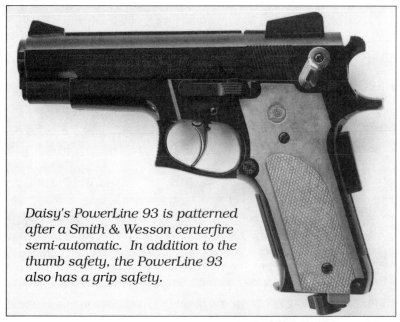

Daisy's PowerLine 93 is patterned after a Smith & Wesson centerfire semi-automatic. In addition to the thumb safety, the PowerLine 93 also has a grip safety.

The magazine release is located in front of the rear sight between the protective ears.

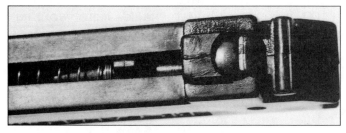

Pressing downward on the ridged tab opens the port for loading BBs in the magazine of a PowerLine 93 or 693.

plastic and the grips are brown plastic with imprinted checkering. A second version known as the PowerLine 693 has a shiny nickel finish on the frame but black plastic slide and grips. Otherwise, the Models 93 and 693 are identical.

The PowerLine 93 can be fired only in the double-action mode. Pulling the trigger com-pletely cycles the action and fires the gun. The hammer is a fake that is a molded lump at the back of the fake slide. The only external parts of the pistol that move are the trigger, thumb safety, and the grip safety. Although not often found on CO_2 pistols, the PowerLine 93 has a functioning grip safety, a bar in the rear of the grip that must be depressed in order for the pistol to fire. The trigger can be pulled without the grip safety being depressed but the pistol does not fire. A Model 93 weighs only 17.6 ounces.

BBs are held in an in-line magazine located on top of the barrel. A serrated magazine release is located just behind the magazine and in front of the rear sight between its protective ears. Pulling the release to the rear allows the rear end of the magazine to pop up out of the recess where it resides. After the magazine is lifted out of its opening on top of the barrel, BBs are loaded in the following manner.

When the magazine is turned bottom side up, a groove is visible in which the spring-loaded follower moves to push BBs to the rear during firing. Pushing the follower forward by means of a small protruding tab allows it to be locked in the forward position when the tab is positioned in a locking notch. After the follower is locked in the forward position, pushing down on a small bar at the rear of the magazine moves a tab that normally covers the BB port. This allows BBs to be dropped into the hole that loads the magazine. The spring-loaded bar must be held down during the loading process to keep the BB port open. After the BBs are loaded, pushing the magazine follower tab out of its locking notch allows it to apply pressure to the BBs for proper feeding. When the magazine is placed in the gun, the bar at the rear of the magazine is forced upward uncovering the BB port so that BBs can drop down to enter the rear of the barrel.

Sights on the Model 93 consist of a square-topped ramp front and a blade rear with a square notch. The rear sight has protective "ears" and the front ramp is serrated. The sights afford an excellent sight picture, but there is no adjustment possible other than possibly to change the height of either sight by filing off some plastic.

To load a CO_2 cylinder in the gun, the left-hand grip panel is removed by pushing outward on the tab at the base. After the grip panel is removed, a CO_2 cylinder can be inserted into the metal chamber inside the grip. Turning the screw with a winged head in the bottom of the grip forces the cylinder up to the piercing pin. With a loaded magazine and a fresh CO_2 cylinder in place, the PowerLine 93 is ready to fire.

The thumb-operated safety consists of a rotating lever at the rear left-hand side of the slide. When it points down, the safety is on. Rotating the safety upward takes it off, and the pistol is ready to fire. The main drawback to achieving good accuracy with this pistol is the long, heavy, uneven trigger pull. As the trigger is pulled, the barrel moves to the rear inside the fake slide to position it at the CO_2 valve. This requires a lot of trigger pressure. Then, the actual firing occurs, which requires an even greater pull. The result is that these double-action-only pistols have long, heavy trigger pulls. For my Model 93, the Lyman trigger pull gauge showed an average pull of 8.5 pounds, and my Model 693 required 9.7 pounds. The Models 93 and 693 are by no means alone with this fault and more will be

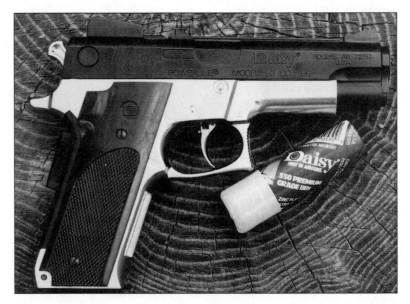

The PowerLine 693 is an attractive CO_2 pistol that functioned flawlessly during testing.

described in the sections dealing with other pistols. With fixed sights and rough trigger action, this pistol would normally be considered as a plinking or fun gun. With an advertised muzzle velocity of 400 ft/sec (which the gun just about equals), it definitely is not a toy. The results obtained during the velocity tests are shown in the tables below.

As mentioned earlier, the PowerLine 93 and 693 are identical except for colors of the plastic parts. Therefore, it is interesting to compare how two identical BB pistols compare mechanically. As the data shows, the velocities are very close with each type of BB used in the tests. The advertised muzzle velocity of 400 ft/sec is almost exactly what you can

Velocity Data for the Daisy PowerLine 93 at 73-75°F

Type of BB	Ave.	High	Low	Std. Dev.
		Velocity, ft/sec		
Daisy Max Speed	393	400	388	5
Crosman Copperhead	393	398	389	4
Crosman Premier	396	400	394	2

Velocity Data for the Daisy PowerLine 693 at 73-75°F

Type of BB	Ave.	High	Low	Std. Dev.
		Velocity, ft/sec		
Daisy Max Speed	397	401	393	3
Crosman Copperhead	401	405	397	3
Crosman Premier	402	405	400	2

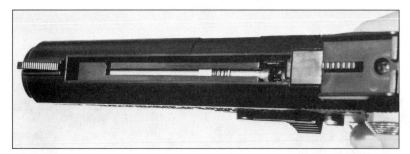

The 15-shot inline magazine is held in a recess along the top of the barrel.

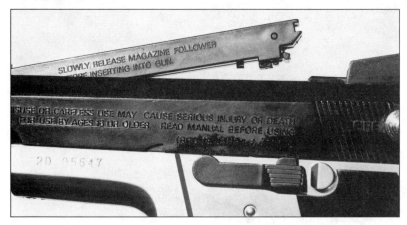

A magazine is placed in the PowerLine 693 front end first and locked in place by pressing it down into the frame.

expect from these fine guns. For CO_2 pistols that sell in the $40-$50 range, I was pleasantly surprised by the uniformity of velocity.

The magazine used in the Daisy PowerLine 93 and 693 is an in-line device that is held in a recess along the top of the barrel. I had wondered about the reliability of the magazine to feed, but my concern was misplaced. Feeding with both pistols throughout the tests involved absolutely no malfunctions, even with the Crosman Premier BBs that have a slimy black coating. This was not true for some of the other pistols.

The Crosman Auto Air II

For several years, a pistol was available in 22 Winchester Magnum Rimfire (WMR) caliber from AMT. The Crosman Auto Air II has a styling that imitates that pistol. The Auto Air II is a 17-shot BB pistol that fires semi-automatically in double action. Pulling the trigger accomplishes the complete firing process. In some ways, the AutoAir II is an offspring of the earlier Crosman 454 and 1600 models that were made of metal (see Chapter 10).

Do not be misled by the rather cosmic appearance of this CO_2 pistol. Despite the fact this pistol is listed as weighing 13 ounces (mine weighs 12.7 ounces on my postal scale without a CO_2 cylinder in place), it has a 10.75-inch barrel. As a result, the advertised velocity for the Auto Air II is 480 ft/sec. This is a real BB launcher! Moreover, the long, smooth bore barrel tips up at the rear so that pellets can be loaded in a single-shot fashion. Advertised velocity with pellets is a respectable 430 ft/sec.

BBs are loaded in the Auto Air II by pulling forward the magazine follower by means of a pin that protrudes from a groove on the right-hand side of the barrel and rotating it to engage the pin in the retaining notch. With the spring-loaded magazine follower locked in its forward position and the pistol turned upside down, BBs can be dropped into a hole in front of the trigger guard. Releasing the magazine follower pin from its retaining notch allows it to move to the rear to place pressure on the BBs in the magazine.

Pellets are loaded by grasping the two grooved plastic barrel releases on either side of the breech and pinching inward. This unlatches the spring-loaded barrel. Being pivoted at the front end, the barrel is tipped up to elevate it out of the frame. A single pellet can be inserted into the breech and the barrel depressed until it latches in place. We

The lightweight Crosman AutoAir II BB pistol provides reliable performance at a low price.

Pinching inward on the flexible ridged knobs releases the barrel.

then have a 177-caliber smooth bore pellet launcher.

The fake hammer is a plastic lump. The serrations on the slide are purely cosmetic. Everything visible is black plastic except the wing-headed piercing screw and the screws that hold the piece together.

Loading a CO_2 cylinder involves removing the right-hand grip panel. A small recess at the base of the panel allows a finger hold to apply pressure. When the grip panel is off, insert a CO_2 cylinder neck up into the grip. Replace the grip panel and turn the piercing screw to push the CO_2 cylinder up onto the piercing pin.

A raised portion sits astride the barrel just in front of the trigger guard. There is a flat-topped rectangular portion that can be used to mount a red dot or laser sight. The sides of this raised area have grooved sections that function as the barrel release. These sections are flexible and pinching them toward each other causes the latches to disengage.

Having discussed the general features of the Auto Air II, we are brought to the subject of sights. Here we find excellence in airgun sights on a pistol of modest cost. The front sight is a wide ramp with a red highlighted face. The rear sight is a blade with an outstanding square notch having white dots on

After the barrel is unlatched, it tips up at the rear.

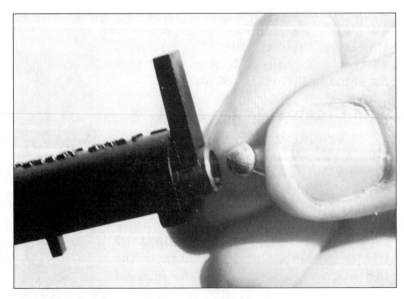

Any type of pellet can be inserted in the breech after the barrel is tipped upward.

Velocity Data for the Crosman AutoAir II at 73-75°F

Type of BB	Velocity, ft/sec			
	Ave.	High	Low	Std. Dev.
Daisy Max Speed	459	468	455	5
Crosman Copperhead	435	442	428	6
Crosman Premier	385	400	375	10

The AutoAir II has excellent sights. The rear sight is fully adjustable.

either side. As a final touch of class, the rear sight is fully adjustable! The sights on this pistol make me realize just how bad the sights are on some other CO_2 pistols. There are no gimmicks, just excellent target sights.

The safety on the Auto Air II is of the cross-bolt type and it is located at the front of the trigger guard. Pushing it to the right puts the safety on and pushing it to the left takes it off and exposes a red firing indicator. At least on my specimen, it is not likely the safety will change positions accidentally because considerable pressure is required to move it. The rather long double-action trigger pull measured 7.6 pounds on my AutoAir II, which is rather light for a double-action pistol. The trigger pull is better than on some of the pistols that cost much more when they are also fired double action.

Velocity determinations for the Crosman AutoAir II gave the results shown in the accompanying table.

The velocity data shown in the table illustrate an important principle. Never assume your air

or CO_2 gun will perform equally well with every type of ammunition you feed it. My AutoAir II did not like Crosman Premier BBs and it showed that fact by giving velocities much lower than either the Crosman Copperhead or Daisy Max Speed BBs. I have absolutely nothing to offer by way of explanation. That is just the way it turned out. Incidentally, the advertised velocity is up to 480 ft/sec with BBs and up to 430 with pellets loaded one at a time. I measured the velocity of the Crosman Copperhead wadcutter at 400 ft/sec. With either BBs or pellets this lightweight pistol shoots hard and costs $30-$35 at Crosman dealers.

During the firing of many shots with the AutoAir II, it became apparent the trigger does not fit my finger. It actually became uncomfortable to pull the trigger in the long double-action mode. As mentioned earlier, sights on the AutoAir II are excellent, and the in-line magazine is easier to load than those on most other BB pistols. This is a competent BB pistol that is also easy on the budget.

The Gamo P-23

Small, sleek, and sturdy are terms that characterize the Gamo P-23 CO_2 BB pistol. Its profile is similar to that of the famous Walther PPK pistol. There are various fake parts molded into the gun to make it have a realistic appearance.

The Gamo P-23 is 7.5 inches long, weighs 16 ounces and has a 4.25-inch barrel. It can be fired only in a double-action mode. The position of the safety is unique. It is located on the left-hand side of the pistol very near the front. A rotating safety lever points to the rear when the safety is on and toward the front when the safety is off. Rotating the lever downward to make it point forward takes the safety off and readies the pistol for firing. Both the location of the safety and the fact

The Gamo P-23 is an attractive CO_2 pistol that is a comfortable size for carry and use.

that it must be rotated 180° are unusual features.

Loading a CO_2 cylinder in the Gamo P-23 involves removing the left-hand grip panel, inserting a CO_2 cylinder neck up in the grip, and turning the folding-head piercing screw to force the CO_2 cylinder upward. Like some of the other BB repeaters, BBs are held in an in-line magazine with pressure applied by a spring-loaded follower. But that is where the similarity to other BB pistols ends.

The Gamo P-23 has a metal barrel and barrel shroud, which tip up as a unit. The magazine that holds up to 12 BBs is located in the frame under the barrel. A barrel latch is located on the rear of the shroud on the left-hand side. Pulling the latch forward unlocks the barrel so it can be raised at the rear. With the barrel tipped up, a raised rib that runs the length of the frame is visible. A red plastic tab is located on the right-hand side of the rib. That red tab is attached to a red, spring-loaded rod that is the magazine follower. Pushing the red tab to its forward

On the Gamo P-23, the safety is a rotating lever on the left-hand side near the front of the frame.

position brings it to a slot in the top of the rib. Turning the red tab upward into the slot locks the magazine follower in its forward position. In this position, the magazine follower is in front of the hole in the top of the rib where BBs are loaded. The magazine can now be loaded with BBs and the magazine follower can be released from its retaining notch to place pressure on the BBs. If you forget to release the magazine follower from its notch, closing the barrel pushes the red tab out of

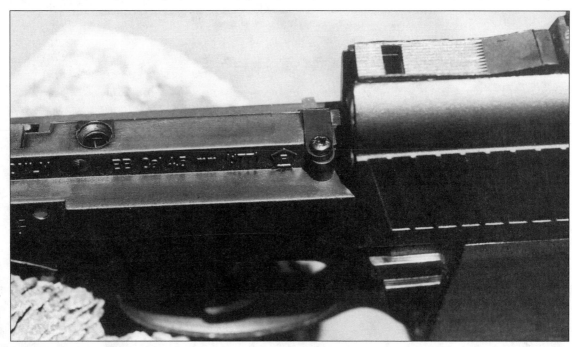

The magazine is located in the frame under the barrel on the Gamo P-23.

the notch automatically. Loading BBs was somewhat awkward because the barrel has a tendency to close on your fingers when you tip the muzzle upward to allow the BBs to slide into the magazine. The Gamo Auto 45 (discussed next) also shares this problem.

When the barrel is tipped up, a small, rectangular, fixed prong projects downward from the right-hand side. As the barrel is closed, you can see this prong enters a rectangular recess in which there appears, just below the surface, a small, rectangular, spring-loaded tab. When the barrel is closed, the fixed prong pushes downward on the spring-loaded tab in the recess. When the barrel is raised, the reverse action occurs. The moving tab in the recess is connected to a safety that prevents the trigger from being pulled while the barrel is raised. This safety prevents the discharge of a blast of CO_2 while the action is open. Of course, the pistol cannot be fired when the safety lever points toward the rear (the "on" position) even when the barrel is closed.

Sights on the Gamo P-23 are missing only one feature to be almost ideal for a pistol of this type. That feature is elevation adjustment in the rear sight. The rear sight is adjustable for windage by sliding it laterally in its dovetail notch after loosening the Allen head locking screw. Overall, the square post and square notch give an excellent sight picture. On top of the barrel shroud is a rib that

has grooves along the edges so that a red dot or laser sight can be mounted.

Even though the Gamo P-23 can be fired double action only, it has a moving, recessed metal hammer. Most of the pistols of this type have no visible hammer or have a fake one.

Finally, there is one other feature of the P-23 that impresses me. Unlike other BB pistols, it has a rifled barrel. Because the barrel can be tipped up at the rear, a 177-caliber pellet can be inserted and the pistol becomes a single-shot pellet pistol. The Gamo Auto 45 (described next) also has this feature. The Crosman Auto Air II can also be used as a single-shot pellet pistol, but it has a smooth bore.

Double-action firing of the Gamo P-23 requires considerable pressure on the trigger. According to my measurement, the weight of pull is 7.1 pounds. For me, the trigger is too small and has a tip that is too sharp, so I do not find it comfortable. Also, when the trigger releases at the end of its travel there is a rather violent release because of the tension applied and that invariably jerks the muzzle laterally. In spite of this, the Gamo P-23 is a well-designed pistol.

Problems were encountered during the velocity testing. Although there is a statement to use only lead BBs in this pistol, they would not load or feed properly. While it functioned flawlessly with Daisy Max Speed BBs, my Gamo P-23 would not feed reliably with either

The Gamo Auto 45 functioned flawlessly in tests.

Crosman Copperhead or Premier BBs. I managed to get only three Crosman Copperhead rounds to feed from the magazine and with those the average velocity was 399 ft/sec, but the shots varied in velocity from 381 to 422 ft/sec. I have no doubt that this is due to some problem with this particular specimen. On the other hand, with Daisy Max Speed BBs, the average velocity was 410 ft/sec with a standard deviation of 8 ft/sec. This is about what I expected based on other reports I have read on this CO_2 pistol. Otherwise, I like the Gamo P-23 very well, and I wish I had a second specimen because the overall construction of the pistol is excellent for its approximately $60 price.

The Gamo Auto 45

While the Gamo P-23 is a sleek, stylish BB pistol, the Gamo Auto 45 is anything but. It is a box with a handle. Even the grip is a box. I suppose it resembles a Glock 23. The slide consists of two portions. The rear portion, as well as the frame and grip, are made of black plastic. The front section of the slide is a metal shroud that contains the barrel. Oper-

ating the Gamo Auto 45 is much the same as the Gamo P-23 described earlier.

Although the 18.1-ounce Gamo Auto 45 is a BB pistol, it has a rifled 4.25-inch barrel. Because the barrel tips up at the rear, it is possible to load a 177-caliber pellet and use the Gamo Auto 45 as a single-shot pellet pistol. The manufacturer states it is possible to fire 12 BBs in 2.4 seconds. If you were inside a barn, you might be able to hit the side of a barn shooting like that. Personally, I would rather that rate of fire not be used as an advertising ploy.

A small rectangular tab protrudes from a slot on the left-hand side of the slide. Pushing the tab forward releases the barrel so that the rear pops up. Because the barrel is hinged at the front, it can be tipped up to expose the magazine located in the frame. Loading the magazine is done in exactly the same way as for the Gamo P-23 described in the previous section. The tab attached to the magazine follower is pulled forward and turned into a recess to lock it in the forward position. BBs are dropped into a hole on top of the magazine and the magazine follower is released to

The inline magazine is accessed by tipping the barrel upward at the rear. The magazine follower is pushed forward and locked in a retaining notch. BBs are dropped into the loading port.

apply pressure on the BBs to make them feed properly. Pressing the rear of the barrel down into the frame until it latches readies the pistol for use.

Like the Gamo P-23, the safety is a rotating lever located near the front of the frame on the left-hand side. When the lever points to the front, the safety is on and when it points to the rear, the safety is off. The safety rotates upward when its position is being changed.

Sights on the Gamo Auto 45 provide a good sight picture. The front sight is a low triangular protrusion that has a white dot on its rear face. The rear sight has a square notch and it is adjustable for windage by means of a slotted screw on the right-hand side.

Removal of the left-hand grip panel allows a CO_2 cylinder to be inserted neck up in the grip. Piercing the CO_2 cylinder is accomplished by turning the piercing screw, which has a large, folding head.

Firing the Gamo Auto 45 is by double action only. The trigger pull is long and heavy at best, but the initial pull is smooth with no roughness. Only at the end of the pull is there a significant increase in force required. The trigger pull measured 8.8 pounds on my Auto 45. As the trigger is pulled, it moves

The safety on the Auto 45 is a rotating lever on the left-hand side of the frame.

backward but just before firing, it stops. When it does let off, it does so crisply, but because of the heavy pull required, the muzzle tends to jump unless the pull is directly to the rear. The trigger is too short for my trigger finger, and it is uncomfortable with so much force required. I think this pistol would be very difficult for youngsters or women to

Velocity Data for the Gamo Auto 45 at 73-75°F

| Type of BB | Ave. | Velocity, ft/sec | | Std. Dev. |
		High	Low	
Daisy Max Speed	452	456	445	4
Crosman Copperhead	450	456	444	5
Crosman Premier	461	465	457	3

shoot accurately. The accompanying table shows the results of the velocity testing.

My Gamo Auto 45 seems to have no preference when it comes to BBs. It gave high, uniform velocities with all three types of BBs tested. While the trigger action did not seem comfortable during preliminary examination, actual firing was pleasant. I was impressed with the overall behavior of this boxy gun. It functioned flawlessly. While I was rather negatively disposed toward this pistol without having ever fired it, it became one of my two favorite BB pistols with the advantage of being able to function as a single-shot pellet pistol. Despite not having the sleek lines of the P-23, my Auto 45 performed significantly better. If

they all work as well as mine does, get a Gamo Auto 45 if you want a CO_2 BB pistol.

The Walther PPK/S

One of the most attractive designs in BB pistols is the Walther PPK/S introduced in 2000 and marketed by Crosman Corporation. Not only does this little pistol mirror the image of the famous Walther firearm, it probably goes further toward duplicating the function than does any other BB pistol. When fired, the slide moves backwards and then goes forward in the same way as an auto-loading pistol does. The result is a very realistic action and feel.

The PPK/S is available in two versions. One is all blue while the other has a nickel finish

The Walther PPK/S BB pistol is elegant, small, and a true semi-automatic.

on the slide. I chose the latter since I thought it had a more elegant appearance, and elegant is one way to describe the PPK/S. This little pistol is only slightly more than 6 inches long and weighs 19.6 ounces. Sights are fixed and rather rudimentary. Barrel length is 3.5 inches, which is supposed to give BBs a velocity of 295 ft/sec. My Daisy Red Ryder gives almost exactly 300 ft/sec, so the little Walther has about the same power as a traditional lever-cocking BB gun. That means it is also the least powerful of the BB pistols tested.

Up to 15 BBs are held in an in-line magazine. What is unusual is that the magazine is held in the front part of the grip. A magazine release button is located on the left-hand side of the frame just in front of the top edge of the grip panel. Pressing the release button inward (to the right) allows the magazine to drop out of the base of the grip. With the magazine removed, the spring-loaded follower is pushed toward the base of the magazine, which allows BBs to drop in the hole at the forward (top) end of the magazine. There is no notch for locking the magazine follower in place while BBs are being loaded. It must be held in the depressed position during loading.

In the base of the left-hand grip panel there is a generous cut out to admit a thumb so that pressure can be applied outward to remove the grip panel. A CO_2 cylinder is placed in the grip frame, and the piercing screw is turned to push the cylinder up to the piercing pin. The head of the piercing screw is a large plastic wing nut that allows for easy turning by hand. In spite of the grip containing both the magazine and the CO_2 cylinder, it is the smallest of any of the BB pistols tested.

The 15-shot magazine is contained in the grip in the Walther PPK/S.

The lever on the left-hand side of the slide at the rear is a fake. The real safety is a lever on the right-hand side of the frame between the grip and the trigger. When the vertically traveling safety lever is in the lower position, the pistol is on safe, and when in the upper position, the pistol is ready to fire.

During the firing cycle, the slide moves backward and forward in a realistic manner during which the gun is cocked for the next shot. And are you ready for this? The Walther PPK/S has a hold-open feature that holds the slide back after the last BB is fired! In the single-action mode, the trigger pull measures a crisp 2.9 pounds.

Velocity testing with the Walther PPK/S was conducted with three types of BBs. The results obtained are shown in the table.

The Walther PPK/S gives average velocities very close to the 295 ft/sec advertised for the little pistol. The velocities also show good reproducibility. However, velocity is not the important issue with this attractive little pistol. Realism is the main point. The blowback

Velocity Data for the Walther PPK/S 70-72°F				
		Velocity, ft/sec		
Type of BB	Ave.	High	Low	Std. Dev.
Daisy Max Speed	287	294	277	7
Crosman Copperhead	296	301	289	5
Crosman Premier	297	299	294	2

action gives a very realistic feel during firing. Every feature worked flawlessly. Feeding of BBs was positive, and the slide remained back after the last BB was fired, exactly as it is supposed to. If the slide is back after the last shot or as a result of pulling it back, it can be released to move forward if the magazine is removed.

After the velocity tests were conducted, we enjoyed filling the magazine and shooting at random targets. A couple of magazines of BBs were fired in rapid fashion with perfect performance. This is a delightful little pistol. The Walther PPK/S excels in the subjective area known as handling. The grip is small even though it contains a CO_2 cylinder and the mag-

azine. It and the Daisy PowerLine 15XT found favor with my wife in the shooting sessions.

Although the owner's manual is printed in German, English, French, and Spanish, the Walther PPK/S has "Made in Japan" stamped on the side. Particularly obnoxious is the reference in the owner's manual to this BB pistol as a weapon. While it is not a toy, it is not a weapon and we do not need that kind of connotation. Although it is a low-powered gun, it is one of the neatest BB pistols I have ever used. It sells for approximately $70 as a kit that contains the pistol, two CO_2 cylinders, packet of BBs, shooting glasses, and a couple of targets.

When the PPK/S is fired, the slide moves backward to simulate the feel of a firearm.

CHAPTER 6

EVALUATION OF LOW-PRICED 177-CALIBER PISTOLS

IN CHAPTER 5, a discussion of some of the currently available CO_2 pistols that shoot BBs was presented. However, the number of such pistols is rather limited and they generally include only the low-end, basic models. In this chapter, we will review a substantial number of CO_2 pistols that fire 177-caliber pellets. The range of pistols of this type is enormous and it includes models that sell for less than $30 to models that cost over $200. In fact, the 177 pistols are by far the most popular type of CO_2-powered guns. Because of the number of such pistols and the wide range of prices and features, the evaluation of 177-caliber pistols will be the subject of two chapters. In this chapter, we will discuss the pistols that comprise the lower end of the price spectrum. While the chapter title labels them as low-priced CO_2 pistols, they have a lot to offer in terms of performance and value. In fact, one of

these relatively inexpensive pistols may meet your needs so well that you may never want to have one of the more expensive models, which are referred to as "elite" for the sake of the title of the next chapter.

The types of tests performed and data collected for the BB pistols were described in Chapter 2. Similar data was collected for the 177-caliber pellet pistols reviewed in this chapter, but in addition, more emphasis was placed on pellet velocity because of the number of pellet types available. There is an enormous number of types of pellets available while the number of types of BBs is rather limited. Also, BBs are all spherical, steel projectiles of the same profile. To evaluate the velocity produced by each of the 177-caliber pistols, six types of pellets were selected for use with each pistol. Velocities were determined with five-shot strings fired with each

The six types of pellets used in the velocity tests are (left to right) the Dynamit Nobel Meisterkugeln, Gamo Match, Daisy Wadcutter, Crosman Wadcutter, Dynamit Nobel Club, and Eley Target.

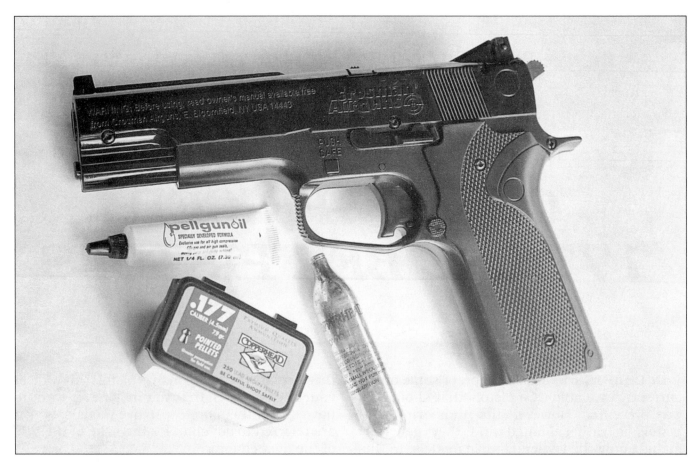

Although made largely of plastic, the Crosman 1008 is patterned after a Smith & Wesson Model 1006.

type of pellet. In an exhaustive accuracy test, a given pistol would be fired with every type of pellet available to determine the very best pellet to use in that particular pistol. I did not feel this level of testing was warranted, especially considering the number of pistols to be evaluated. The results are shown for velocity as High, Low, and Standard Deviation (in ft/sec). The results give an adequate indication of what each pistol can be expected to deliver, especially since more than one specimen was tested in some cases.

In the descriptions that follow, instructions are given for installing a CO_2 cylinder and loading ammunition in each model. Although is it not stated explicitly in the discussion of each model, the safety should always be in the "on" position before loading propellant or projectiles in any CO_2 gun. There is danger in piercing a CO_2 cylinder in a gun that might already have pellets in it or in placing pellets in a gun that is pressurized with a pierced CO_2 cylinder. Read the owner's manual and follow all safety instructions.

The Crosman 1008 RepeatAir

After producing several models of CO_2 pistols over a long period of time, Crosman introduced the 177-caliber Model 1008 RepeatAir in 1992. The version known as the 1008SB, which has a silver exterior and black grips, was introduced in 1994. For several years, Smith & Wesson produced a large frame semi-automatic pistol chambered for the 10 mm Auto cartridge. With many Smith & Wesson handguns, model numbers ending in 6 signify stainless steel construction. The 10 mm semi-auto was known as the Model 1006 while the pistol chambered for the 45 ACP was designated as the Model 4506. Because the Crosman CO_2 pistol resembles the 10 mm firearm and because it holds eight pellets, Crosman designated the pistol as the Model 1008. For the 1008SB, the S signifies silver finish and the B signifies black grips. The 1008B is all black in external finish.

Crosman 1008 pistols (this designation will be used for both 1008B and 1008SB models)

Although it looks like a semi-automatic, the Crosman 1008 holds pellets in a revolving cylinder.

are not crafted in the image of the legendary Crosman Model 600 (see Chapter 10). That 22-caliber pistol was a true semi-automatic made of metal and weighing 41.6 ounces. The 1008 has almost nothing external made of metal except the head of the piercing screw at the bottom of the grip. A 1008 weighs only 17 ounces, is 8 5/8-inches long, and has a 4 1/4-inch rifled steel barrel. Muzzle velocity is specified as up to 430 ft/sec, and the owner's manual indicates that a CO_2 cylinder provides power for an average of 60 shots.

Externally, the Crosman Model 1008 bears a strong resemblance to the Smith & Wesson 1006 from which its name is derived. Plastics are wonderful materials, and it is possible to produce almost any shape during the molding process. As a result, the Model 1008, like other CO_2 pistols, has fake parts and features that make the pistol look like a firearm. The Crosman 1008 has a fake ejection port, slide release lever, magazine release, etc. molded on the external surface in locations where the actual parts would be found on a firearm. Even the checkering pattern on the grips is the same as on the Smith & Wesson 1006. The result is a CO_2 pistol that bears a strong resemblance to a firearm. Unlike the Smith & Wesson 1006, which has a black front sight, the 1008SB has a silver post.

The Crosman 1008 "semi-automatic" is actually a revolver made with the external configuration of a semi-auto. It makes use of a revolving cylinder that holds eight 177-caliber pellets. Both single- and double-action firing are possible. The cylindrical magazine does not rotate as the hammer is cocked during single-action shooting. It rotates as the trigger is pulled during both single- and double-action shooting. Unlike a typical revolver, the cylindrical magazine is completely enclosed in the frame so rotation cannot be seen.

The barrel is hinged at the front and tips up at the rear to give access to the cylinder. On top of the barrel is a small, ridged, black tab that functions as the barrel release.

Pushing the tab forward allows the barrel to tip upward at the rear. The barrel lock is a projecting plastic chisel that locks in a recess in the shroud just to the rear of the barrel. When closing the barrel, I recommend pushing the release tab forward so that the lock does not have to force its way over the edge of the frame. While it is certainly of appropriate size, the lock is not overly robust.

The plastic cylinder that holds the pellets measures 0.280 inches in thickness, which is sufficient to accommodate almost any 177-caliber pellet. A loaded magazine is placed in the pistol so that its center hole fits over the shaft on which it rotates.

Although fake safety levers are molded on the rear portion of the fake slide, a cross-bolt safety is located just above the trigger. Pushing it to the right places the safety on while pushing it to the left takes the safety off. The words "push fire" appear on the right-hand side of the frame and "push safe" appears on the left-hand side.

The rear sight on the Crosman 1008B and 1008SB is outstanding. It is a sturdy plastic unit that is adjustable for windage and elevation by means of two screws. Turning the screw on the side of the sight clockwise moves the point of impact to the right while turning the screw on top clockwise raises the point of impact. The front sight on the Model 1008SB is a silver-colored post, which is not easy to use with a rear sight that is black. A little black paint will quickly make the front sight have the same color as the rear. Overall, the sights on the 1008B and 1008SB are more than adequate.

The barrel on the 1008 has a low rib that runs from just forward of the latch almost to the front sight. This rib has grooved edges so that a red dot or laser sight can be mounted if desired.

Trigger action in the single-action mode involves a take-up motion followed by the actual let-off. On my three 1008 specimens, let-off is crisp and light. However, the take-up motion is mushy and jerky. The reason for this is that cocking the hammer does not rotate the cylinder. The cylinder is rotated during the first stage of the trigger action even in single-action shooting because the trigger operates the linkage that rotates the cylinder. Trigger motion in double-action firing is quite short. Pulling the trigger moves the hammer to the rear, rotates the magazine, and fires the piece. All of this occurs as the result of the trigger moving only about 1/4-inch. The result is a double-action trigger pull that is rather heavy although smooth for a CO_2 pistol. I have three Model 1008 pistols and the average single-action pull is 4.2 pounds while the double-action pull averages 9.4 pounds. Overall, I would describe the trigger action of the Crosman 1008 as good, certainly for a pistol that sells for around $40-$50.

Installing a CO_2 cylinder in the Model 1008 requires the removal of the right-hand grip panel by pushing outward on the bottom edge. A CO_2 cylinder is inserted neck up and the grip panel snapped in place. Turning the piercing screw completes the process.

Over the years, my shopping at various places has provided me with three of the Model 1008 pistols. Two are the black version (designated as (1) and (3) in the table) and the third is the silver version (designated as (2) in the table). In the velocity tests, all three of the Crosman 1008s were fired with the same six types of pellets used throughout the velocity determinations for the 177-caliber pistols. The data from all of the pistols were included to provide an indication of how much difference can be expected to exist between pistols that are nearly identical. The results of the velocity determinations are shown in the accompanying table.

The advertised maximum velocity for the Crosman 1008 is up to 435 ft/sec. None of my pistols will give a velocity that high. Firing a very light pellet on a hot day would probably give a velocity approaching that value.

When I see the results of tests conducted with a particular gun, I often wonder if the data presented are representative of that model and how much difference would be seen if another specimen of the same model were tested. With that in mind, I tested the three Crosman 1008 pistols. The data show that with most of the pellets, the average velocity given by all three guns does not vary by more than approximately 15 ft/sec. Keep in mind these pistols use cylinders that hold eight pellets. It is possible in loading pellets in the cylinders to have slight differences in seating depth. The interchangeable cylinders have

Velocity Data for the Crosman 1008 at 70-72°F

Pellet		Velocity, ft/sec			
		Ave.	High	Low	Std. Dev.
D.N. Meisterkugeln	(1)	369	374	364	5
D.N. Meisterkugeln	(2)	354	358	351	3
D.N. Meisterkugeln	(3)	359	368	351	10
Gamo Match	(1)	385	391	379	5
Gamo Match	(2)	378	380	375	2
Gamo Match	(3)	369	382	360	10
Daisy Wadcutter	(1)	384	391	372	8
Daisy Wadcutter	(2)	381	386	377	4
Daisy Wadcutter	(3)	373	384	366	10
Crosman Wadcutter	(1)	369	376	362	6
Crosman Wadcutter	(2)	361	364	359	2
Crosman Wadcutter	(3)	350	358	340	7
D. N. Club	(1)	389	391	384	5
D. N. Club	(2)	382	388	370	7
D. N. Club	(3)	380	399	360	14
Eley Target	(1)	375	389	363	11
Eley Target	(2)	375	380	368	4
Eley Target	(3)	362	383	348	15

(1), (2), and (3) refer to three different specimens of the Crosman 1008.

slight differences in thickness and dimensions of the individual chambers. There are slight differences in the CO_2 valves and tension of the hammer springs. In view of these factors, it is perhaps surprising three different guns give approximately the same velocity.

During the tests, two minor problems were encountered, neither of which indicates anything wrong with the pistols. First, the pellets must be forced into the cylinder in order to assure they do not protrude from the rear face of the cylinder. If they do, they will hang up and prevent the cylinder from turning. In the process, the base of the pellet will become

battered. Second, make sure the barrel latch is seated securely. If it is not, firing the pistol will cause the rear of the barrel to flip up and send pellets flying out of the cylinder. Needless to say, this is rather distracting. If my wife and I had not experienced this, I would not be cautioning against it. Careful, consistent handling of this and all other CO_2 guns will give trouble-free shooting.

The Marksman 2001

It is not necessary for a CO_2 pistol to be as elegant as the Colt 1911 or Smith & Wesson 586 in order to function. If it were, the Marksman 2001 wouldn't have a chance. This large, black, plastic pistol has white insets along the grips, a large white grip cap that functions as a piercing screw, and a visible white magazine. The trigger and safety lever are also white. Furthermore, this CO_2 handgun really doesn't know what it is. Shaped loosely like a cosmic semi-automatic, the Marksman 2001 has a pump handle that functions in shotgun fashion and a non-removable rotating cylinder like a revolver. In terms of looks, it reminds me

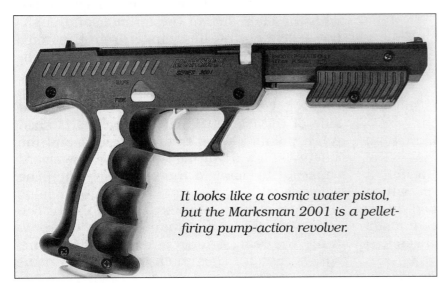

It looks like a cosmic water pistol, but the Marksman 2001 is a pellet-firing pump-action revolver.

The Marksman 2001 is cycled for each shot by pulling back on the pump lever below the barrel.

The Marksman 2001 makes no pretense. The cylinder is clearly visible and not removable.

Loading a CO_2 cylinder in the Marksman involves removing the large, white cap at the base of the grip and inserting a CO_2 cylinder neck first. Replacing the cap and tightening it pierces the CO_2 cylinder. The process is simple but effective with no levers, adjustable tensioning devices, etc. You don't even have to remove a grip panel.

Pellets are loaded in the white cylindrical magazine one at a time while rotating the magazine clockwise. A groove in the right-hand side of the frame behind the cylinder exposes one chamber at a time as the cylinder is rotated. Rotating the cylinder can be accomplished by pushing on it with a thumb or operating the pump handle. Pellets must be seated flush with the back face of the cylinder so it can rotate freely. The cylinder measures 0.295 of an inch in thickness, which means it should accommodate almost any 177-caliber pellet. However, I do not use pointed pellets in this pistol. If a pellet slips forward, a pointed pellet is more likely to engage the barrel breech and prevent the cylinder from turning. If a hang up does occur, the damaged pellet must be pushed back into the cylinder and the cylinder rotated to align it with the loading groove so the pellet can be pushed out from the front. The Marksman comes with rod for pushing a pellet from the barrel. It also comes with a plastic tool for seating pellets flush with the back face of the cylinder and pushing pellets out of the cylinder from the front. The rifled steel barrel measures approximately 4.3 inches in length.

The safety on the Marksman 2001 is a rotating white lever located on the right-hand side of the frame. When the lever is pushed up, it points toward the word "safe", and the safety is on. Rotating the lever downward causes it to point to the word "fire", and the safety is off.

Sights on the Marksman are fixed. The front sight is a nicely shaped square-top post while the rear sight is a thick blade with a square notch. The notch is too wide com-

more of a water gun than a pellet launcher. There is an old saying that a camel is a horse designed by a committee. I believe the Marksman 2001 is clearly the result of a design committee that may not have ever met.

Having humorously bashed the Marksman 2001, it is necessary to give an appraisal of this unique and somewhat bizarre pistol. It certainly does not resemble a firearm, which from a safety standpoint may be a good thing. The Marksman 2001 is a low-priced pistol that actually functions quite well. In fact, it has a number of commendable features.

Velocity Data for the Marksman 2001 at 70-72°F

Pellet	Ave.	Velocity, ft/sec		Std. Dev.
		High	Low	
D.N. Meisterkugeln	306	309	303	2
Gamo Match	305	306	303	1
Daisy Wadcutter	284	287	281	3
Crosman Wadcutter	276	283	265	7
D. N. Club	285	293	277	5
Eley Target	272	275	268	3

Simplicity is a characteristic of the Marksman 2001. Other than the sliding handle, the safety and the trigger are the only controls.

pared to the width of the front sight, which gives too much open space on either side of the front sight when aiming. A ridge along the top of the frame has grooves that permit attaching red dot, laser, or scope sights. Trigger pull on the Marksman 2001 is long, heavy, and mushy.

While the Marksman 2001 is certainly not going to be mistaken for an art object, it works. In fact, it works quite well for a CO_2 pistol with a price of less than $30. Did I mention that I bought mine on a clearance sale for $12? I got my money's worth. Seriously, the Marksman 2001 is intended to provide pellet gun fun at the lowest possible price. In terms of this objective, it is successful.

While the Marksman 2001 did not give very high velocities, they were about as reproducible as those given by any other CO_2 pistol. The pistol gave a very low report and simply

kept on shooting. Although no record was kept of the number of shots per CO_2 cylinder, the number is large. During the firing of this pistol, no malfunction of any kind occurred. However, loading the non-removable cylinder was found to be slow. The low powered Marksman 2001 could easily be used indoors where it is desirable to keep noise to a minimum level. As stated earlier, the Marksman 2001 works even though it is a rather cosmic piece.

The Gamo PT-80

Weighing 15.9 ounces and measuring a little over 7 inches in length, the Gamo PT-80 is a very convenient and well-made 177-caliber CO_2 pistol that sells for approximately $70. It has a very realistic appearance. With a 4-inch rifled barrel, the advertised muzzle velocity is 400 ft/sec.

Like many other CO_2 pistols, the Gamo PT-80 makes extensive use of plastics although the barrel and its shroud are metal. This gives the pistol a weight distribution that provides more weight toward the muzzle, which is an advantage for steady holding. The PT-80 holds eight pellets in a magazine that is 0.357 of an inch from front to back. A magazine of this length will accommodate virtually any pellet in 177 caliber since most pellets are shorter than 0.300 of an inch long. It is therefore possible to use pointed or domed pellets in the PT-80. One unique feature of the PT-80 is a small hole in the top of the barrel shroud about an inch in front of the rear sight. Through that hole it is possible to watch the cylinder as it rotates. A plastic finger inside the extension of the barrel shroud rests above the cylinder. As the cylinder turns, the plastic finger engages the grooves on the outside edge of the cylinder. The grooves on the cylinder are spaced so that when the finger engages one of them, one of the chambers is directly aligned with the bore. This arrangement provides a more precise and rigorous lock of the cylinder in alignment with the bore than most of the lower-priced pistols obtain.

The plastic grip panels are finely checkered and provide an excellent gripping surface. There are grooves on the front and back of the grip frame and the front of the trigger guard.

My major criticism of the PT-80 is in regard to the action of the trigger. In single action, the trigger is a two-stage affair. After the take-up motion, the let-off is very heavy with the trigger pull gauge registering 9.5 pounds. With the hammer cocked, pulling the trigger to fire the pistol causes the hammer to move back slightly just at let-off. This indicates there is not a correct position of the sear with respect to trigger motion. The double-action trigger pull is somewhat rough, and the pull measured 9.9 pounds. The fact the trigger pull is about the same in either single- or double-action firing shows that the hammer must be forced to the rear in either firing mode. I suspect this is a defect in my individual pistol, and the trigger pull did improve slightly with use as the testing was carried out.

The safety lever is on the left-hand side of the "slide". An identical lever on the right-hand side is a totally inoperative feature that is purely cosmetic. Also cosmetic is the "magazine release" button behind the trigger guard. A dummy lever is located at the front of the trigger guard on the left-hand side. The slide release is also a fake.

The rear sight of the Gamo PT-80 is adjustable for windage by moving the sight laterally in its dovetailed groove after loosening the locking screw. The front sight is a low, forward-tapered ramp with a white dot on the back face. White dots also appear on either

The Gamo PT-80 is a compact 177-caliber pistol that is constructed to high standards.

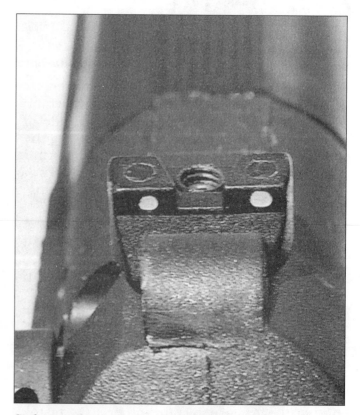

Sights on the Gamo PT-80 give an excellent sight picture.

The ribbed slide just above the front of the trigger guard allows the barrel to be tipped up at the rear for loading a pellet cylinder.

Like most other CO_2 pistols, the CO_2 cylinder is held in the grip of the Gamo PT-80, but the piercing screw is recessed.

side of the square notch in the rear sight. The sight picture is as good as that provided by any of the inexpensive CO_2 pistols. The plastic grip panels are nicely checkered and the front of the grip and trigger guard are grooved.

The barrel on the PT-80 is hinged at the front and tipping the barrel upward exposes the eight-shot rotary magazine. Two ridged slides are located on the frame just above the front of the trigger guard. Placing the thumb on one slide and the forefinger on the other allows them to be pulled forward. This action moves a rectangular lock out of its matching recess under the barrel, and the spring-loaded

barrel then moves upward exposing the cylindrical magazine. When the barrel is latched in place, the lock up is very rigid and secure.

A CO_2 cylinder is loaded in the grip by forcing the left-hand grip panel outward at the bottom causing it to snap off. The CO_2 cylinder is inserted neck up and a screw having a pivoting wing-nut head is rotated clockwise to force the CO_2 cylinder upward to pierce it. A deep recess in the butt of the grip hides the folding head of the wing nut. This gives a clean profile with no protruding piercing screw head.

This is a very attractive pistol. The two halves of the molded plastic frame are well mated and held together with several Phillips-head screws. The barrel housing is metal, which gives the pistol a weighted forward end.

Velocity testing of the Gamo PT-80 was carried out with the same types of pellets used in all of the pistols evaluated in this chapter. The results obtained are shown in the accompanying table.

Velocity Data for the Gamo PT-80 at 70-72°F

| Pellet | Ave. | Velocity, ft/sec | | Std. Dev. |
		High	Low	
D.N. Meisterkugeln	340	343	335	4
Gamo Match	362	366	354	5
Daisy Wadcutter	377	382	371	5
Crosman Wadcutter	352	359	346	5
D. N. Club	386	399	376	3
Eley Target	367	375	358	7

During the testing procedures, the Gamo PT-80 performed flawlessly. It functioned exactly like it was supposed to and gave velocities that were quite uniform. With its 4-inch barrel, velocities were slightly lower than those given by some of the other guns, which was expected. If I can get the single-action trigger pull improved, this gun will hold its own against any inexpensive pistol of its type. It is a very well made pistol that is a pleasure to use.

The Daisy PowerLine 45

From a casual glance, the Daisy 45 resembles a large-frame Smith & Wesson centerfire autoloader. Fake safety/decocking levers, magazine release button, and slide release lever add to the realistic look. The rear sight (nonadjustable on the Daisy 45) has the protective "ears" as found on Smith & Wesson autoloaders that have adjustable sights. Even the checkering pattern on the plastic grip panels resembles that on the real thing. However, that is where the similarity ends. The PowerLine 645 is identical to the Model 45 except the 645 has a silver colored frame. Although listed in Daisy catalogs as the Model 45, my pistol has the number 4500 on the frame.

Several years ago, the Daisy PowerLine 45 was made with the external look of a Colt 1911, but the current version has the outward appearance of a Smith & Wesson auto. While the two versions have quite different appearances because of their molded plastic shells, they function in the same manner. My PowerLine 45 weighs 20.4 ounces. The advertised muzzle velocity for the PowerLine 45 is up to 400 ft/sec.

This gun uses a 13-shot in-line clip that rests in a recess on top of the pistol directly behind the front sight. The magazine has a spring-loaded follower that forces the pellets

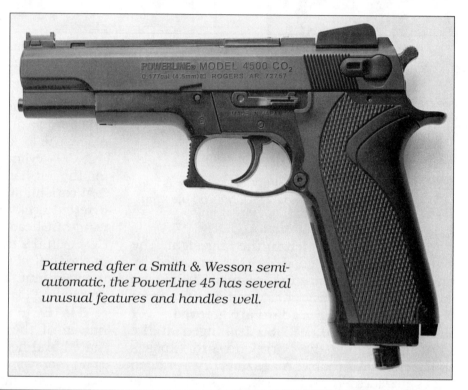

Patterned after a Smith & Wesson semi-automatic, the PowerLine 45 has several unusual features and handles well.

The magazine release is the button just below the muzzle. Pushing in on the button allows the front end of the magazine to snap up out of the recess.

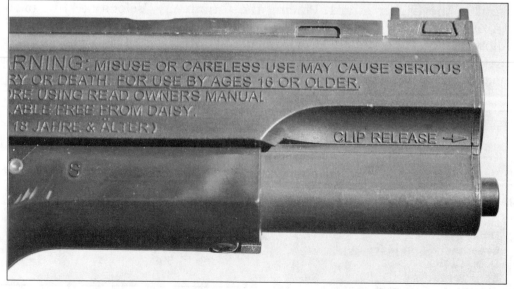

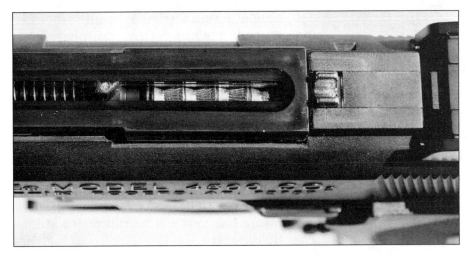

Up to 13 pellets are held in an in-line magazine that is held in a recess along the top of the barrel.

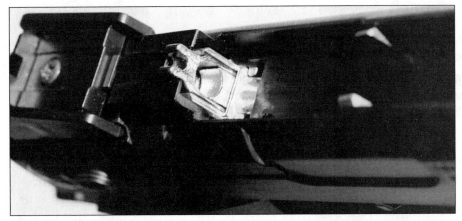

Pellets are moved downward from the rear of the magazine by this carrier to bring them into alignment with the breech as the trigger is pulled.

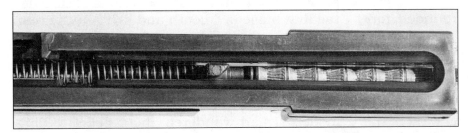

Pellets are loaded into the magazine of the PowerLine 45 by pulling the magazine follower forward and dropping pellets into the loading port.

pulled down will hang up in the hollow skirt of the pellet in front of it.

The magazine can be loaded while it is contained in the pistol by pulling the spring-loaded follower forward and turning it so the lock pin engages a recess. With the follower in the forward position, pellets can be dropped one at a time into the opening at the forward end of the magazine. When the magazine is loaded, turning the pin out of its retaining notch allows the follower to move back to make contact with the pellets. The magazine can be removed by pushing the button just below the muzzle and grasping the forward end of the magazine and lifting upward. Replacing the magazine requires the rear end to be started in the frame first, making sure the end of the magazine matches the recess in the frame. The front end of the magazine is pressed downward into the recess in the frame until it snaps into place.

The PowerLine 45 has a somewhat unusual safety. The lever is located on the right-hand side of the frame just above the front end of the trigger guard. When the lever points forward, the safety is on. Turning the lever so it points downward takes the safety off. However, before the safety lever can be rotated downward, it must be pressed into the frame slightly against spring pressure. When the safety is on, the lever is locked to prevent its rotation accidentally. The safety can be taken off only after the lock is disengaged by pushing it inward (to the left).

Sights on the PowerLine 45 consist of a square-topped front post with a red fiber optic insert and a square-notch rear that is nonadjustable. I could easily get along with-

to the rear. When the trigger is pulled, a pellet is removed from the rear of the magazine by a dropping pellet carrier that pulls it down to align with the barrel at the time of firing. Because each pellet is removed by sliding down out of the magazine while in contact with the base of the pellet in front of it, only flat-nosed pellets can be used. If pointed pellets are loaded, the point of the pellet being

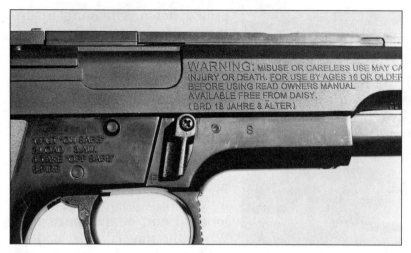

The safety on the PowerLine 45 is a rotating lever on the right-hand side of the frame just above the front of the trigger.

single-action trigger pull at 5.2 pounds while the double-action mode required a pull of 9.5 pounds. Trigger function on the PowerLine 45 is very good for a pistol of this type.

Overall, this is a very nice pistol. Although the CO_2 cylinder is contained in the grip, it is considerably slimmer than those on almost all of the CO_2 pistols. This provides a very good grip. Grip panels are well checkered and the front of the grip frame has vertical serrations to aid in holding the pistol. The front of the trigger guard is deeply checkered, which also aids when using a two-hand hold. The data obtained during velocity testing are shown in the accompanying table.

Although the advertised velocity for the PowerLine 45 is up to 400 ft/sec, my pistol exceeded that velocity with all of the types of pellets tested. Moreover, the velocities were very reproducible as shown by the very low standard deviations. With some of the lighter pellets like the Daisy wadcutter and Gamo Match, the average velocity was nearly 35 ft/sec higher than the advertised maximum.

When firing the PowerLine 45 single action, the first stage of the trigger action moves the pellet carrier downward, taking a pellet from the magazine to align it with the breech. Although this mechanical action is occurring, the first stage is smooth and light. At the rear of its travel, the trigger is now poised for releasing the sear. The trigger was predictable and smooth. I found the PowerLine 45 to have the best "feel" during the cocking and firing sequence of any of the lower-priced models. I had wondered about pellet feeding from the in-line magazine, but my concern was misplaced. During the firing of dozens of

out the fiber optic insert, the end of which generates a red dot about half way up the front of the sight. I suspect a novice will not be sure whether to put the top of the front sight even with the top of the rear sight or to put the red dot there or somewhere else. The fiber optic sight inserts may have high visibility, but they certainly do not make for more accurate aiming.

Loading a CO_2 cylinder in a PowerLine 45 consists of pushing on a tab at the bottom of the left-hand grip panel to remove it, inserting the cylinder (neck up) and turning the large screw in the base of the grip to force the cylinder upward to pierce it. Inside the grip frame, the CO_2 cylinder is surrounded fore and aft by a metal frame or box.

Double-action firing requires a normal force on the trigger, and the force increases as the firing point is reached. Single-action firing takes place with a crisp let-off after a long, soft first stage pull during which the pellet carrier moves downward to place a pellet in position at the breech. I measured the

Velocity Data for the Daisy PowerLine 45 at 70-72°F

Pellet	Velocity, ft/sec			
	Ave.	High	Low	Std. Dev.
D.N. Meisterkugeln	415	417	412	2
Gamo Match	435	436	434	1
Daisy Wadcutter	434	440	428	5
Crosman Wadcutter	404	408	399	4
D. N. Club	432	438	427	5
Eley Target	431	436	426	4

The Gamo R-77 Combat is a realistic revolver patterned after a Smith & Wesson 586.

On the Gamo R-77, the entire cylinder swings out of the frame for loading pellets.

The gas release pin and transfer bar are located where they can be struck by the hammer.

shots, functioning of this pistol that sells for $40-$45 was flawless. I was so impressed with the PowerLine 45 that I may order a 645 just to have a choice of colors!

The Gamo R-77 Combat

While the major emphasis in CO_2 handguns is focused on those resembling autoloaders, revolver fans have not been forgotten. One of the most realistic revolvers in both looks and function is the 177-caliber Gamo R-77. There are actually four models in the series. Three of them are the R-77 Combat with a 4-inch barrel, the R-77 Classic with a 6-inch barrel, and the R-77 2.5, which has a 2.5-inch barrel. The fourth model, the 4-inch-barreled R-77 Laser, has a laser sight, which is activated by a pressure sensitive switch in the grip backstrap, built into the barrel lug. While the Classic has checkered walnut grips, the other models have rubber grips of Santoprene® with finger grooves. An outstanding "feel" is provided by the surface of the soft grips. All models have full-length lugs below the barrels. My R-77 Combat, which sells for $70-$75, weighs 21.2 ounces.

Most CO_2 revolvers hold pellets in a short cylinder (actually a disk) that is located in front of a larger fake cylinder. Only that disk containing the pellets rotates during firing. A unique feature of the Gamo R-77 family of revolvers is the fact the entire cylinder rotates, not just a small portion of it. This rotating cylinder gives the revolvers a very realistic appearance, and since the cylinder stays in the gun, there is no dinky little pellet holder to get lost. Of course, it is not possible to reload as quickly by dropping in a pre-loaded cylinder, but that is the way real revolvers work. I like it. The cylinder holds eight pellets.

The Gamo revolvers can be fired both double and single action. As the hammer is cocked, the cylinder rotates (counterclockwise) approximately one-half of the distance between chambers. Pulling the trigger causes the cylinder to rotate the remaining amount needed to align a chamber with the barrel. The cylinder is opened for loading by swinging it out of the frame to the left after pulling forward on the latch pin that is located on the left-hand side of the barrel lug. Pulling the latch forward moves a pin out of a recess on the forward edge of the crane allowing the cylinder to swing open. There is a fake cylinder latch located on the left-hand side of the frame behind the cylinder that has the appearance of the latch on Smith & Wesson revolvers.

The trigger on the R-77 is broad and finely grooved. Firing single action, I measured the trigger pull to be 4.6 pounds and in double-action firing it was 7.5 pounds. The hammer is broad and has grooves although the surface of the hammer spur has a smooth feel. A cross-bolt safety is located at the top of the frame just behind the rear sight. When pushed to the right, the safety is on and the hammer is blocked from striking the gas release valve. When pushed to the left a red firing indicator shows and the gun can be fired. If the hammer is in the fully down (forward) position, the safety can be moved from on to off, but if the safety is off, it cannot be moved to the on position without forcing the hammer back slightly, which requires considerable force.

Sights on the Gamo R-77 provide a sight picture that is outstanding. The front sight is a square-topped blade on a ramp and it closely resembles that on my Smith & Wesson Model 15 Combat Masterpiece. The rear sight consists of a fully adjustable square notch with slotted screws controlling the adjustments. Unfortunately, the entire rear sight assembly is made of plastic and it has a considerable amount of flex to it. Also, the windage adjustment screw has a rather large head with a slot that can accommodate a small coin. It turns easily enough that it can be turned with finger pressure only.

Although the construction of the sights leaves something to be desired, the sight picture is second to none. I am very glad there is no round-topped fiber optic sight on this gun that must be aligned with a square notch rear sight. That is something difficult to do, at least for me.

Loading a CO_2 cylinder in the R-77 is a simple task. The right-hand grip panel has a large recess in the bottom and pulling outward (to the right with the muzzle pointed away) causes the grip panel to snap off. The butt of the grip has a screw with a folding head that controls the movement of the plate that supports the bottom of the CO_2 cylinder. The screw is backed out enough to insert a CO_2 cylinder (neck up), and after the grip panel is replaced, the screw is turned clockwise to force the CO_2 cylinder upward to cause it to be pierced.

Velocity testing of the Gamo R-77 yielded the results shown in the table. Although velocities showed satisfactory uniformity, they were not quite as uniform as those given by some of the other models. Part of this is undoubtedly due to the fact that the eight chambers in the cylinder must have some variation in dimensions. Unless the face of the cylinder is perfectly uniform, there would be slight differences in the barrel-to-cylinder gap when different chambers are aligned. Even with these factors considered, the velocity uniformity is quite good. With a 4-inch barrel, the advertised velocity is 380 ft/sec. The data show that at a temperature of 80°F, the Gamo R-77 will exceed that velocity with most pellets.

One minor problem occurred while firing the Gamo R-77. This revolver has no bolt or

Velocity Data for the Gamo R-77 Combat at 80-82°F

Pellet	Velocity, ft/sec			
	Ave.	High	Low	Std. Dev.
D.N. Meisterkugeln	387	393	378	5
Gamo Match	391	400	388	5
Daisy Wadcutter	398	405	392	6
Crosman Wadcutter	402	407	394	4
D. N. Club	398	409	393	6
Eley Target	397	404	392	4

lock to hold the cylinder aligned with the barrel. The hand that rotates the cylinder moves it into alignment while the shot is being taken, but between shots, the cylinder can be rotated. If the cylinder is moved accidentally, a pellet may be skipped or an empty chamber may next be brought into alignment. I would prefer that the Gamo R-77 have a locking bolt to hold the cylinder to prevent accidental rotation between shots.

Because of having a size that is very close to that of many popular firearms, the Gamo R-77 serves well for practice. That practice could include handgun hunting or combat training. In any event, the Gamo R-77 is a convenient, attractive CO_2 handgun. Because it has a full-size rotating cylinder, it provides realistic training for persons becoming familiar with these types of firearms.

The Crosman RepeatAir 1710

Take a Crosman RepeatAir 1008, add a barrel extension with a fake compensator and a funky fiber optic front sight and you have a Crosman RepeatAir 1710. To paraphrase the late Jack O'Connor, that front sight is "straight from the chamber of horrors!" While the RepeatAir 1008 is available with either black or satin shiny finish, the 1710 is available only with the simulated stainless steel finish.

Basically, this is a plastic pistol with a lot of nice features. It can be fired either single or double action and it utilizes an eight-shot rotary magazine. Except for the long barrel and fake compensator, it has the styling of a large-frame Smith & Wesson centerfire pistol. Even the wrap-around grip panels are checkered in the Smith & Wesson pattern. The RepeatAir 1710 weighs 17.1 ounces and has a 7.24-inch barrel. Retail price is in the $40-$45 range.

Plastic magazines that hold eight pellets are inserted by tipping the barrel up at the rear. The barrel release is a small, ridged protrusion on top of the slide at the rear of the fake ejection port. Pushing the catch forward allows the spring-loaded barrel to pop up smartly, exposing the shaft on which the magazine rotates. A loaded magazine can be placed on the shaft and the barrel depressed to lock it in place. Because the plastic latch is forced forward a considerable amount as the barrel is closed, I recommend pushing the latch forward as the rear of the barrel is pressed downward then releasing it when the barrel is in place. This will prevent excessive wear and possible breakage of the latch. The latch moves forward as the barrel is closed and it must withstand considerable force even though the bottom edge of the latch is beveled.

The Crosman 1710 is a long-barreled 177-caliber pistol that gives high velocity.

A cylinder holding eight pellets fits inside the frame of the Crosman 1710.

Cocking the hammer for single-action shooting requires a light pull on the ridged hammer spur. Cocking action is smooth. When the pistol is fired single action, the trigger requires a slight take-up motion after which let-off is rather light. Firing double action requires a rather heavy pull, but it is fairly smooth. The measured trigger pull in the single-action mode is 3.6 pounds while that in double action is 9.6 pounds for my pistol. The total trigger travel in double-action firing is noticeably shorter than for some of the other CO_2 pistols.

The black rear sight on the Crosman 1710 is excellent. It has a square notch and is fully adjustable for windage and elevation by means of two slotted screws. It is of sturdy and excellent design. As mentioned earlier, I find the front sight to be "straight from the chamber of horrors." It is silver in color, has a rounded top, and is too wide for proper sighting in the rear notch. The green fiber optic insert does nothing to enhance the sight picture. I have threatened many times to simply cut it off, make an appropriate black ramp, and glue it in place. I am still not sure that I won't!

Prior to the tests that gave the velocity data shown in the table, the only measurements I had made with the Crosman 1710 were at a temperature of 86°F. At that temperature, I obtained an average velocity of 464 ft/sec with the Crosman wadcutter pellet. Keep in mind the Crosman 1710 is essentially a Model 1008 with a longer barrel, so it should produce higher velocities.

The data show the 1710 produces velocities approximately 50-60 ft/sec higher than the Model 1008. Such a difference is directly attributable to the 3-inch-longer barrel of the 1710. A velocity of approximately 425 ft/sec with the very sturdy Crosman Copperhead wadcutter and pointed pellets indicates the

The safety is of the cross-bolt type and pushing it to the right places it on while pushing it left takes it off. The safety is located just above the front end of the trigger guard.

A CO_2 cylinder is placed in the grip after removing the right-hand panel by pressing it outward at the bottom. The cylinder is inserted neck up, and the piercing screw is tightened to force the cylinder upward. The piercing screw has a folding wire loop head and it is recessed in the bottom of the grip.

Velocity Data for the Crosman RepeatAir 1710 at 70-72°F

Pellet	Velocity, ft/sec			
	Ave.	High	Low	Std. Dev.
D.N. Meisterkugeln	423	428	414	7
Gamo Match	434	446	411	13
Daisy Wadcutter	432	437	426	4
Crosman Wadcutter	425	433	419	7
D. N. Club	442	449	439	3
Eley Target	432	439	422	7

1710 would be a logical choice if you wish to dispatch small pests with a pistol of this type.

When the barrel is opened on the Crosman 1710, the barrel extension tips forward until it almost touches the front edge of the frame. The spring that tips the barrel upward is quite strong, so it is possible to receive a pinch if a finger or part of a hand is located at the front edge of the frame when the barrel flips up. This model has recently been discontinued and does not appear in Crosman's 2003 catalog. It will probably still be found available from some dealers so it is included in this chapter. Incidentally, I did not cut off the front sight on this pistol. I reserved that treatment for a Model 2210. The result of that modification can be seen in Chapter 8.

The Crosman 357

Crosman has offered a CO_2 revolver designated as a Model 357 since 1983. Although numerous changes have been made over the years, the current version of the Model 357 is all black and is made with the styling to resemble the classic Colt Python. However, the resemblance ends there.

The Crosman 357 uses a short rotating cylinder that occupies a position in front of the fake cylinder. Unlike the Daisy PowerLine 44 (see Chapter 10) and the Gamo R-77 that have swing-out cylinders, the Crosman 357 is a top-break revolver. On the top of the frame just above the short cylinder that rotates is a square-button release. Depressing this catch disengages a hook that catches a recess in the top part of the barrel shroud. When the hook is disengaged, the barrel tips forward. The magazine can then be lifted off the shaft on which it turns.

Because of the way the hook catches in a recess in the barrel, lock-up is not perfect. As a result, there is a small amount of vertical play in the barrel even when it is latched. In order to keep the locking arrangement as tight as possible, I recommend the release button be depressed during closing rather than just pushing the barrel up and allowing the latch hook to snap into place. The locking mechanism is not overly fragile, but neither is it made like a tank. Under no conditions should the barrel be snapped up smartly to close it. I have seen more than one of these revolvers with a broken latch or latch spring. If the opening and closing of the barrel are done with some care, there is no reason why the mechanism should not last indefinitely.

One unique feature of the Crosman 357 is that it will function with cylinders holding either six or 10 pellets. Both types of cylinders are still available. Until recently, Crosman offered accessory packs of cylinders that contained two 10-shot cylinders and one 6-

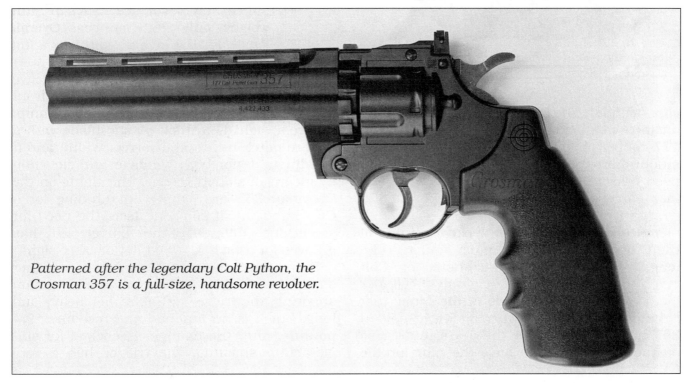

Patterned after the legendary Colt Python, the Crosman 357 is a full-size, handsome revolver.

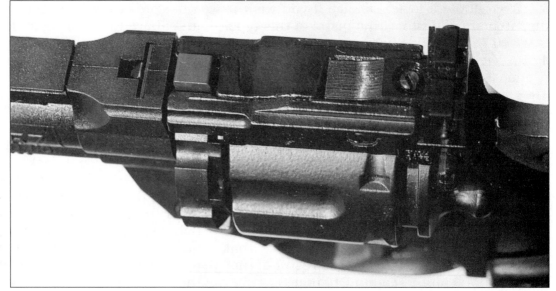

The Crosman 357 is a top-break revolver and depressing the square button on top of the frame unlatches the barrel.

Although the cylinder shown here holds 10 pellets, cylinders that hold 6 pellets can also be used in the Crosman 357.

shot cylinder. The cylinders measure 0.355 of an inch in thickness so almost any type of 177-caliber pellet can be used since they are much shorter than the cylinder. The advertised velocity for the Crosman 357 with a 6-inch barrel is up to 435 ft/sec and up to 375 ft/sec with a 4-inch barrel.

A ventilated rib adorns the barrel shroud of the Crosman 357. The hammer spur has the long, gentle curve characteristic of Colt revolvers. There is a fake Colt-style cylinder latch on the left-hand side of the frame just behind the cylinder. Grips on the Crosman 357 have changed over the years, but those on the current version have the same profile

as the famous Hogue grips. They have finger grooves and a rough surface to give a secure hold. Also, they extend below the grip frame far enough to completely enclose the folding wing head of the piercing screw. Therefore, the bottom of the grip is smooth and rounded with no protruding piercing screw.

The Crosman 357 is currently available with either a 4- or 6-inch barrel length. Although the Crosman catalog lists the weight of the Model 357 with a 6-inch barrel as 32 ounces, my postal scale says my gun weighs only 26.3 ounces. Overall length is 11.4 inches, so this is a full size revolver with a large grip.

Sights on the Crosman 357 leave nothing to be desired. The front sight is a long, serrated, square-topped ramp. The rear sight is a thick plastic blade with a square notch having the correct width, and it is adjustable for both windage and elevation by means of slotted screws. The sights on the Crosman 357 are simply outstanding for a CO_2 handgun. If someone feels the need for something different, the barrel rib has grooves for attaching a red dot or laser sight.

Firing the Crosman 357 can be done either single or double action. In double-action shooting, the trigger pull is rather heavy and long, but it is not too bad and measures 9.4 pounds. After the hammer is cocked for single-action shooting, the trigger has a very

A CO_2 cylinder is held in the grip of the Crosman 357, but the grip panels enclose the piercing screw.

Velocity Data for the Crosman 357 at 70-72°F				
		Velocity, ft/sec		
Pellet	Ave.	High	Low	Std. Dev.
D.N. Meisterkugeln	432	442	423	8
Gamo Match	441	449	434	6
Daisy Wadcutter	446	453	439	6
Crosman Wadcutter	432	441	424	7
D. N. Club	467	478	456	8
Eley Target	436	442	429	5

short take-up motion followed by a crisp let-off and the trigger pull is only 5.1 pounds. Although it is slightly heavy, the trigger pull in the single-action mode is quite acceptable.

Although the advertised velocity for the 6-inch barreled Crosman 357 is up to 435 ft/sec, I found this velocity was exceeded with several pellets. The Crosman 357 produces enough power to be a useful tool for dispatching small varmints. In fact, with every type of pellet tested, the Crosman 357 gave slightly higher velocities than did the Model 1710,

which has a barrel approximately 1.25 inches longer. I had not expected that, but that is what the chronograph registered. The Crosman 357 handled well, functioned reliably, and exceeded my expectations. I had planned to use a Model 1710 as a training piece for handgun varmint hunting, but the Model 357 is causing me to reconsider. It is a classic American CO_2 handgun and represents excellent value at its usual selling price of $40-$45.

CHAPTER 7

EVALUATION OF ELITE 177-CALIBER PISTOLS

WHILE THE MANY inexpensive CO_2 pistols give good performance and are functionally very reliable, it is not appropriate to compare them to the models that cost up to $200. The high-end models have a quality of construction, fit and finish that more closely approximate the characteristics of firearms. As a result, the upper-end models that sell for approximately $100 or more are designated in this book as "elite" models, and they will be evaluated separately in this chapter.

In the descriptions that follow, instructions are given for installing a CO_2 cylinder and loading ammunition in each model. Although is it not stated explicitly in the discussion of each model, the safety should always be in the "on" position before loading propellant or projectiles in any CO_2 gun. There is danger in piercing a CO_2 cylinder in a gun that might already have pellets in it or in placing pellets in a gun that is pressurized with a pierced CO_2 cylinder. Read the owner's manual and follow all safety instructions.

The Beretta 92FS

A CO_2 pistol with the name PIETRO BERETTA GARDONE on the side would be expected to be special and the Beretta 92 FS certainly is. There are actually four versions of the Beretta 92 FS that have different fin-

The Beretta 92 FS bears an incredible likeness to the famous 9 mm Beretta.

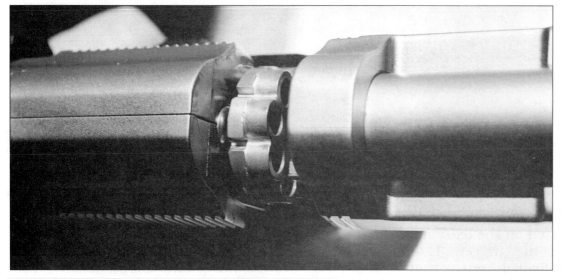

While the Beretta 92 FS looks like an autoloading pistol, it holds eight pellets in a metal cylinder that is completely enclosed in the frame.

Dual safety levers are located on the upper rear portion of the fake slide.

ishes, sights, and grip materials. My version of this pistol with its nickel finish that resembles satin stainless steel accented by its black grips, trigger, sights, hammer, and safety levers, is beautiful. In my opinion, in terms of realism its appearance is unsurpassed among CO_2 pistols. In size and weight, the Beretta 92 FS is equal to the famous military sidearm. Its weight is 45.7 ounces, overall length is 8 inches, and the barrel length is 5 inches. The basic blue and nickel versions sell in the $175-$200 range and are marketed by Crosman Corporation.

The Beretta 92 FS, and other models of this CO_2 family, use eight-shot, metal magazines. A cylindrical magazine is inserted by moving the front portion of the slide forward. The

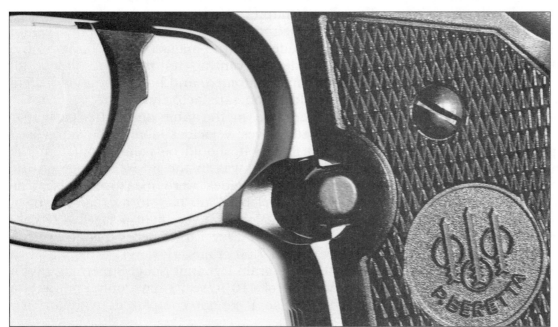

The button on the left-hand side of the frame behind the trigger is not a magazine release. Pressing it inward pushes the right-hand grip panel away from the frame so it can be removed to load a CO_2 cylinder.

Velocity Data for the Beretta 92 FS at 80°F

Pellet	Velocity, ft/sec			
	Ave.	High	Low	Std. Dev.
D.N. Meisterkugeln	424	428	420	4
Gamo Match	428	436	424	5
Daisy Wadcutter	436	437	435	1
Crosman Wadcutter	445	449	440	3
D. N. Club	479	483	476	3
Eley Target	463	471	456	6

slide is released by pushing downward on the rotating lever located on the left-hand side of the frame above the trigger. This action allows the spring-loaded front portion of the slide to move forward. The spring is quite strong and the barrel and slide slam forward smartly. The magazine is placed in the open area between the two sections of the slide and pushing the forward section to the rear closes the slide over the magazine. As this occurs, a shaft passes through the center hole in the magazine and it rotates on that shaft during firing. When the action is open, the trigger cannot be pulled, and the hammer cannot be moved to the cocked position.

Dual safety levers are provided at the rear of the slide. However, the safety levers are not decocking levers. Placing the safety on does not lower the hammer. The lever on the left-hand side of the frame that resembles the slide release on the centerfire Beretta firearm is a fake. The button behind the trigger that is the magazine release on the firearm pushes the right-hand grip panel away from the frame to permit access to the area where the CO_2 cylinder is located. A CO_2 cylinder is placed in the grip frame with the neck up. A lever pivoted at the rear forms the bottom of the grip, and it is used to pierce the cylinder. With the lever pulled down and a CO_2 cylinder in place, a brass screw with a large knurled head is positioned against the base of the cylinder. Then, with the cylinder placed snugly between the piercing pin and the base screw, returning the lever to its position flush with the grip frame pierces the CO_2 cylinder.

Sights on the Beretta 92 FS are excellent, and they consist of a square-topped blade front sight and a square-notch rear. The rear sight is adjustable for windage only by loosening the locking Allen-headed screw and moving the blade laterally. The sturdy black sights give an excellent sight picture.

Single-action trigger pull on my Beretta 92 FS is rather heavy and there is some creep. My Lyman trigger pull gauge indicated the pull to be 5.7 pounds. There is a short take-up in the two-stage pull before the actual let-off is approached. In the double-action mode, trigger pull is moderately heavy and it increases about two-thirds of the way through the motion. The gauge indicated a double-action pull of 8.6 pounds.

Partially because this is a pistol with a lot of class, I was anxious to see how the Beretta would perform. The advertised muzzle velocity is 393 ft/sec, but the velocity depends on pellet weight and temperature. Because of the short length of the cylindrical magazine, the instruction manual recommends only pellets shorter than 0.256 inches in length be used. Most 177-caliber pellets are shorter than that, but several of the pointed pellets measure from 0.260 to 0.275 inches in length (see Chapter 3). The longer pellets should not be used in this pistol because they would protrude from the magazine and hang up the cylinder preventing its rotation. Almost all wadcutter, domed, and hollow pointed pellets will function satisfactorily.

The data in the table show this particular Beretta gives velocities above the advertised 393 ft/sec. It should be pointed out that the temperature was in the 80-82°F range on the day the velocities were measured. Also, the Dynamit Nobel Club has an average weight of only 6.98 grains, a very light pellet in 177 caliber, and the Eley Target pellet has an average weight of 7.50 grains. However, two shots with the 9.36 grain Dynamit Nobel Supermag gave a velocity of 410 ft/sec. I have only one Beretta 92 FS so I cannot compare it with another

Outwardly, there is little to distinguish the CO_2 pistol from the legendary Colt 1911 firearm. Elegant is an appropriate way to describe these elite pistols.

specimen. This particular Beretta is quite fast and the velocities for the five-shot strings were very uniform as indicated by the extreme spread of only a few ft/sec in velocity and standard deviations that average only 3.7 ft/sec.

The Colt 1911 A1

Probably the two most recognizable auto-loading pistols in the world are the Colt 1911 and the Beretta 92. The first of these was the official military sidearm for about 75 years and the latter currently holds that distinction. It was inevitable that CO_2 pistols with these configurations be made. And made they have been, with the resemblance between them and the firearms that inspired them being astounding. The Beretta 92 was discussed earlier and this section deals with the Colt 1911.

Along with several other CO_2 pistols, the Colt 1911 A1 is produced by Umarex in Germany and imported by Crosman Corporation. Several versions are available. In blued finish, models are available with grips made of black plastic, simulated ivory, and wood. Nickel-plated models are available with wood or plastic grips. My Colt CO_2 pistols all have the plastic grips that

The lever above the trigger is the release that lets the front section of the slide and barrel move forward.

have the feel of rubber, and they give an excellent feel. Other versions of the Colt 1911 A1 having compensators and combat-type sights and grips are also available.

Retail list prices for the Colt 1911 A1 models start at $199 and go up a long way for the combat versions, although the actual selling

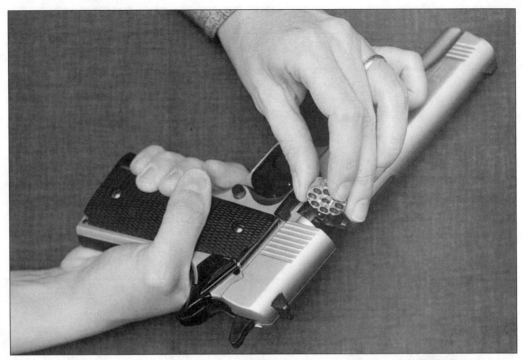

A metal 8-shot cylinder is held inside the frame of the Colt 1911 A1.

prices are somewhat less. At this price level, one would expect a lot in a CO_2 gun. The Colt 1911 A1 delivers a lot. The level of fit and finish is outstanding. Blue models are highly polished and given a deep blue finish. Nickel-plated models are likewise very highly finished. These pistols do not carry the most prestigious name in handguns for nothing. In my opinion, the Colt CO_2 pistols are among the two or three most elegant and realistic models available.

Outwardly, the resemblance between the Colt CO_2 pistol and a real Colt 45 auto is impressive in its detail. The Colt pistol has a functioning grip safety that must be depressed before the pistol will fire. The thumb safety is a large lever located at the left rear of the slide, exactly as on the Colt 1911 firearm. Other cosmetic features are included to enhance the realistic appearance.

The button on the left-hand side just behind the trigger that serves as a magazine release on the Colt 45 serves a different function on the CO_2 pistol. Pushing the button inward (to the right) forces the right-hand grip panel to snap off giving access to the chamber where the CO_2 cylinder is contained. The lever above the trigger on the left-hand side of the frame is the slide release on a Colt 45. It is also the slide release on the CO_2 pistol, but pushing the lever downward releases the spring-loaded front section of the slide,

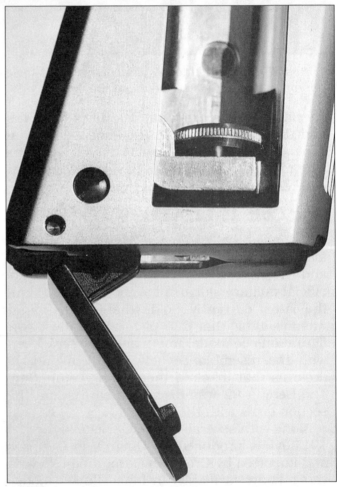

Piercing the CO_2 cylinder is accomplished by pushing the lever against the bottom of the grip frame. The large knurled screw is used to position the cylinder correctly before the lever is moved.

Only the ridges on the front end of the slide suggest that the front section must be gripped securely to move it into the locked position. The Colt firearm has no such ridges at the front end.

which is the barrel housing, allowing it to move forward. This is how access to the magazine is afforded. The magazine is a metal cylinder that holds eight 177-caliber pellets. The owner's manual makes it clear that diabolo lead pellets are the only acceptable ammunition for use in this pistol.

Sights on the Colt 1911 A1 are true to those on the firearm. The front sight is a small square-topped ramp and the rear sight is a blade with a square notch. The rear sight is adjustable for windage after loosening a lock screw with an Allen wrench (supplied with the pistol). The sights provide an excellent sight picture. A replacement set of sights consisting of a higher front sight and an adjustable rear is available as aftermarket accessories.

Charging the pistol is accomplished by removing the right-hand grip panel to gain access to the interior of the grip. A CO_2 cylinder is inserted neck up in the grip frame. Piercing of the CO_2 cylinder is caused by moving a lever that forms the bottom of the grip. After the lever is pulled down, a CO_2 cylinder is placed in the chamber inside the grip frame. A tensioning screw with a large head rests against the base of the cylinder and is turned to move the cylinder upward against the piercing pin. Pushing the lever up against the bot-

tom of the grip frame causes the CO_2 cylinder to be pushed against the piercing pin.

Both single- and double-action firing of the Colt 1911 A1 CO_2 pistol are possible. In single-action firing, the hammer is cocked for each shot. For double-action firing, the trigger is pulled until the hammer moves back and is then released. In single-action firing, the trigger let-off is light and fairly crisp. The average trigger pull for my three Colt pistols averaged only 2.7 pounds in single-action firing. In double-action firing, the pull seems to increase as the trigger moves to the rear and gets quite heavy near the end of the trigger movement (which is known as stacking). For my Colt guns, the average trigger pull in double-action shooting was just over 10 pounds. While the three specimens that I have some experience with do not impress me in double-action firing, the single-action trigger movement is unexcelled by any other CO_2 pistol I have tested.

Overall length of the Colt 1911 is 9 inches and the rifled steel barrel is 5 inches long, dimensions that equal those of the famous firearm. Weight is specified as 38 ounces, but mine weighs 39.3 ounces on my postal scale. The owner's manual indicates approximately 60 shots can be obtained from a CO_2 cylinder. A muzzle velocity of 393 ft/sec is also specified, but the weight of the pellet that gives that velocity is not. Each pistol comes in a padded plastic case with two pellet cylinders, a cleaning brush, a can of pellets, a CO_2 cylinder, and an Allen wrench that fits the locking screw in the rear sight. It makes an elegant package indeed.

Velocities were measured at 80°F with six different types of pellets. Five-shot strings were fired with the results displayed in the table.

While the specified muzzle velocity for the Colt 1911 is 393 ft/sec, the owner's manual does not specify the temperature or pellet weight with which that velocity was obtained.

Velocity Data for the Colt 1911 A1 at 80°F

Pellet		Velocity, ft/sec Ave.	High	Low	Std. Dev.
D.N. Meisterkugeln		418	420	416	2
D.N. Meisterkugeln	(2)	390	398	379	8
Gamo Match		430	436	428	3
Gamo Match	(2)	394	402	391	5
Daisy Wadcutter		436	439	431	3
Daisy Wadcutter	(2)	374	384	359	10
Crosman Wadcutter		448	450	447	1
D. N. Club		484	491	474	6
Eley Target		466	467	464	1

(2) indicates data from a second Colt 1911 with velocities measured at 70°F

In the data obtained with my Colt on a day in which the temperature was slightly over 80°F, the velocity was over 400 ft/sec with all pellets chosen for testing. The very light Club pellet (6.98 grains) gave an average velocity almost 100 ft/sec higher than the advertised velocity for this pistol. I know for a fact that not all Colt 1911 pistols will give velocities this high, even when allowance is made for the temperature and pellet weight. To demonstrate this, a second Colt 1911 was tested on a day when the temperature was 10 degrees cooler than when the first testing was conducted. The data obtained with three of the same types of pellets used earlier are shown in the table. The second Colt gave average velocities 30-50 ft/sec lower than the first. While the difference in temperature accounts for part of the difference, it appears the second Colt gives lower velocities anyway. This is expected due to difference in valves, hammer spring stiffness, etc.

It is interesting to compare the data for the Colt 1911 with that for the Beretta 92 FS since both pistols are made by Umarex, have the same barrel length, and use the same eight-shot metal magazines. As expected, the data show the velocities from these two fine CO_2 pistols are nearly identical (but not for the second Colt).

When I first started shooting targets with the Colt and a lightweight wadcutter pellet, I found that with my usual six o'clock hold, the gun fired approximately 3 inches high at 10 yards. Since there is no vertical sight adjustment, I was unable to move the point of impact. At that point I switched to the Dynamit Nobel Supermag wadcutter pellet, which

has a weight of 9.36 grains. This resulted in a lower point of impact on the target at 10 yards. I then fired eight three-shot groups that averaged only 0.81 inches. In my opinion the Colt is capable of outstanding accuracy, but I wish it had a fully adjustable rear sight. As mentioned earlier, a set consisting of a higher front sight and a fully adjustable rear are available as accessories.

I suppose it is inevitable that one would ask whether the Colt 1911 or the Beretta is a better choice. Let me say from the beginning, the factors that enable one to make such a decision are subjective. There are some things I like better about one than the other. For example, the Colt 1911 has a smaller grip and weighs almost 6 ounces less so it has a better feel in my hand. Sights are virtually identical and both have very good single-action trigger pull although that of the Colt is much lighter. However, I have no real affection for the grip safety on the Colt. Ease of loading and insertion of CO_2 cylinders is identical. Based on my experience with all the models discussed in this chapter (and I own all of them), I would have no hesitation about picking either of these elite CO_2 pistols. Some of the other models discussed in this chapter are fine pistols and have a lot to offer at prices significantly lower than the Colt or Beretta. As you read the rest of this chapter you will see what I mean.

The Crosman C40 and CB40

Crosman produced the classic Model 600 22-caliber semi-automatic in 1960-1970. It was a durable gun made of metal and it is described in detail in Chapter 10. Following

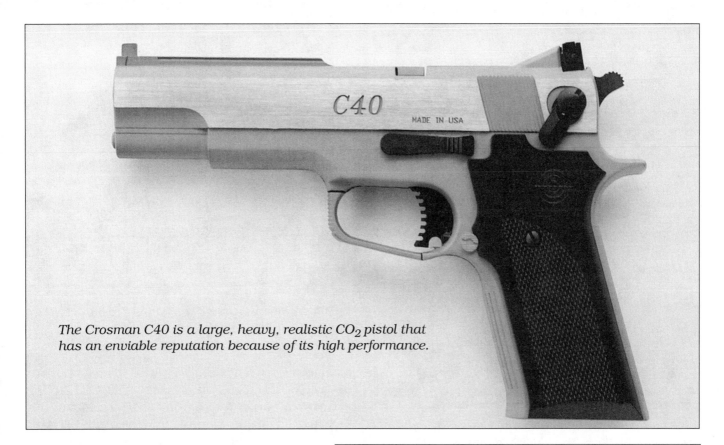

The Crosman C40 is a large, heavy, realistic CO$_2$ pistol that has an enviable reputation because of its high performance.

the production of the Model 600, single-shot CO$_2$ pistols made of metal were also marketed, but there was no repeater of similar construction for a considerable time. With the appearance of the Repeat-Air 1008 in 1992, Crosman again had a repeating CO$_2$ pistol that resembled a semi-automatic; but the Model 1008 was made largely of plastic. As nice as it is, the 1008 is not a classic in the same sense as are earlier models like the 600.

I am sure that through the years many Crosman fans wanted to see the production of a metallic repeating pistol. That wish came true in 1998 when Crosman introduced the C40 (silver finish) and CB40 (black finish) pistols in 177 caliber. Of course, I would have preferred a 22-caliber version also being available. All features except color are identical for the two models. As of early 2003, the black CB40 is being discontinued. Retail price of the C40 or CB40 is in the $100 range.

While the C40 represents a return to classic Crosman quality in a CO$_2$ pistol, it is not a Model 600. The Model 600 was a true semi-automatic in that after cocking the pistol for the first shot, subsequent shots required only

The lever on the left-hand side just below the "MADE IN USA" is the release that allows the barrel to tip upward at the rear.

pulling the trigger (single action) because the pistol reloaded and recocked itself. The Model C40 can be fired by simply pulling the trigger, but the pistol is not recocked by an action caused by gas pressure. Pulling the trigger again causes the hammer to move to the rear, but it is not moved to the rear (cocked position) by the previous shot. In other words, to make a C40 fire by pulling the trigger, the firing is double action. In that sense, it is actu-

Like many other CO_2 pistols, the C40 holds eight 177-caliber pellets in a plastic cylinder that is identical to those used in the Model 1008.

The fully adjustable rear sight on the Crosman C40 is excellent, but I believe the front sight should also be black instead of the light-colored metal.

ally more like firing a double-action revolver. Also, the C40 makes use of a revolving cylinder contained inside the frame. Pulling the trigger fires the piece, but it does not stay cocked between shots because the hammer rests in the down position. Of course, the pistol can be cocked manually and fired by pulling the trigger (single action) also.

Weighing 40 ounces and measuring 8.63 inches in overall length, the Crosman C40 very closely resembles a large-frame Smith & Wesson centerfire semi-automatic. It is an extremely well made piece that is very highly regarded by shooters of CO_2 pistols. Having a rifled steel barrel of 4-1/4 inches, the C40 is capable of fine accuracy, and Crosman advertised the muzzle velocity as up to 425 ft/sec. Although it shares similar dimensions with the Crosman 1008, that is where the similarity ends.

Unlike the Crosman 1008, which has a cross bolt safety, the C40 has a rotating lever on the left-hand side of the frame in the upper rear position. While most of the Smith & Wesson firearms that it resembles have safety levers on both sides, the C40 has a

lever only on one side. When the lever points down, the safety is on.

Controls on the Crosman C40 are straightforward in their operation. Located on the left-hand side of the frame just behind the trigger is a raised "button" that would be the magazine release button on a Smith & Wesson semi-automatic. On the C40 it is a fake. Located on the left-hand side of the frame just above the trigger is a sliding lever. The rear surface of the lever is ridged for applying pressure to move the lever to the rear. When the lever is moved to the rear, it releases the barrel lock and the barrel and its housing tip up at the rear. A cylindrical magazine holding eight pellets can be placed on the shaft located just below the barrel. Interestingly, even though the C40 is a heavy, metal pistol, it uses the same plastic cylinders used in the Model 1008 RepearAir.

Sights on the Crosman C40 are excellent. The front is a square-topped post with excellent shape although on the C40 it is gray colored. The rear sight is a black plastic assembly held between two large metal bosses. It is fully adjustable for windage and elevation by means of two slotted screws. Although I would prefer a black front sight (it is a simple matter to make it so), the factory sights are as good as those on any of my CO_2 pistols. Additionally, the rib along the top of the barrel assembly has grooves along the edges for easy mounting of auxiliary sights.

The piercing lever is pivoted at the bottom and outward from the frame.

The hammer is deeply grooved permitting positive thumb action during cocking. While the grip is rather large, the grip panels are deeply checkered and provide for secure holding of the pistol. The front and back straps are grooved, as is the front of the trigger guard. Even the rotating safety lever (located on the left-hand side of the frame at the rear) is ridged for a good grip.

Loading a CO_2 cylinder in the C40 involves removing the right-hand grip panel by applying outward pressure at the notch on the top edge. The piercing lever is pivoted at the bottom, and it swings outward away from the frame. Pushing the lever inward at the top moves the base screw against the bottom of the CO_2 cylinder by cam action, which causes piercing of the cylinder.

Located in the bottom of the grip frame is an adjustment screw that controls how far upward the CO_2 cylinder will move as the piercing lever is pushed back into the grip. If the cylinder moves too far, it will place too much pressure on the piercing pin, and if it moves too little, piercing may not be achieved or a gas tight seal may not result. The correct amount of movement is established by first placing a CO_2 cylinder neck up in the grip. Start moving the piercing lever toward the frame. When pressure is felt, the CO_2 cylin-

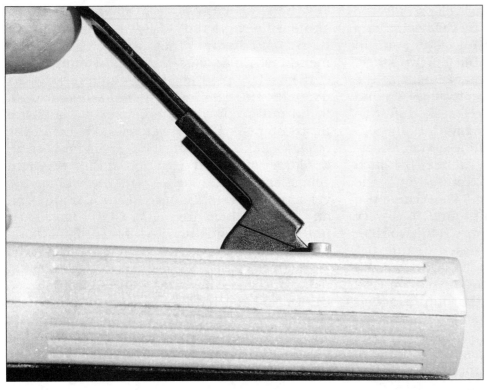

An index line on the piercing lever is aligned with the outside edge of the grip frame to show how much movement the lever should have to correctly pierce the CO_2 cylinder.

Velocity Data for the Crosman CB40 at 80°F

Pellet		Velocity, ft/sec			
		Ave.	High	Low	Std. Dev.
D.N. Meisterkugeln		376	382	372	4
D.N. Meisterkugeln	(2)	395	396	394	1
Gamo Match		395	402	387	7
Gamo Match	(2)	402	406	398	3
Daisy Wadcutter		393	401	386	6
Daisy Wadcutter	(2)	383	388	378	4
Crosman Wadcutter		402	411	389	11
D. N. Club		446	450	443	3
Eley Target		427	433	420	7
Gamo Match		395	402	387	7

(2) indicates data obtained with a Crosman C40 fired at 70°F

der is in contact with the piercing pin and the support base. Looking at the lever from the rear, one can see a line running diagonally across its back edge. That index line should align with the outer edge of the grip frame while there is contact of the CO_2 cylinder with both the piercing pin and the base support. If it does not, the position of the base support can be adjusted by means of a slotted-head screw in the base of the grip. By turning that screw, adjust the distance between piercing pin and the base support so that the index mark on the lever aligns with the edge of the grip frame. With that adjustment made, pushing the piercing lever the rest of the way into the grip will provide the correct amount of travel of the CO_2 cylinder.

Trigger action on my C40 is very good. In single-action firing, the pull is two-stage. There is a rather long, soft movement of the trigger and then resistance is felt. At that point, let-off is light and crisp. Let-off was measured at 4.0 pounds for my C40 and 4.3 pounds for my CB40. In double-action shooting, the trigger moves only about 1/4 inch during which the cylinder rotates and the hammer moves to the rear. That causes a rather short, heavy pull although it is very smooth on both my C40 and CB40. Double-action pull on the C40 was measured at 10.1 pounds while that for the CB40 was 10.8 pounds. Frankly, none of the triggers on CO_2 pistols are outstanding in the double-action mode, but that on my Crosman C40 is as good as most.

Although the other CO_2 pistols in the elite category carry names of American firearms manufacturers, they are foreign made. The Crosman C40 has stamped "Made in U.S.A." on the left-hand side of the frame. It is a sturdy, attractive handgun that is fully the equal of any other of its type.

Crosman advertises a velocity of up to 430 ft/sec for the C40 with no temperature or pellet weight specified. The data show that when the temperature is in the low 80s and with pellets weighing around 7 grains, the C40 will actually exceed that velocity. All of the velocities are in accord with those expected for the weight of the pellets used. The standard deviations are not quite as low with the types of pellets chosen, but they are still reasonable. For the Crosman Copperhead wadcutter, the standard deviation of 11 ft/sec is much larger than that for any other pellet. It should be mentioned this pellet has a skirt diameter of 0.181 inch while the Gamo Match has a skirt diameter of 0.186 inch. In my particular C40, it did not seem that the Crosman wadcutter fit in the magazine as well as did some of the other pellets. That may have contributed to the larger standard deviation in the measured velocities for that pellet. On the whole, the velocity performance of the C40 is quite good and the velocities are higher than I have seen published in some reviews of this pistol.

At a later date when the temperature was 10 degrees cooler, a Crosman C40 was tested using three of the same pellets used in the CB40. As expected, the velocities were somewhat different with the two pistols, but the effect did not seem to be one caused by the temperature. In fact, the average velocities were higher even though the C40 was fired at

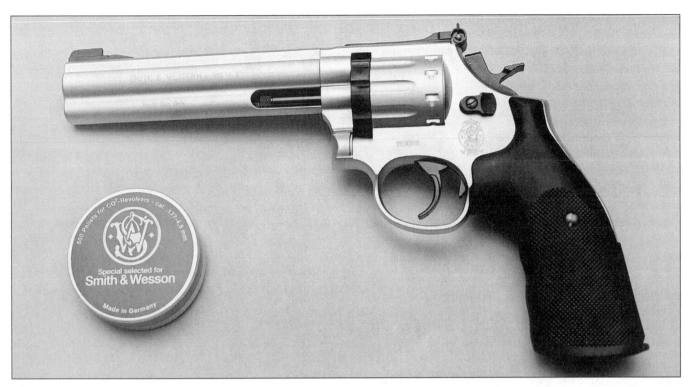

The elegant appearance of the Smith & Wesson 586 and 686 CO_2 revolvers is matched by their performance.

70°F while the CB40 was tested when the temperature was 80°F. The differences were not great, but it appears the C40 gives higher velocities than my particular CB40.

The Smith & Wesson 586 and 686

Founded in 1852, Smith & Wesson is one of the most respected names in firearms. My interaction with Smith & Wesson revolvers has been a long one, and for a brief period about 30 years ago, I had a Smith & Wesson Model 15 Combat Masterpiece for occasions when I was on duty with a sheriff's reserve unit.

For several years, the legendary Smith & Wesson name appeared on a variety of air rifles and pistols. In the interim, manufacturers like Crosman and Daisy have produced numerous CO_2 pistols that mimic various Smith & Wesson models, and they are described in this book.

After an absence of 20 years, pellet guns are again available bearing the prestigious Smith & Wesson name. The new CO_2 guns are made in Germany by Umarex and marketed by Crosman Corporation. Smith & Wesson revolvers are made in four sizes that are known as J-, K-, L- and N-frames (in the order of increasing size). The N-Frame is the one used for the very large revolvers such as

Pushing forward the release behind the cylinder unlatches it on the Smith & Wesson CO_2 revolvers. The cylinder swings out of the frame to the left.

the 44 Magnum. Several popular revolvers chambered for cartridges such as the 357 Magnum are based on the L-frame. The new Smith & Wesson CO_2 revolvers are faithful reproductions of the L-frame firearms. Barrel lengths offered include 4-, 6-, and 8-inch

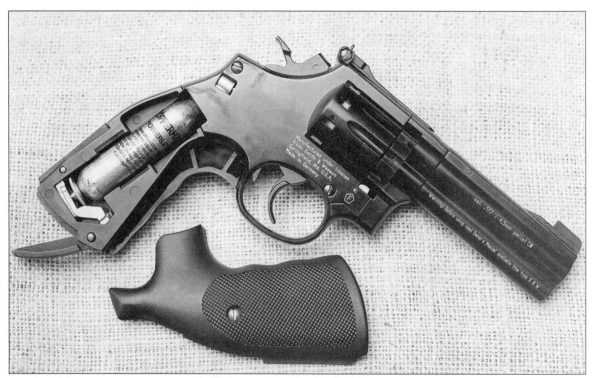

A positioning screw and hinged lever are used to pierce the CO_2 cylinder.

lengths and black (Model 586) and nickel (Model 686) finishes are available. My Smith & Wesson specimens include a 4-inch Model 586 and a 6-inch Model 686, both of which were evaluated during the testing.

Barrels of different lengths for the Smith & Wesson have matching shrouds and they are interchangeable. Each revolver comes with a special tool that has a hexagonal head to match a hexagonal recess in the front end of the barrel shroud. By loosening the retaining plug, the barrel and shroud can be easily removed.

When you pick up one of the Smith & Wesson revolvers, you are immediately impressed with its weight. These metal guns have full lug barrels and beautifully checkered rubber grips so the weights are 39.9, 44.6, and 49.4 ounces for revolvers with 4-, 6-, and 8-inch barrels, respectively. These 10-shot revolvers are realistic! Although they sell for $150-175, fit and finish of these guns leave nothing to be desired.

Cylinders of the Smith & Wesson revolvers have a large fake (but very realistic) portion and the actual rotating magazine that constitutes the forward section. Oddly, the cylinders that hold the pellets are all blue, so they contrast with the nickel finish revolvers. The cylindrical magazine matches the appearance of the larger fake rear portion very well, so the combined "cylinder" looks authentic on the blue models. Moreover, the "magazine

cylinder" swings out of the frame on the left-hand side when the latch is pushed forward. Located on the left-hand side of the frame just behind the cylinder, the latch functions exactly as it does on Smith & Wesson firearms. The latch is finely checkered and fits the right-hand thumb very well. With the cylinder rotated fully out of the frame, 10 pellets can be inserted, or the cylinder can be lifted off its supporting spindle and a previously loaded cylinder can be installed. The cylinder measures 0.370 inch in thickness so any type of 177-caliber pellet can be inserted in the chambers without protruding from the front of the cylinder.

As with other CO_2 repeating pistols, the CO_2 cylinder is contained in the grip. The right-hand grip panel can be lifted outward away from the frame by means of a recess at the bottom. Swinging the piercing lever downward causes the bottom support screw to move downward slightly. A CO_2 cylinder is inserted neck up into the grip and the tensioning screw is turned until it meets the bottom of the cylinder, which moves upward until its neck makes contact with the piercing pin. After replacing the grip panel, the piercing lever is moved upward until it is flush with the bottom of the grip.

When fired single action, let-off was crisp and the trigger pull on my Model 586 mea-

Velocity Data for the Smith & Wesson 586 (4-inch) at 80°F

| Pellet | Ave. | Velocity, ft/sec | | Std. Dev. |
		High	Low	
D.N. Meisterkugeln	367	372	363	4
Gamo Match	386	390	382	6
Daisy Wadcutter	395	398	393	2
Crosman Wadcutter	390	395	379	7
D. N. Club	441	447	432	6
Eley Target	411	416	408	3

Velocity Data for the Smith & Wesson 686 (6-inch) at 80°F

| Pellet | Ave. | Velocity, ft/sec | | Std. Dev. |
		High	Low	
D.N. Meisterkugeln	437	441	431	4
Gamo Match	457	464	447	8
Daisy Wadcutter	457	465	446	8
Crosman Wadcutter	460	466	451	6
D. N. Club	503	510	494	8
Eley Target	475	481	470	4

sured 5.6 pounds while that of my Model 686 measured 6.1 pounds. In the double-action mode, the pull weights were 10.0 and 9.0 pounds, respectively.

I almost run out of superlatives when I describe the sights on the Smith & Wesson 586 and 686 revolvers. In my opinion, the sights are the best on any CO_2 gun I have. A beautiful square-topped post-on-ramp front sight is matched with a blade rear sight having a square notch. The rear sight is fully adjustable by means of two slotted screws. The sights are very similar to those on Smith & Wesson firearms. Indeed they are first-class sights, but it doesn't end there. Since three barrel lengths are available, the front post needs to be of different width for each barrel length in order to correctly match the square notch of the rear. Otherwise, with the longest barrel the front sight will be farther from the eye and appear to be thinner. This situation would cause more space between the front sight and the edges of the notch in the rear to appear. To deal with this problem, each Smith & Wesson comes with three ramp front sights that have widths of 2.5, 2.8, and 3.2 mm. Since the front sight is held to the barrel with a single screw, it is a simple matter to interchange the front sights and place the sight

with the widest post on the longest barrel, and vice versa. In this way, a consistent, uniform sight picture is afforded even when barrels having different lengths are used. The factory sights on the Smith & Wesson Models 586 and 686 are simply outstanding.

Velocity data for the Smith & Wesson 586 show that with pellets of normal weight, the maximum muzzle velocity is approximately the advertised 396 ft/sec. However, with lighter pellets such as the Club and Eley Match, the velocity is considerably higher than the advertised value when the temperature is 80-82°F.

The real surprise was when the Model 686 with a 6-inch barrel was fired across the chronograph. With the advertised muzzle velocity being 426 ft/sec, it was expected that most pellets would give velocities this high or slightly higher since it was a warm day. However, even the Meisterkugeln, which weighs 8.225 grains, went across the chronograph at 437 ft/sec! The very light Club pellet actually gave an average velocity that was over 500 ft/sec! With the very sturdy Crosman Copperhead wadcutter, the average velocity was 460 ft/sec. Even with the 9.36 grain Dynamit Nobel Supermag, the Model 686 the velocity was 424 ft/sec. There is no question that the

Smith & Wesson 686 has sufficient punch to be useful for dispatching small pests. It would be an excellent choice for a CO_2 handgun to be used as a practice arm for handgun hunters. It has the size and weight to match a firearm having of the same label and model. My Model 686 is a superb handgun, and I hope to spend a lot of time with it.

In the velocity tests, two of the fine Smith & Wesson revolvers were used. It was expected that since the advertised velocities for the 4-inch and 6-inch barreled models are specified as 396 and 426 ft/sec, respectively, the velocities with each pellet would differ by about 30 ft/sec. In fact, the difference was about 50-70 ft/sec in favor of the longer barrel. After much of the testing had been completed, it was found that the cylinder in the Model 586 had much tighter chambers and the pellets had to be forced in during loading. It is possible this accounted for at least part of the difference in velocity with some pellets. However, the cylinder from the Model 686 was loaded with Crosman Copperhead wadcutter pellets and placed in the Model 586 and the velocity was not significantly different.

The Walther CP99

The Walther name is one of the most celebrated names in the world of firearms. Walther pistols include such legendary models as the P38 and PPK. It is no surprise that a Walther CO_2 pistol would represent a significant entry in the field. The German company, Umarex, is the parent company for Walther, and many of the fine CO_2 pistols described in this book are produced by Umarex for marketing under other brand names. Crosman Corporation markets the Walther and several other brands made by Umarex.

Like other CO_2 pistols, the Walther CP99 holds the CO_2 cylinder in the grip. However, that is where the similarity ends. At the rear of the trigger guard, there is a short, curved, black lever that has serrated top edges. Pulling down on this lever allows the release of the "magazine" from the grip except in this case the "magazine" is the entire housing and piercing mechanism for the CO_2 cylinder. The bottom of this device rotates 90° on a spiral bevel that moves the adjustable brass base support and CO_2 cylinder upward to pierce the cylinder. Then, the entire assembly is inserted into the grip until it clicks into place. Interestingly, the upper section of the assembly also contains the CO_2 valve. As a safety feature, the rear portion of the slide (that cocks the gun for single-action shooting) cannot be moved to the rear to cock the gun when the CO_2 assembly is removed.

The Walther CP99 has a large sliding safety lever located on the right-hand side of the frame. Each end of the lever is serrated and moving the lever to the rear exposes "F" and a large red dot. Moving the lever forward exposes an "S" showing that the safety is on. This is a very positive safety and only filling in the "F" and "S" with white paint to make them more visible would improve it slightly.

The Walther CP99 matches the appearance of the Walther P99 firearm in almost every detail.

Unique to the Walther CP99 is the fact the CO_2 cylinder and valve assembly are removed as a unit. Piercing of the CO_2 cylinder is carried out before the assembly is replaced in the grip.

The variant I bought, the CP99 Military, has an olive green composite frame but the entire slide is made of heavy metal. Retail prices for the various CP99 models are in the $110-120 range. Excellent ergonomics are provided by the raised knobs and grooves on the grips and the front of the trigger guard. Front and rear sights have no white dots but the front sight is a thick square-topped ramp and the rear sight has an excellent square notch. The rear sight is adjustable for windage in a most unusual way. Pulling the rear half of the slide back (as in cocking the gun for single-action shooting) exposes two Phillips screws on the underside of the slide just below the rear sight. These screws hold the rear sight in place. After loosening them, the rear sight can be moved laterally in its slot. There is no elevation adjustment.

The Walther CP99 has a total length of only 7 inches and it has a 3-inch rifled barrel. Weight of the pistol is 25.9 ounces and it has an advertised muzzle velocity of 360 ft/sec. Unlike most other CO_2 pistols, the CP99 has a two-part slide. The front slide section contains the barrel and it moves forward when the release lever (located on the left-hand side of the frame) is depressed. Moving the front part of the slide forward exposes the eight-shot metal cylinder. The rear half of the slide

The safety on the Walther is a sliding lever on the right-hand side of the frame.

can be pulled back to cock the piece for single-action shooting. If the piece is cocked and you want to decock it, depressing the decocking lever (located just forward and to the left of the rear sight) decocks it and also engages a firing pin safety.

Trigger action of the Walther CP99 is among the best for pistols of this general type. In single-action shooting, the trigger was crisp and measured 3.6 pounds. Double-action trigger pull was 9.1 pounds but it was smooth. Overall, I would rate the trigger action as very good for my pistol.

The front section of the slide on the CP99 moves forward to gain access to the pellet cylinder.

The Walther CP99 is unusual in that there is only one screw visible (just under the front end of the barrel), and it releases the barrel assembly for removal (Don't!). It is a remarkably clean design with only five pins visible. The grip has a replaceable backstrap inset so that the size of the grip can be altered. At the bottom rear of the grip is a recess with a cross pin for attaching a lanyard. The forward portion of the frame has a mount for attaching accessory sights. This pistol represents an exceedingly well-thought-out design, and outwardly, it is nearly an exact copy of the Walther P99 Military model. The results of testing the CP99 with six types of pellets are shown in the table.

The velocity data show the Walther CP99 gives velocities in excellent agreement with the advertised value of 360 ft/sec. Lighter pellets such as the Dynamit Nobel Club exceed that value while velocities with heavier pellets like the 8.2-grain Meisterkugeln are slightly lower. Measured velocities and their uniformity are certainly satisfactory for this small pistol.

My wife found the Walther CP99 to fit her hands better than some of the other pistols with large grips.

Velocity Data for the Walther CP99 at 68-70°F

Pellet	Ave.	Velocity, ft/sec		Std. Dev.
		High	Low	
D.N. Meisterkugeln	353	356	348	3
Gamo Match	365	367	363	2
Daisy Wadcutter	362	365	358	3
Crosman Wadcutter	362	369	354	7
D. N. Club	378	385	369	6
Eley Target	367	375	355	9

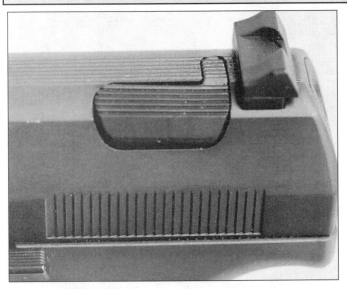

Pressing downward on the lever in front of the rear sight decocks the pistol.

In Chapter 4, a discussion of how many shots could be expected from a CO_2 cylinder was presented. The data show that the Walther CP99 gave very uniform velocities at least for about the first 30 shots. The average velocity with the Crosman Copperhead wadcutter was approximately 365 ft/sec. At 10 yards, I was able to get five-shot groups of 1.23 and 1.81 inches with the Gamo Match and D. N. Meisterkkugeln pellets, respectively.

The RWS C225

Rheinisch Westaflische Sprengstoff-Fabriken (abbreviated RWS) took over the marketing of airguns manufactured by Dianawerke in the 1980s. Since that time, the RWS-Diana airguns have become some of the most successful and widely accepted models. Not surprising is the fact that some of the finest CO_2 pistols carry the RWS label. The basic model was the 177-caliber RWS C225. There were four variants having differ-

ent barrel lengths and finishes. Originally, models were available with 4-inch barrels having blue or nickel finish. Later, blue and nickel finishes were available on pistols having 6-inch barrels. Models having 6-inch barrels were designated as target models. Retail prices are in the $175-200 range depending on finish and sight options.

A rotary magazine (cylinder) holding eight pellets is used in the C225 just as in the case of several other CO_2 pistols. Overall length of the 4-inch model is 7 inches and the weight is 37.6 ounces. Muzzle velocities are specified as 393 and 426 ft/sec for pistols with 4- and 6-inch barrels, respectively. A kit was offered so that 4- and 6-inch barrels could be interchanged. Also, a scope base was available, which permitted a scope, red dot, or laser sight to be mounted. An accessory sight kit was also available that consisted of a fully adjustable rear sight and a front sight with a higher blade. The C225 was, in fact, the basis for a system approach to customizing a CO_2 pistol.

While the RWS C225 shares several design features with other CO_2 pistols that resemble semi-automatic firearms, it also has unique features. The C225 features a slide that consists of a rear stationary part and a movable front section. A pivoted lever on the left-hand side of the frame just above the trigger is the latch that opens the magazine compartment. When the rear portion of the lever is rotated downward, the front section of the slide springs forward, which allows a magazine to be inserted. The magazine is placed into the recess between the two sections of the side, and the front portion is pushed to the rear while making sure the magazine pivot shaft enters the center hole in the magazine. The cylindrical magazine measures 0.277 inch in thickness, which is adequate to accommodate

The RWS C225 is a well-designed pistol that functioned reliably in the tests.

all but the longest 177-caliber pellets. However, the instruction manual states that diabolo pellets with a maximum length of 6.5 mm (0.254 inch) should be used.

The serrations on the rear (stationary) portion of the slide serve only a cosmetic function. Serrations on the sides of the slide near the muzzle are there to aid in getting a good grip on the slide when forcing it to the rear to close it.

A lever that forms the bottom of the grip is used in piercing the CO_2 cylinder. Pushing to the right on the button located on the left-hand side of the frame behind the trigger forces the right-hand grip panel away from the frame. The rear-pivoted lever is pulled down away from the grip frame. With the grip panel removed, a CO_2 cylinder is inserted neck up and the brass tensioning screw is turned to take up the slack so that the CO_2 cylinder is against the piercing pin. Then, after the grip panel is replaced, the piercing lever is rotated upward, which pushes the CO_2 cylinder onto the piercing pin.

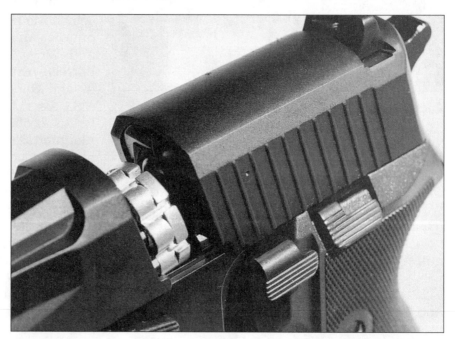

Releasing the front section of the slide gives access to the cylinder that holds pellets.

While a fake lever is found on the left-hand side of the frame just above the grip, a functioning control is located just above the trigger. That lever is the decocking lever.

When the hammer is cocked, depressing the decocking lever allows the hammer to fall part way down. Allowing the lever to return to its original position lowers the hammer com-

As with other elite CO₂ pistols, the piercing system of the C225 consists of a tensioning screw and a swinging lever.

locking screw is loosened. An Allen wrench of the correct size comes with the pistol. An excellent sight picture can be obtained with these sights.

Trigger action on the RWS C225 is about all one could expect from a CO_2 pistol of this type. After the hammer is cocked in single-action shooting, let-off is very crisp, although it is a little heavy with my trigger pull gauge registering 6.0 pounds. Double-action trigger pull is smooth with some increase in force required at the end of the trigger movement. The double-action pull measured 9.3 pounds for my RWS 225. Overall, the trigger is among the best to be found on the CO_2 pistols I have tested. On the negative side, I find the trigger to be uncomfortable because of its shape. The square-edged frame above the trigger causes my finger to ride low on the trigger, and I find the shape of the lower end of the trigger does not fit my finger well. This became clear during the extensive testing of the pistol. The results of the velocity tests are shown in the accompanying table.

The data obtained during velocity testing show the RWS C225 gives velocities that are

pletely. This action also engages a firing pin safety. When the slide is open, the trigger is blocked and cannot be pulled.

Sighting equipment on the RWS C225 is very good. The front sight is a low, square post while the rear sight is a thick, sturdy blade. The rear sight is adjustable for windage by moving it laterally after the Allen-head

There are three levers on the left-hand side of the frame of the C225. The front releases the moving portion of the slide, the middle is the decocking lever, and the rear is a fake.

Velocity Data for the RWS C225 at 73-75°F

Pellet	Ave.	Velocity, ft/sec High	Low	Std. Dev.
D.N. Meisterkugeln	358	362	354	3
Gamo Match	372	375	369	3
Daisy Wadcutter	376	380	374	2
Crosman Wadcutter	386	391	383	3
D. N. Club	408	415	404	4
Eley Target	395	398	393	2
D. N. Supermag	345	351	339	5

excellent with regard to uniformity. One reason for the velocities being slightly lower than those obtained with other pistols of this type is that the temperature was almost 10 degrees lower on the day these tests were conducted. Also, this pistol has a 4-inch barrel rather than the 5-inch tube on most other models. Velocity with the Supermag pellet was determined in case there is a need to use a heavier pellet (9.4 grains) to make the point of impact coincide with the point of aim.

Metal surfaces on the RWS 225 are finished in matte black. The black rubber-like grips have an outstanding feel due to the fine-checkered surface. This pistol represents a very high level of fit and finish. It comes in a

Sights on the C225 are quite acceptable, and I found the pointability of this pistol to be outstanding.

foam padded plastic case along with a cleaning brush, sight wrench, two magazines, and a can of pellets. Overall, this is one of the truly outstanding CO_2 pistols in the elite category. The RWS C225 has very recently been discontinued, but it should still be available from some dealers.

The Crosman CK92

What weighs 42 ounces, has a length of 8.5 inches, looks like a Beretta 92 and is made in Italy? The answer is the Crosman CK92. This 177-caliber, eight-shot pellet pistol is essentially all metal except for the grip panels, which are made of black plastic. This fine pistol is another of those real firearm "look alikes" that certainly looks authentic. Crosman marketed the CK92 in 2000-2002 and sold it in the $110-120 range.

This pistol has a 4.25-inch rifled steel barrel. It has a square-post type front sight and a square-notch rear sight that is adjustable for elevation and windage. Like others of the autoloader type, it utilizes an eight-shot cylinder that is exposed when the barrel is tipped up at the rear. On the Crosman CK92, the barrel latch is where the slide release is on a firearm and it slides forward to release the barrel. Even though the CK92 has the appearance of having the frame cut out to expose a round barrel, the frame and barrel shroud are one piece. Along the bottom edge of the rounded barrel there are grooves that

The Crosman CK92 is a well-made pistol that resembles the famous Beretta 92 firearm.

panel. However, this pistol has a novel means of loosening the panel. The transverse bolt latch that functions as a magazine release on an autoloading firearm can be pushed from right to left. In so doing, it engages the left-hand grip panel to force it away from the grip frame. This allows the grip panel to be grasped and removed.

Inside the grip, one finds a lever hinged at the bottom that swings to the left away from the frame. After the lever is swung outward, the curved plate that engages and supports the base of the CO_2 cylinder can be moved downward. The CO_2 cylinder is placed inside before the lever is forced back in place, where it forms the left-hand side of the grip frame. Forcing the lever back in the frame causes the plate against the bottom of the CO_2 cylinder to move upward to pierce the cylinder. Moreover, an adjustment screw that is accessed from the bottom of the grip frame is available to regulate the distance the CO_2 cylinder travels to adjust the tension. Thus, this pistol has a lever piercing mechanism that uses cam action to load the CO_2 cylinder in the pistol.

enable auxiliary sights to be attached by means of an intermount.

The safety is of the rotating lever or "decocker" type although rotating the safety when the hammer is cocked does not drop the hammer. The dual levers function only as the safety.

As with other guns of this type, the CO_2 cylinder is held in the grip. Access to the chamber is made by removing the left-hand grip

The CK92 has dual safety levers and a fully adjustable rear sight.

Velocity Data for the Crosman CK92 at 72°F

| Pellet | Ave. | Velocity, ft/sec | | Std. Dev. |
		High	Low	
D.N. Meisterkugeln	394	397	388	4
Gamo Match	418	421	414	3
Daisy Wadcutter	425	428	423	2
Crosman Wadcutter	391	400	384	8
D. N. Club	437	447	429	7
Eley Target	422	429	418	5

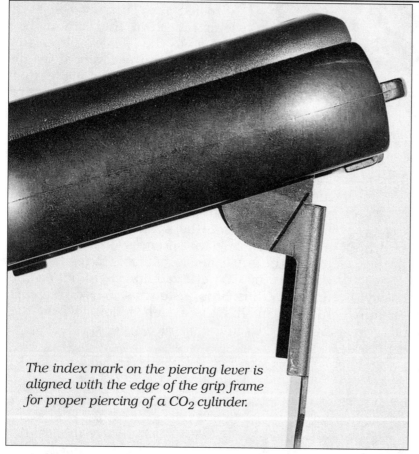

The index mark on the piercing lever is aligned with the edge of the grip frame for proper piercing of a CO_2 cylinder.

using a two-hand hold. Data from the velocity testing are shown in the following table.

Although it was offered only in 2000-2002, the CK92 probably suffered from being in direct competition with the Crosman C40. I obtained my CK92 in a store after it had been returned for some reason. I do not know what the reason was because I found the pistol to perform very well. The velocities with the six types of pellets were in the range advertised and they were uniform. The CK92 uses the same eight-shot cylinders as the Crosman Models 1008, 1710, and C40. I found them hard to load with the tiny 177-caliber pellets, especially the ones with thin, ridged skirts. This is no fault of the pistol.

The Crosman CK92 is a heavy, full-sized pistol that has a great deal of realism. It was the first of the upper-end pistols I bought and it has not been a disappointment. Only the fact that it fires 177-caliber pellets, uses CO_2 as the propellant, and uses a hidden rotary cylinder makes it differ from the real thing. I chased a rattlesnake with mine but couldn't catch up with the rascal before he disappeared in some high grass. He was warming himself on an asphalt road at dusk when I spotted him. When he realized he was being stalked, he literally exploded off the road, and I could not get an accurate shot although I emptied the magazine fast enough to show me the CK92 will fire very rapidly. I don't think the snake was in any real danger, but I meant to do him harm; maybe next time.

Trigger pull on the Crosman CK92 is among the best for pistols of this type. I measured the single-action pull at 4.7 pounds and the double-action pull was 6.3 pounds. Let-off was quite good when shooting in either mode.

There are several other small features that add to the authentic nature of the pistol. These include a hole through the hammer and a lanyard loop in the grip. Serrations are located on the sides of the "slide" and the frame has the appearance of being cut out to expose the barrel as on the Beretta 92 firearm. The front and back of the grip are smooth, but the front of the trigger guard has grooves as an aid to holding the piece when

CHAPTER 8

EVALUATION OF 20- AND 22-CALIBER PISTOLS

I'M NOT SURE how many different models of 177-caliber pistols there are but the number is large. They are made to resemble many of the most popular centerfire pistols and revolvers. In comparison, the number of models of 20- and 22-caliber CO_2 pistols is almost insignificant. From my perspective, this is unfortunate because I believe the 22-caliber pistols are just as much fun to shoot and are

more versatile. The velocities produced by the 177- and 22-caliber pistols are not greatly different because the pressure in a CO_2 cylinder is determined by its temperature. As a result, the pistols operate at approximately the same pressure regardless of caliber. Because of their firing heavier pellets, the 22 pistols can be useful for control of small pests. It is also easier to handle and load the

The Daisy PowerLine 622X has the lines of a Beretta 92, but it relies heavily on plastics in its construction.

larger pellets. This chapter is devoted to the evaluation of some of the 22-caliber pistols and the only current 20-caliber CO_2 gun readily available.

In the descriptions that follow, instructions are given for installing a CO_2 cylinder and loading ammunition in each model. Although it is not stated explicitly in the discussion of each model, the safety should always be in the "on" position before loading propellant or projectiles in any CO_2 gun. There is danger in piercing a CO_2 cylinder in a gun that might already have pellets in it or in placing pellets in a gun that is pressurized with a pierced CO_2 cylinder. Read the owner's manual and follow all safety instructions.

The Daisy PowerLine 622X

It was with considerable interest that I heard of the availability of the Daisy Power-Line 622X in March 1999. As would be expected, a CO_2 pistol today must resemble a firearm and the PowerLine 622X is no exception. In this case, it has the outward appearance of a Beretta 92. All of the external shell of the Model 622X is made of black plastic that has the various levers, slides, and buttons of a Beretta firearm molded in their places. This is a rather realistic looking pistol.

As soon as I unpacked and handled the PowerLine 622X, I liked it. Weighing in at 21 ounces, it has a comfortable feel. Like most other CO_2 pistols, the CO_2 cylinder is contained in the grip. The left-hand grip panel is removed by pulling outward on a protruding tab at the bottom. When the grip panel pops off, a CO_2 cylinder can be inserted neck up into the metal grip frame. Piercing the CO_2 cylinder is accomplished by turning a large screw clockwise, which forces the cylinder upward onto the piercing pin. In this regard, the Model 622X is very similar to many of the other current CO_2 pistols.

Like several other CO_2 pistols, the PowerLine 622X uses a rotating cylinder, but in this case, it holds six pellets. It is removed and replaced by tipping the barrel upward at the rear. The latch that releases the barrel is located just in front of the rear sight. Pulling the tab to the rear causes the latch to slide backward releasing the barrel, which springs upward. The cylinder rotates on a pivot located just below the barrel. Unlike the short cylinders used in some CO_2 pistols, the cylinder of the 622X, which measures 0.355 inch, is long enough to accommodate pointed pellets.

An ambidextrous safety has a rotating lever on each side of the rear portion of the slide. A

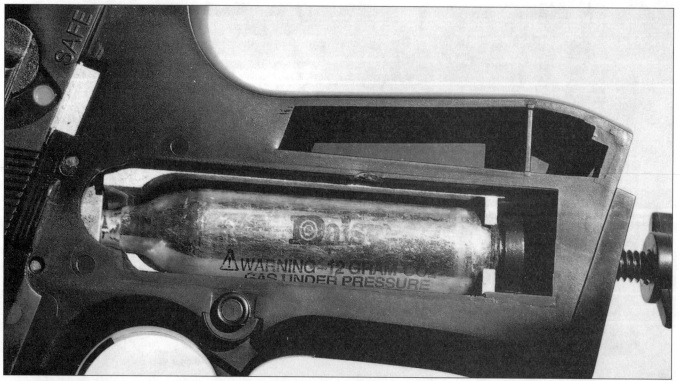

A CO_2 cylinder is held in a metal frame within the grip of the 622X.

The latch in front of the rear sight is pulled to the rear to allow the barrel to tip up.

Pellets are held in the PowerLine 622X in a cylinder that holds six pellets.

large red dot firing indicator is visible on the left-hand side of the slide when the safety is off. If the hammer is cocked with the safety off, placing the safety on does not allow the hammer to fall. The safety levers are safety

levers only, not decocking levers. However if the safety is placed on when the pistol is cocked, the hammer can be let down by holding it with the thumb and letting it down while pulling the trigger. If the safety is on, pulling the trigger allows the hammer to fall without firing the gun.

The PowerLine 622X can be fired in either single-action or double-action mode. After the hammer has been cocked for firing single action, the trigger is of the two-stage type. After the initial take-up, the let-off is crisp with a trigger pull of 5.7 pounds. The double-action pull is smooth, and although the force required increases slightly near the end of trigger travel, the force required is only 7.7 pounds. Overall, trigger action is excellent for a pistol of this type, which sells in the $65-$70 range.

Sights on the PowerLine 622X consist of a square-topped post front sight with a red fiber optic insert and a nonadjustable rear sight with a square notch. Ignoring the red fiber optic portion of the front sight allows the formation of the "square post in a square notch" sight picture.

Grips on the Model 622X consist of black plastic panels that are nicely checkered. The front and back of the grip have vertical grooves to prevent slipping in the hand, and the front of the trigger guard has horizontal grooves. While not made of metal like some of

Dual safety levers are located on the rear of the fake slide of the PowerLine 622X.

In my opinion, the PowerLine 622X is second to no other CO_2 pistol in handling characteristics. I could do without the fiber optic insert in the front sight, but an adequate sight picture is possible with the 622X.

the other expensive CO_2 pistols and not quite as realistic in appearance, this is nonetheless a nice pistol. The results of the velocity tests with the PowerLine 622X are shown in the accompanying table.

The Daisy PowerLine 622X is advertised to give up to 400 ft/sec. With some of the lighter pellets, this velocity could certainly be achieved with a fresh CO_2 cylinder on a warm day. Since the muzzle energy is approximately 4.6 ft-lbs, this is a rather powerful CO_2 pistol for a repeater.

Velocity Data for the Daisy PowerLine 622X at 80-82°F

Pellet	Ave.	High	Low	Std. Dev.
		Velocity, ft/sec		
D.N. Meisterkugeln	388	393	383	4
Gamo Match	386	389	377	5
D.N. Super-H-Point	369	374	360	6
Crosman Wadcutter	389	395	381	6
Beeman Silver Sting	342	354	331	9
Crosman Pointed	341	351	333	8

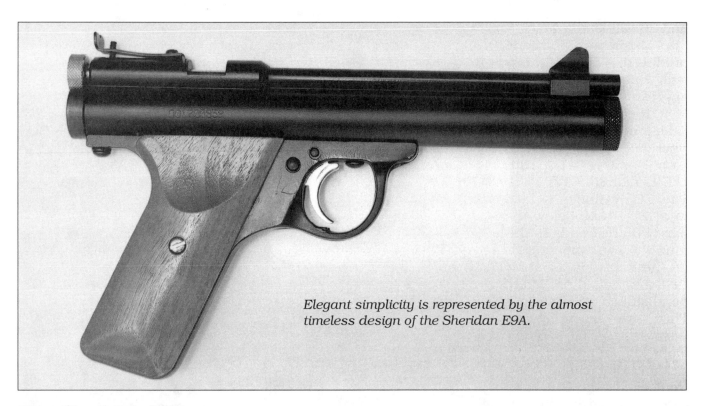

Elegant simplicity is represented by the almost timeless design of the Sheridan E9A.

The Sheridan E9A

With the merger of the Benjamin and Sheridan companies in 1992, the multi-pump rifles became known as Benjamin/Sheridan rifles. Design changes were made and the stock of the Benjamin rifles was redesigned so the two lines had the same appearance. At some time, it seems that the 20-caliber rifles again became designated as Sheridans and those in 177 and 22 calibers were designated as Benjamins, which reestablished their historical identities. The Benjamin rifles are the 397 (177 caliber) and the 392 (22 caliber) while the Sheridan models are CB9 (Blue Streak) and C9 (Silver Streak). However, it took a little longer to get things sorted out with the CO_2 pistols. The 2003 Crosman Catalog shows only the 177-caliber Model EB and 20-caliber EB20 on a page labeled "Benjamin/Sheridan Air Pistols" at the top. My 20-caliber pistol, which was made in the late 1990s, is stamped E9A, which is the older Sheridan model number. The current Model EB20 is identical to the older E9A. The nickel-finished models formerly produced are now discontinued.

For many years, Benjamin and Sheridan have offered single-shot CO_2 pistols of the same basic design represented by the E9A and EB17. Although currently available in 177

Until recently, the 20-caliber pistol was designated as the Sheridan E9A. It is now known as the EB20.

and 20 calibers, a 22-caliber pistol was formerly produced. These excellent pistols sell for approximately $100.

If there is a classic design in CO_2 pistols, the Sheridan E9A (and the corresponding 177-caliber Benjamin E17) is it. The CO_2 cylinder is held in a large tube below the barrel that extends to the muzzle. The appearance of these pistols is such that they would not likely be mistaken for firearms. They are essentially a retro design that actually looks like an airgun.

A knurled cap on the front end of the CO_2 tube can be removed and a CO_2 cylinder inserted. Replacing and tightening the cap pierces the CO_2 cylinder.

Smooth walnut grips are standard on the Sheridan E9A and Benjamin E17 (not tested) pistols. Sights consist of a blade front and a rear sight with a square notch adjustable for windage and elevation. For my eyes, the front sight blade is too thin and it is difficult for me to center it in the rear sight notch. Elevation adjustment is accomplished by means of a vertical screw that extends through the rear sight base. Loosening the front mounting screw allows the rear portion of the sight to be moved laterally to adjust for windage. A cross-bolt safety with a red firing indicator is located behind the trigger.

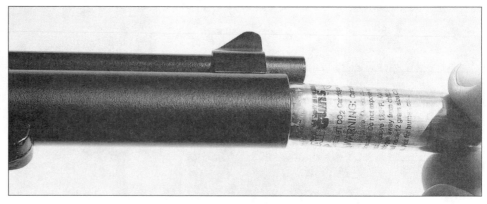

A CO_2 cylinder is inserted in the large tube below the barrel.

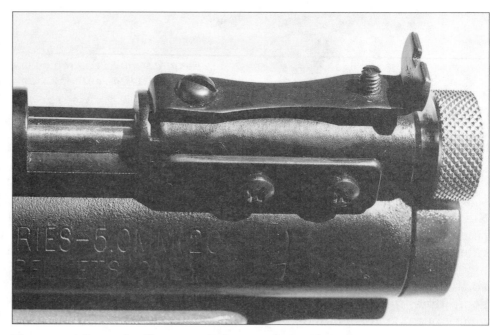

The rear sight on the Sherican E9A is simple but fully adjustable. The knurled knob is the bolt handle.

One pellet can be loaded in the single-shot E9A pistol.

Occasionally, a drop of oil should be placed on the O-ring seal at the front of the bolt of this and other Crosman models that use this type of seal.

The pistol has a single-shot bolt action, the operation of which is simplicity itself. A large knurled bolt head is located at the rear of the action. It is rotated counterclockwise and withdrawn until two clicks are heard. The pistol is now cocked. A single pellet is placed in the loading track and the bolt pushed forward and turned clockwise to lock it. When the cross-bolt safety is pushed to the left, the safety is off and the pistol is ready to fire. Because the pistol is cocked manually, trigger action involves releasing the sear, so let-off is crisp; it measured 4.8 pounds.

These pistols offer the simplest, most uncluttered design available in a CO_2 pistol. However, that does not mean they are short on performance. In 177 caliber, the EB17 is advertised to give up to 500 ft/sec and the 20-caliber E9A has a velocity of up to 425 ft/sec listed for it. These are high-powered CO_2 pistols, the result of their closed-breech design and the 6.38-inch barrels. Barrels are rifled with the 20 caliber having a twist of one turn in 12 inches and the 177 caliber having a one-turn-in-14-inch twist.

In terms of construction, it is hard to fault these fine pistols. They are made of black finished brass, a traditional material for air and CO_2 guns because of its resistance to corrosion. These are CO_2 pistols of classic design and construction. Weight is 28 ounces and the overall length is about 9 inches. Velocity measurements with the E9A gave the results shown in the table.

Examination of the velocity data for the Sheridan E9A shows the outstanding uniformity that comes from the pistol having a closed breech. There are no cylinders with chambers differing slightly in dimensions or gaps between the cylinder and the barrel. While such features assure that velocities should be uniform, the advertised velocity of up to 425 ft/sec is easily eclipsed with all but the heaviest pellets. The Crosman Premier, Sheridan cylindrical, and Sheridan diabolo pellets all weigh 14.3 grains and with them the average velocity is almost exactly what is advertised. For the seven types of pellets tested, the average standard deviation in the velocities is only 2.1 ft/sec. To expect any more uniform velocities is unreasonable.

The Beeman Silver Bear has a weight of 10.00 grains so the velocity should be high. However, I was somewhat surprised that the average velocity approached 500 ft/sec. The Beeman H&N Match, which weighs 10.32

Velocity Data for the Sheridan E9A at 80-82°F				
	Velocity, ft/sec			
Pellet	**Ave.**	**High**	**Low**	**Std. Dev.**
Crosman Premier	429	431	426	2
Sheridan Cylindrical	421	424	419	2
Sheridan Diabolo	419	421	417	2
Beeman Silver Bear	487	490	484	3
Beeman Silver Sting	478	480	477	1
Beeman Ram Jet	466	468	461	3
Beeman H&N Match	493	494	490	2

The Crosman 2210 is a competent 22-caliber pistol at a modest price.

grains, gave a very high velocity also. Both the Beeman Ram Jet and Silver Sting are in the 11.0-11.5 grain range and the velocities with these pellets are between those obtained with the heavier and lighter pellets.

Given that the Sheridan E9A produces muzzle energies of approximately 6 ft-lbs, this pistol would be a very good choice for use on pests. Keep in mind that a 20-caliber pellet that weighs 14.3 grains (such as the Sheridan cylindrical or Crosman Premier) will retain its velocity slightly better than will a pellet of the same weight in 22 caliber. The difference is not great, but nonetheless the 20 caliber is a good choice for use on critters. In my opinion, only the Crosman 2240 is better suited for use as a hunting CO_2 handgun. This little gun measures only 9 inches in length and mine weighs 27.9 ounces. There is no way to get more performance in a CO_2 handgun of this size. If you want to shoot eight shots in 2.4 seconds, this is not the gun to choose. However, if you want the most power and accuracy from a CO_2 handgun in a very convenient size, this should be one of your two choices. The other will be discussed later in this chapter. The 22-caliber Model EB22 has been discontinued. After my experience with this little 20 caliber, I regret not getting a 22 when they were available.

The Crosman 2210

While the Crosman 1710 discussed in Chapter 6 has a shorter counterpart in the Model 1008, the Crosman 2210 has no such companion piece. The 1710 differs from the 1008 by having a rather cosmic looking barrel extension and a front sight with a round top and a fiber optic insert. I wish that a 22-caliber shorter version made just like the 1008 were available. However, what we do have is the 2210, which has the barrel extension and fake compensator. This interesting pistol has a retail price in the $40-$50 range.

While it is not designed according to my specifications, the 2210 is a very nice pistol. It is made almost entirely of silver-colored plastic, and the only visible metal parts are the hammer and the piercing screw in the bottom of the grip. A later variant of the Model 2210 had the barrel extension and front sight made of black plastic. But true to the Crosman tradition, this pistol works and it works very well. The rear sight is made of black plastic, and it has a square notch that is fully adjustable. It provides all that could be desired in a low-cost pistol. It is the front sight that causes me problems with its silver-colored plastic, rounded top, and bright green fiber optic insert about halfway up. It is

The small, ridged black tab on top of the frame above the trigger releases the rear of the barrel of the Crosman 2210. You can also see from this photo that the 2210 has an excellent, fully-adjustable rear sight.

The light-colored, rounded front sight with a fiber optic insert does not allow a good sight picture when used with the black, square-notch rear sight.

impossible to get a good sight picture on a paper target with this sight.

The general operation of the Model 2210 is identical to that of the Models 1710 and 1008, which were discussed in detail in Chapter 6. There's no need to repeat those instructions here.

Single-action trigger pull on my three 2210 pistols measure 4.6, 4.7 and 4.9 pounds after a rather long and motion jerky take-up motion. With the Model 2210, the trigger is linked to cylinder rotation so cocking the hammer does only that. As a result, the first stage of the trigger motion even after the hammer is cocked is not very smooth because of the motion of the hand. Double-action trigger pull can only be described as long, rough, and heavy. On my 2210 pistols, the double-action pull measures 10.4, 10.9 and 11.0 pounds. This is not a pistol I can shoot with any degree of accuracy in the double-action mode.

My preliminary velocity measurements with the Model 2210 were with the 14.3-grain Crosman Copperhead wadcutter pellets, and I found an average velocity of 380 ft/sec with a standard deviation of 6 ft/sec. Switching to the 12.0 grain RWS Hobby pellets, I found an average velocity of 405 ft/sec with a standard deviation of 8 ft/sec. This is a pistol with considerable power that produces a muzzle energy of 4.6 ft-lbs. With different sights, this pistol is one that I like for dispatching small pests.

In conducting the tests on the Crosman 2210, I used all three of the specimens available. Therefore, the table shows data for all three guns.

In general, there is no significant difference in the velocities given by the three pistols with most pellets. It appears that gun (1) does not yield velocities as high as the other two with the Meisterkugeln pellet. The difference is not great, but no reason for this behavior is readily apparent since the three pistols were nominally the same. The muzzle energy is approximately 4.7 ft-lbs, which is sufficient for

Like many other CO_2 pistols, the Crosman 2210 is a revolver disguised as semi-automatic. The cylinder holds seven pellets.

To install a proper front sight, I began by removing the factory sight with a craft saw.

taking small pests within the range at which they can be hit reliably. Note that specimen (1) gave an average velocity of 406 ft/sec with the relatively light Dynamit Nobel Hobby pellet.

I currently have three of the Model 2210 pistols, which indicates my fondness for this model. It should be noted that the Model 2210 does not appear in the 2003 Crosman catalog, but it should still be available from some dealers.

When I got my first Crosman 2210, it did not take long for me to realize I did not like the front sight. Did I make that point earlier? From the beginning, I thought about what I could use to fabricate a front sight that would provide a nice black outline with a square top. I knew getting the original sight off would be no problem. While spending some time in a hardware store, I realized one entire wall was covered with a drawer unit having hundreds of drawers containing every imaginable type of screw, fitting, pin, tube, spring, seal, etc. Then I found the drawer containing numerous types of keys used to lock pulleys on shafts by sliding in grooves in both. There it was—a metal, half-moon key that was just the right size and shape. That key, known as a Woodruff key, was going to be a front sight. Woodruff keys come in a variety of sizes. The

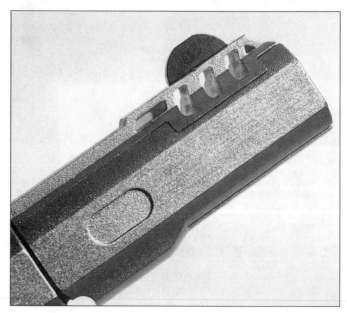

The Woodruff key was attached with a strong bonding adhesive.

one used in this project is 0.125 inch thick, 0.236 inch high, and 0.600 inch long.

My dissatisfaction with that factory front sight finally got to the point of no return. Since I have two of the all-silver versions of the 2210, I knew I had to get a better front sight on one of them. I started by using a fine-toothed craft saw to remove the three vertical posts at the base. Then, I smoothed

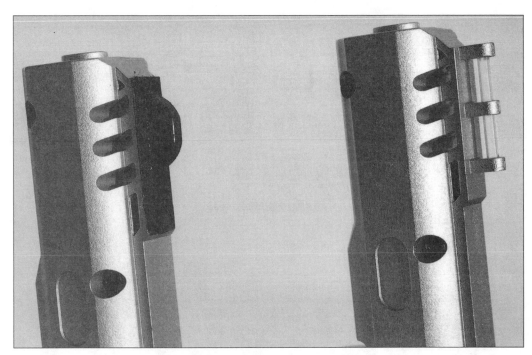

Viewed through the rear sight, the black metal post gives a vastly improved sight picture.

Velocity Data for the Crosman 2210 at 80-82°F					
			Velocity, ft/sec		
Pellet		Ave.	High	Low	Std. Dev.
D.N. Meisterkugeln	(1)	351	357	342	8
D.N. Meisterkugeln	(2)	372	393	362	12
D.N. Meisterkugeln	(3)	375	383	364	8
D.N. Super-H-Point	(1)	367	372	359	5
D.N. Super-H-Point	(2)	374	376	371	2
D.N. Super-H-Point	(3)	365	369	362	3
Crosman Wadcutter	(1)	371	372	368	2
Crosman Wadcutter	(2)	370	376	368	4
Crosman Wadcutter	(3)	361	366	356	4
Gamo Match	(1)	367	374	362	5
Gamo Match	(2)	378	380	375	2
Gamo Match	(3)	371	377	365	4
Crosman Pointed	(1)	382	387	376	4
Crosman Pointed	(2)	385	399	368	12
D. N. Hobby	(1)	406	411	395	8

Numbers in parentheses identify the three pistols used.

off the stumps to make a flat surface on which to mount a front sight. Attaching the Woodruff key required an adhesive of considerable strength and I had just the right one. I coated the bottom of the key and set it on the base. It is a good thing I got it on reasonably straight because the glue set up immediately and I couldn't move it. After allowing the glue to harden, I took a flat-black touch-up paint pen and painted the sight and the top of the base. When I held the pistol and sighted along the barrel, I knew I had done the right thing. I can shoot this 2210 considerably better than I can my other two.

The Crosman 2240

One type of firearm used in hunting is a single-shot bolt-action handgun with a long barrel chambered for a cartridge normally used in rifles. Although they are called "handguns" or pistols, they are really short rifles with the stocks cut off. They bear no resemblance to the typical revolver or semi-automatic handgun. The Crosman 2240 is

Power and accuracy are the strong points of the single-shot Crosman 2240 pistol.

comparable to this type of single-shot handgun except it is a 22-caliber CO_2 pistol. A shoulder stock can be attached when the grips are removed, which indicates this pistol is capable of performing like a rifle. Because of its high power, it is a true magnum among CO_2 pistols with an advertised muzzle velocity of 460 ft/sec.

Since the Crosman 2240 bears almost no resemblance to a firearm pistol, it looks like the typical air or CO_2 pistol of 40-50 years ago. Because it is a single shot, it is very simple. The receiver, grips, barrel band, and sights are plastic. The rest of the pistol is metal. A Crosman 2240 has a 7.25-inch barrel and weighs 29 ounces. Because the sight radius is longer than that of almost any other CO_2 pistol and the barrel is held rigidly in place, high accuracy is virtually assured. If your idea of fun is to fire eight shots in 3 seconds, this is not the CO_2 pistol for you. If you want an accurate and powerful CO_2 pistol to shoot targets or dispatch pests, this pistol is unsurpassed by any other currently manufactured CO_2 pistol.

The CO_2 cylinder is held in a large tube below the barrel. The front-end cap is checkered for ease of gripping, and it has a slot large enough to accommodate a coin.

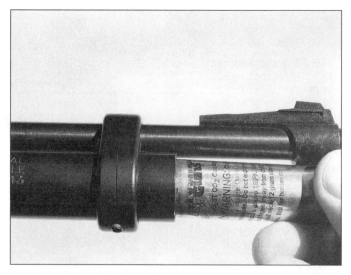

A CO_2 cylinder is inserted neck first in the large tube below the barrel.

Unscrewing the end cap opens the tube so that a CO_2 cylinder can be inserted neck first. Replacing and tightening the end cap pierces the cylinder.

A single 22-caliber pellet of any type is loaded by raising the bolt handle and pulling the bolt back until the gun is cocked. With the bolt open, the pellet is placed in the groove that leads into the chamber and the bolt is closed. Located just behind the trigger is a safety of the cross-bolt type. When the

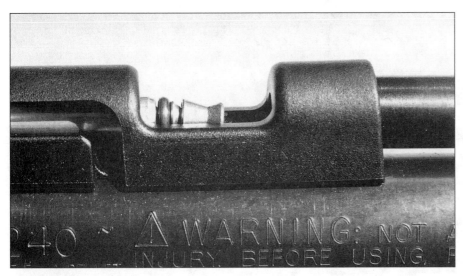

Loading the 2240 consists of opening the bolt, putting in a pellet, and closing the bolt.

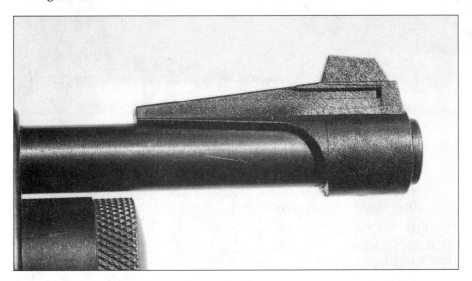

The square-topped post front sight on the 2240 has a very good shape to be used with a square-notch rear sight.

While this rear sight does not work well on the Crosman 2260 rifle, it is quite acceptable on the 2240 pistol.

safety is pushed from right to left, the pistol is ready to fire. Pushing it to the right places the safety on. The bolt and trigger on the Crosman 2240 are brass but the remainder of the metal surface is black.

Sights on the Crosman 2240 are adequate. The front sight is part of a plastic nose cap on the barrel. With its rectangular profile, it is well shaped. The rear sight is the same as that found on several other Crosman pistols and rifles. On a pistol, this rear sight works adequately because with the piece held at arms length the square notch appears to have about the correct width. On a rifle, where the rear sight is much closer to the eye, the notch appears several times as wide as the front sight blade. In this case, such a sight is almost worthless on a rifle, as will be discussed further in Chapter 9.

The rear sight consists of a plastic base to which a metal blade is attached by means of a single screw. Upon loosening the screw, the blade can be moved up or down (the elevation adjustment). In addition to the square notch, the blade has a tiny hole on the end opposite the notch. Removing the screw allows the blade to be removed and reattached with this tiny hole on top instead of the square notch. Presumably, this would constitute a sort of peep sight, but to see the front sight through a hole less than one-sixteenth inch in diameter would require it to be very close to the eye. This not a practical situation on a hand-gun and the "peep sight hole" is absolutely worthless on a

The Crosman 2240 the author is testing in this photo is the most powerful and accurate of the CO_2 handguns tested.

pistol. Because of it being much closer to the eye, it works marginally well on a rifle. My advice is to use the square notch only on a pistol and the peep sight only on a rifle. Of course with the sight base being made of plastic and the screw holding the blade to it being so small, you will strip the threads unless you are very careful.

Sight adjustment is made by trial and error. Windage adjustment is made by loosening the screw that holds the sight base to the receiver and simply sliding the whole sight in the desired direction. Elevation adjustment is made by loosening the tiny screw that holds the sight blade in place and sliding the blade up or down. There are no graduations or reference marks of any kind on the rear sight. A two-piece intermount that clamps on the barrel is available. The grooves on the top edges of the intermount allow scope mounts or optical sights (red dot or laser) to be attached. My preference is to put the blade with the square notch up and to mount nothing on the barrel. However, if the 2240 is used with a shoulder stock

attached, a compact scope would be the best means of taking advantage of the inherent power and accuracy of this pistol.

The black, checkered plastic grips are comfortable and there are ambidextrous thumb rests. On my Crosman 2240, the trigger has some creep, but the let-off requires 4.8 pounds. The brass trigger is too thin for comfortable shooting with the 2240. Several types of pellets were used in the velocity tests since this versatile pistol is applicable for many types of shooting. The table shows the results obtained.

Several things stand out from the velocity data for the Crosman 2240. First, the velocities are high. This is a high-powered pistol that generates muzzle energies over 7 ft-lbs. Second, the velocities are remarkably uniform with some pellets giving five shots with an extreme spread of only 2 ft/sec, and the average standard deviation in velocity for all the pellets is only 2.4 ft/sec. The effects of the manual cocking bolt action and closed breech are evident with the high, uniform velocities. This is a pistol to pick if you want

Velocity Data for the Crosman 2240 at 80-82°F

| Pellet | Ave. | Velocity, ft/sec | | Std. Dev. |
		High	Low	
D.N. Meisterkugeln	459	464	454	4
Gamo Match	470	470	469	1
D.N. Super-H-Point	460	463	457	2
Crosman Wadcutter	464	465	463	1
Beeman Silver Sting	457	460	452	5
Crosman Pointed	460	465	458	3
Winchester Hunting	464	465	463	1

to hunt pests or small game with a CO_2 handgun. In my opinion, at a retail price of $40-$50, it is a bargain.

The Crosman 2240 is a sturdy pistol of time-proven design. It is certainly a high-performance, serious pistol. However, in almost any hobby area, there are participants who seek to modify equipment to maximize performance. In the area of CO_2 handguns, the Crosman 2240 is the model most often modified to make a gun that performs in a superlative manner. The factory receiver made of a composite is sometimes replaced with one made of metal. The thin trigger is modified or replaced to improve its function. Sometimes the barrel is replaced with one of a different length and the internal parts are polished to improve gas flow. All of these modifications are undertaken to produce a CO_2 pistol of outstanding power and accuracy. Such custom pistols are often the tools of choice for the hunter of pests and small game. The fact that the Crosman 2240 is the pistol chosen for such modifications speaks well of its basic design. This is not a fast shooting, fun gun. This is a serious pistol, and it seems as if it is almost developing the cult status that the Crosman 600 and Mark I enjoy (see Chapter 10).

CHAPTER 9

EVALUATION OF CURRENT CO$_2$ RIFLES

WHILE HANDGUNS USING CO$_2$ power abound, the number of CO$_2$ rifles is quite small. This may promote the view that CO$_2$ guns are only for fun, but nothing could be further from the truth. There is much to be said for choosing a single-shot CO$_2$ rifle as a training piece for shooters who plan to move up to a 22 rimfire later. Firing a single-shot CO$_2$ rifle requires opening the bolt to cock the piece, inserting a single pellet, closing the bolt, and firing. These are exactly the same steps involved in firing a single-shot bolt-action rimfire rifle. There is no pumping involved with either type of rifle so the procedures are identical. It is easy to make the transition from firing a CO$_2$ rifle to using a firearm.

While CO$_2$ rifles are usually not the first choice of airgunners going after pests, there is nothing to prevent using these rifles in this way. Generally, air or CO$_2$ guns chosen for use as varmint rifles are the more powerful models and this is reasonable. A magnum air rifle is one that generates at least 12 ft-lbs of kinetic energy at the muzzle. None of the unmodified CO$_2$ rifles evaluated will give an energy this high, but some are close. They are entirely suitable for pest control as long as the pests are small ones at short range.

Although the selection of CO$_2$ rifles is not extensive, there is a rifle for almost any use. Even though they were not evaluated in this work, there are some suitable for formal target shooting. The Crosman 2260 is a 22-caliber rifle of considerable power while the

Crosman 1077 is a 177 caliber that can be fired rapidly if there is a reason to do so. There are a couple of choices between these two extremes so the spectrum is covered rather well by the few models available. My extensive testing of these models has given me an appreciation for the capability of rifles of this type. They represent good value for their cost. Crosman pioneered the use of the familiar 12-gram CO$_2$ cylinders as the power source for pellet rifles, and as you will see from the evaluations, Crosman still dominates this field.

In the descriptions that follow, instructions are given for installing a CO$_2$ cylinder and loading ammunition in each model. Although is it not stated explicitly in the discussion of each model, the safety should always be in the "on" position before loading propellant or projectiles in any CO$_2$ gun. There is danger in piercing a CO$_2$ cylinder in a gun that might already have pellets in it or in placing pellets in a gun that is pressurized with a pierced CO$_2$ cylinder. Read the owner's manual and follow all safety instructions.

The Crosman 2260

Crosman pioneered the use of CO$_2$ cylinders as the power source in American pellet rifles. Early models had a large full-length tube below the barrel that was filled from an external cylinder that held 10 ounces of CO$_2$. In 1954, the Model 150 pistol became the first CO$_2$ gun to use the now standard 12-gram cylinders. A year later, the first rifle to

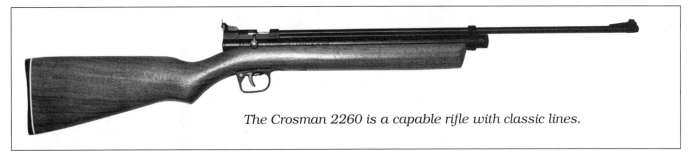

The Crosman 2260 is a capable rifle with classic lines.

use these cylinders as the power source was introduced. That rifle was the legendary 22-caliber Model 160. Three variants of the Model 160 appeared in its 1955-1971 production period. All of the variants used two 12-gram cylinders as the power source.

There are many who believe the Crosman 160 was the finest CO_2 sporting rifle ever produced in this country. Made of metal and having a very nice wood stock, it was an American classic. After the Model 160 was discontinued, Crosman produced a number of 22-caliber repeating rifles, but they never really successfully replaced the Model 160. After a long series of corporate changes and relocation, Crosman returned to the production of a 22-caliber single-shot CO_2 rifle made largely of metal and wood. That model, the Model 2260, was introduced in 1999 and is still in production. It is a very nice rifle that represents a good value for the $90-$100 price range.

Power source for the Crosman 2260 is a single CO_2 cylinder held in a large tube below the barrel. That tube extends only slightly beyond the front of the forearm. Removing a checkered end cap allows a CO_2 cylinder to be inserted, neck first. Replacing the cap causes the cylinder to be pierced.

Crosman designed the bolt action of the Model 2260 in such a way that the same action can be used regardless of the barrel length. Using the same action with a barrel about 7 inches long results in the Crosman Model 2240 single-shot pistol (see Chapter 8). With a barrel slightly longer than 14 inches, you get the Model 2250 compact rifle, which will be discussed later in this chapter. Simply varying the length of the barrel and the tube that holds the CO_2 cylinder allows a family of guns having the same action and function to be produced. Moreover, 177-caliber versions of some of these guns have also been pro-

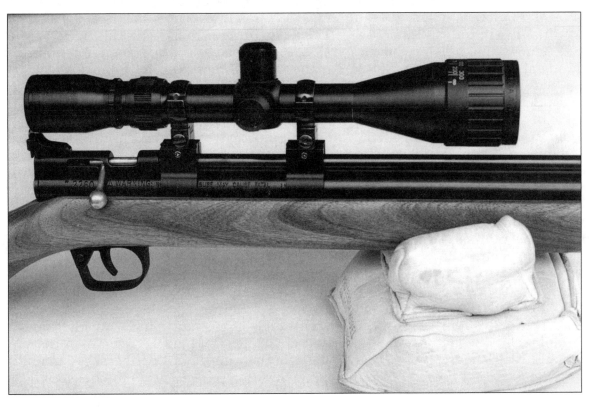

Mounting a scope on the Crosman 2260 requires clamping the intermount to the barrel.

duced. The bolt and trigger on all these models are made of brass.

Operation of the Crosman 2260 is as simple as it gets. It is a single-shot, bolt-action rifle so opening the bolt, drawing it to the rear until it cocks the firing mechanism, and inserting a single pellet in the breech constitutes the loading sequence. Near the front end of the bolt there is the same type of O-ring seal that Crosman has used for many years. A cross-bolt safety is located just in front of the trigger. When pushed to the right, it is on and when pushed to the left, it is off. My two Crosman 2260 rifles have trigger pulls of 3.8 and 4.1 pounds, both with very little creep.

The Crosman 2260 weighs 4 pounds 12 ounces and measures 39.75 inches in length. Barrel length is 24 inches, so the Model 2260 is a full-size rifle. Metal surfaces are nicely blued, but I have found that rusting seems to occur very quickly under damp conditions. I once took my 2260 on a trip during which the rifle stayed in a plastic case in the back of the truck. Condensation on the metal occurred and when I later removed the rifle from the case, there were large areas of the barrel and gas tube that were reddish brown in color. As a result of traveling with a tool kit that included a wide range of materials, the remedy was quickly effected. I used very fine steel wool on the barrel and gas tube to remove the rust. In a few minutes, I also had the thin, easy-to-remove blue finish removed, which gave the metal surface a bright, shiny appearance. I wiped it with a damp cloth and quickly applied Birchwood Casey Perma Blue® with a clean cloth. After the liberal application of bluing solution, I sponged the surface with a damp paper towel and rubbed it lightly with steel wool. The bluing, sponging and rubbing operations were repeated six or seven times. By this time, the metal had a deep, rich blue that was far superior to that on the new rifle. I have reblued several Crosman guns in this way and the result has been guns that looked better than they did when new.

While I have refinished the metal on my Crosman 2260, I have not worked on the stock, but I would like to. The factory stock is not bad but it could easily be improved. It is too thick in cross section and the grip is too fat. Slimming and reshaping the forearm would improve the stock. Reworking the grip area to make a real pistol grip and fluting the comb would also give the stock a sleek appearance. The bottom of the stock between the grip and butt is too thick so I would remove some wood in that area. These steps would convert a somewhat chunky factory stock into a well-shaped sporter.

The front sight on the Model 2260 is a hooded post on a plastic ramp that functions as a muzzle cap. It is a very competent sight even though the entire nose cap came off my rifle as I removed it from a case. I put a couple of drops of super glue around the muzzle and slipped the nose cap back on. It has not come off again. The front sight hood also slips on and off too easily.

The rear sight is another matter altogether. There is no open rear sight located on the barrel in front of the receiver. The rear sight consists of a composite base held on top of the rear part of the action by a single screw. Being mounted on the rear of the action, the sight assembly is placed quite close to the shooter's eye. At the rear of that base is a thin, reversible metal blade held in place by a small screw. One end of the blade has a small hole that lets it be used as a peep sight and on the other end is a square notch. When the blade is turned so that the notch is up, it makes a notch and post alignment possible. The only thing wrong with this idea is the sight is so close to the eye the notch appears many times as wide as the front post. Accurate aiming is not possible. While the rear sight blade works satisfactorily as a peep sight, it is useless as an open sight on a rifle. Furthermore, there are no effective reference marks of any kind so sight adjustment is a "move it and shoot it" proposition. Windage adjustment is made by moving the entire rear sight laterally after loosening the single large screw holding it to the receiver.

While the factory sights leave something to be desired, it is possible to mount a scope on the Model 2260. Because the receiver is made of a plastic composite, it is not feasible to cut grooves for mounting a scope on the receiver. Accordingly, Crosman makes an intermount that clamps to the barrel. Grooves on the top edges of the intermount permit scope mounts made for grooved receivers to be attached.

Velocity Data for the Crosman 2260 at 68°F				
		Velocity, ft/sec		
Pellet	**Ave.**	**High**	**Low**	**Std. Dev.**
Beeman Crow Magnum	475	481	467	5
Crosman Pointed	526	541	516	8
Gamo Match	542	547	533	6

Because the Model 2260 is a CO_2-powered rifle that requires no pumping, a scope does not make the rifle awkward to handle. However, because the intermount clamps to the barrel, a scope mounted in this way is rather far from the shooter's eye. I normally prefer to use most air and CO_2 rifles without a scope if the only means of attaching it is clamping it to the barrel.

Having had two Crosman 2260 rifles for a considerable period of time, I have had more experience with this model than with the others described in this chapter. Velocity measurements were carried out by firing five-shot strings with three types of pellets. The results obtained are shown in the table.

In looking at the velocity data shown in the table, it must be remembered that 68°F is rather low for efficient operation of a CO_2-powered rifle. Also, the Beeman Crow Magnum is a heavy pellet that weighs 18.4 grains, so the velocity would be expected to be low. The advertised velocity for the 2260 is up to 600 ft/sec, which is possible on a warm day with a light pellet. In a series of tests I conducted at 80°F, it was found the velocity with the Crosman pointed pellet was approximately 550 ft/sec for several shots. In the same series, the Dynamit Nobel Hobby pellet gave several shots in the 590-599 ft/sec range from the same CO_2 cylinder. In an endurance test, I found the CO_2 cylinder gave 44 shots with a velocity of 450 ft/sec or greater.

Some informal accuracy tests have also been conducted with a Crosman 2260 at a range of 25 yards using the factory peep sight. In those tests, I found the Crosman pointed pellet gave five three-shot groups that averaged 0.62 inch with the largest being 0.77 inch and the smallest being 0.52 inch. This represents a high level of accuracy for a rifle of this type especially when the deficiencies of the factory peep sight are considered.

When the test was repeated using the Dynamit Nobel Meisterkugeln pellet, the average group size was 0.76 inch with the largest being 0.88 inch and the smallest being 0.59 inch. The Daisy pointed pellet gave an average group size of 0.86 inch with the largest being 0.98 inch and the smallest being 0.69 inch. Although the accuracy testing was not exhaustive, it clearly shows the Model 2260 is capable of fine accuracy. I have been very favorably impressed with the Crosman 2260, which is why I have two of them. I have no doubt that better results could be obtained under better conditions with a scope.

In spite of what I perceive to be deficiencies in sights, the Crosman 2260 is a fine CO_2 rifle. It is not the equivalent of the classic Model 160, but it is still a very fine rifle. I spoke earlier about traveling with one. Even though I have a significant number of other choices available, I chose the Crosman 2260 because I like it.

The Crosman 1760

Having introduced the Model 2260 in 1999, it was a simple matter for Crosman to attach a 177-caliber barrel and produce the Model 1760 in 2000. This rifle is exactly like the Model 2260 discussed above in both appearance and function, and it shares the same strengths and weaknesses as the 2260. It also sells for around $90-$100. Therefore, a description of the features of this rifle is not necessary and we can progress immediately to an evaluation of this model. My Crosman 1760 has a crisp trigger let-off at 4.10 pounds.

The Crosman 1760 gives a velocity up to 700 ft/sec. Velocity data shown in the table indicate that with a pellet of rather light weight, that is almost exactly what the little rifle will give. However, since a single-shot, bolt-action rifle is capable of excellent accu-

Velocity Data for the Crosman 1760 at 75°F				
		Velocity, ft/sec		
Pellet	**Ave.**	**High**	**Low**	**Std. Dev.**
D.N. Meisterkugeln	671	679	666	5
Crosman Premier (7.9 gr)	674	678	670	3
Crosman Wadcutter	674	681	665	6
Eley Target	694	702	684	7

racy, I view the Model 1760 primarily as a pest rifle for small species. In view of this, the velocities of 670-675 with more sturdy pellets like the Crosman Premier and wadcutter mean this rifle has plenty of power and a flat enough trajectory to be a good pest rifle at distances up to 35 yards. During the tests and a great deal of informal plinking afterward, the Crosman 1760 performed as expected.

The Benjamin G397

Although Benjamin airguns are best known in the form of the multi-pump rifles, CO_2 rifles and pistols have been produced for many years. Current CO_2 guns produced by Benjamin include the EB17 pistol and the G397 rifle, both 177-caliber single-shot models. There is also a 20-caliber EB20 pistol that has become equivalent to the former

Sheridan E9A since the merger of Benjamin and Sheridan. It is a single-shot pistol but it is now considered to be a Sheridan because that name has long been associated with 20-caliber airguns.

Following the production of several older models, the Benjamin G397 was introduced in 1992 and it is constructed in the classic style using metal and walnut. To call it a handsome airgun seems almost inadequate. Without the pump handle in front of the forearm, the G397 has only a stock with the barrel and gas tube extending out front. This gives the rifle a trim appearance that makes it resemble a firearm more closely than do the multi-pump Benjamin and Sheridan rifles. The stock on the Benjamin G397 is rather thick in cross section and could have a better-shaped grip area, but it is a real piece of

The Benjamin G397 is an outstanding CO_2 rifle with a well-deserved reputation for durability and accuracy.

This Benjamin from several years ago shows the shotgun-type safety used then.

The open sight on the Benjamin G397 is fully adjustable.

The bolt action on the Benjamin G397 is the same proven design used on the pneumatic rifles. Lifting the bolt handle and drawing it to the rear exposes the loading track. To cock the action, the bolt must be drawn fully to the rear. A single pellet is placed in the track and the bolt is closed to complete the loading process. As with other bolt action and CO_2 guns, the forward end of the bolt has an O-ring gas seal that should be lubricated occasionally.

Benjamin rifles have had two types of safeties in modern times. Current Benjamin rifles have a cross-bolt safety located in the front of the trigger guard, which is a thick casting. Until the latter part of the 1990s, the safety on Benjamin rifles was located just behind the receiver and the trigger guard was a thin metal stamping. Because of where it is located and the fact that it functions by sliding with the thumb, it is sometimes referred to as a shotgun type safety because it resembles the safety on a double-barreled shotgun. My G397 was made around 1996 so it has the shotgun or sliding type of safety.

Sights on the Benjamin G397 are identical to those on the multi-pump Benjamin and Sheridan rifles. The front is a blade while the open rear sight is has a square notch, which is adjustable for elevation and windage. Elevation adjustments are made by turning the vertical screw that passes through the rear sight base. Windage adjustments are made by means of two screws, one on either side of the rear sight at its forward end. These two screws serve to hold the sight base tightly between them. Loosening one of them and tightening the other positions the sight base in a new location. Windage adjustments are made as fol-

nicely finished walnut. Retail price of the G397 is in the $120-$130 range.

The G397 is a simple rifle. The large tube below the barrel holds one CO_2 cylinder that is inserted neck first after removing the end cap. The cap has a knurled surface in order to get a good grasp. Replacing the cap pierces the CO_2 cylinder. Charging a CO_2 gun does not get any easier than that.

The Benjamin G397 can accept a scope after the intermount is clamped in place on the barrel. This places the scope in a rather forward position.

lows. To move the rear sight to the right, loosen the screw on the right-hand side of the sight base and tighten the screw on the left-hand side. Loosening the screw on the right-hand side allows the sight to move to the right when the other screw is tightened. To move the rear sight to the left, loosen the screw on the left-hand side of the sight base and tighten the screw on the right-hand side.

Although the factory sights on the G397 are adequate for short range shooting, the ability to add better sights is important for more accurate work. Benjamin rifles, including the G397, come from the factory with two tapped screw holes on the right-hand side of the receiver specifically for attaching the Williams receiver sight made for these rifles. I have the Williams peep sights on several of my Benjamin and Sheridan multi-pump rifles. Peep sights do not change the weight and handling of the rifles but they allow for more accurate sighting than is possible with open sights.

Perhaps the best way to improve sighting with the Benjamin is to use the Williams peep that is made specifically for Benjamin and Sheridan rifles.

On Benjamin multi-pump rifles, mounting a scope makes them somewhat awkward to pump because the scope is placed where it is most convenient to grasp the rifle. While that is not a problem with the CO_2-powered G397, you still need the same intermount that clamps on the barrel and provides dovetail grooves for scope mounts. While I do not like

Velocity Data for the Benjamin G397 at 68°F				
		Velocity, ft/sec		
Pellet	Ave.	High	Low	Std. Dev.
Beeman Crow Magnum	617	629	611	7
Crosman Premier Light	614	624	608	6
Daisy Pointed	667	681	657	9

scopes on multi-pump Benjamin rifles, I like them fine on the little G397.

Trigger action of my Benjamin G397 is superb. At 2.6 pounds, it is light and crisp with absolutely no take-up motion. I have no air or CO_2 rifle with a better trigger, and it is superior to those on most firearms I shoot.

While I may like looking at the Benjamin G397 and studying its features, it is not its role as an art object that concerns me. Pretty is as pretty does is an old but appropriate axiom. The maximum advertised velocity for the G397 is 680 ft/sec, but velocity will depend on a number of factors that include temperature and pellet weight. As described in Chapter 4, the gas pressure in a CO_2 cylinder increases with increasing temperature. As a result, the propellant will yield higher pellet velocities at high temperatures. For a given gas pressure, lighter pellets will be given higher velocities than will heavier ones.

My first tests with the Benjamin G397 were conducted at 68°F, a rather low temperature for efficient use of CO_2 guns. Five-shot strings were fired with three different types of pellets and the measured velocities are summarized in the table.

Six shots with the 7.9-grain Crosman Premier pellet gave an average velocity of 614 ft/sec with a standard deviation (SD) of 6 ft/sec. The Beeman Crow Magnum in 177 caliber weighs 8.28 grains so the average velocity was lower (617 ft/sec). Average velocity with the 7.14-grain Daisy Max Speed pellet was 667 ft/sec, which is quite close to the advertised velocity of 680 ft/sec even though the temperature was only 68°F. There is no question that on a warm day, the G397 will reach the advertised velocity if the pellet used is rather lightweight. The muzzle energy is approximately 7 ft-lbs, which indicates the use of a G397 as a short-range pest rifle is appropriate.

The Benjamin G397 does not appear in the 2003 Crosman catalog and it is currently being phased out, but it is still available from some dealers. My suggestion is if you want a 177-caliber CO_2 rifle, find one and buy it.

The Crosman 1077

While I am quite content with a single-shot rifle I can load, cock, and fire, many shooters are not. For some reason, speed of fire is deemed important and many of the current models of CO_2 rifles and pistols stress that trait. One such rifle is the Crosman Model 1077, which is a 12-shot repeater that uses rotary pellet magazines. To further stretch the point, the rotary clips are contained in a large rectangular magazine that protrudes from the bottom of the stock just in front of the trigger guard. The clip is removable so that another one containing a loaded 12-shot rotary magazine can be inserted quickly. Personally, I think there is too much emphasis on the rate of fire. Because of cooling due to the expansion of gas, CO_2 guns become cooler and performance diminishes when they are fired rapidly.

The Crosman 1077 comes in two versions that differ in the choice of stock. One is the 1077, which has a black composite stock; and the other is the 1077W, which has a very nice wood stock. I have both although specifications and performance are identical for the two versions. The 1077 has a retail price of $55-$60 while the 1077W sells for about $90-$100.

A more handsome CO_2 rifle than the Crosman 1077 is hard to imagine. The rounded receiver with its clean top, the absence of a bolt handle, and the sporter-style stock make for a rifle of classic proportions and lines. The Model 1077W has the configuration of the famous Ruger 10/22 semi-automatic rimfire or the Winchester Model 100 centerfire rifle of

The Crosman 1077W is a trim 12-shot repeater with a nice wood stock.

The other version of the Crosman 1077 has a composite stock.

days gone by. While the barrel, shroud and gas tube are metal, the receiver, trigger guard, and magazine assembly are made of black plastic. With the overall styling of the Model 1077W, it would be very easy for someone to assume you are using a firearm.

Several features on the Model 1077W are self-evident. First, the CO_2 cylinder is contained in a large tube below the barrel. The end cap is located just in front of the forearm, and the cap is sharply knurled to aid in gripping it. After removing the cap, a CO_2 cyl-

inder is inserted neck first, and replacing the cap pierces the cylinder. Second, the safety is of the cross-bolt type and is at the front of the trigger guard.

Sights on the Model 1077 are excellent even if (or possibly because) they are traditional. The rear sight is a metal blade with a square notch that can be moved vertically by means of the familiar stepped ramp. Lateral movement is possible after loosening the screws that hold the sight to the blade. The front sight on my 1077 is a very well shaped

One CO$_2$ cylinder contained in the tube below the barrel supplies power for the Crosman 1077.

The Crosman 1077 has a sturdy, adjustable rear sight.

that permit the mounting of a scope, red dot, or laser sight.

For me, the weak link in the accuracy capability of the Crosman 1077 is the trigger. There is no means to cock the rifle except by means of the long, heavy trigger pull. The rifle is actually a double-action revolver in terms of its function. Pulling the trigger causes rotation of the clip holding the pellets and brings the hammer back for striking the valve. Both of my Crosman 1077 rifles have a trigger pull of 9.0 pounds. While this rifle is labeled as a semi-automatic, it is in reality a double-action-only proposition. As a result, the trigger pull is characteristic of double-action-only CO$_2$ guns, many of which have been described in earlier chapters. This is a nice little rifle, but it is not a semi-automatic in the sense of the Crosman 600 pistol of yesteryear (see Chapter 10).

Loading the Model 1077 involves removing the large magazine box or clip by pressing inward on the rectangular tabs on the sides. These tabs are attached to movable sections of the magazine having ridges that lock into

square post on a ramp. An excellent sight picture is provided by the factory sights. Although I am at a loss to explain why, the 2003 Crosman catalog shows the current Model 1077 has a front sight with a fiber optic insert. If I were shopping for a Model 1077, I would find one that had been in a store for a couple of years and buy it instead of the latest version. The top of the receiver has a raised bar with grooves on the sides

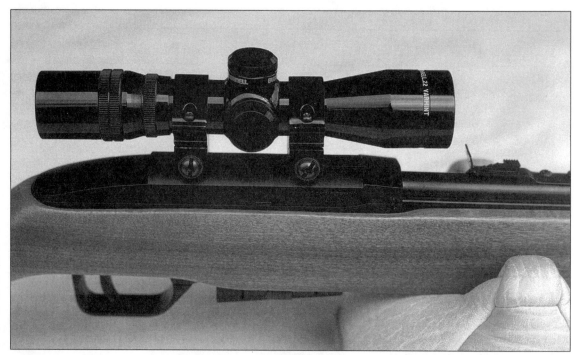

Because it has a raised rib with dovetail grooves, it is convenient to mount a scope on the Crosman 1077.

the receiver. With the clip box removed, a cylindrical pellet magazine holding 12 pellets is inserted in the slot at the top rear section of the clip. The cylindrical magazine rotates on a shaft that protrudes through its center hole. This shaft is attached to a tab that protrudes through a slot in the upper left-hand side of the detachable clip. Pulling the tab forward moves the shaft so the cylinder can be inserted. Pulling the tab backward moves the shaft through the clip to provide the support for the rotary magazine. With the magazine locked in place, it cannot fall out of the clip as it is removed from the rifle.

The Crosman 1077 uses a 12-shot cylinder held in a large detachable magazine.

The detachable clip is constructed with a rounded groove at the top just forward of the front edge of the cylinder that holds the pellets. When the clip is inserted in the rifle, the rear portion of the barrel fits in this groove with the breech at the forward face of the cylinder. In function, this is exactly like the barrel extension in a revolver, which almost makes contact with the front face of the cylinder. It is a clever arrangement that enables the barrel to almost be in contact with the revolving cylinder, which minimizes loss of CO_2 when a shot is fired. After all, the cylinder must rotate, but the gap between the front face of the cylinder and the barrel should be as small as possible.

On either side of the receiver is a small rectangular tab that protrudes from a slot. Each tab resides in a notch at the top of the slot. Pushing downward on the tabs releases them from the locking notches so that pushing forward causes them to move to the front of the

The Crosman 1077W the author is using here makes a convenient, capable plinking rifle.

slots. This motion slides the steel barrel forward about 1/4-inch inside the barrel shroud. Moving the barrel forward slightly may become necessary if a pellet gets hung at the interface between the rotating cylinder and end of the barrel. There is no way to move the cylinder to the rear so removing a stuck pellet can be accomplished only if the barrel is moved forward slightly. The only purpose of the two tabs on the sides of the receiver is to enable the barrel to be moved forward for removing jams. They have nothing to do with the functioning of the rifle or the repeating mechanism. In fact, they may need to be moved very seldom if ever in normal practice. As a safety feature, when the tabs are in the forward position and the barrel is moved away from the clip face, the trigger cannot be pulled and the rifle will not fire. This is an exceedingly well-designed CO_2 rifle. Velocity testing of the Crosman 1077W yielded the data shown in the accompanying table.

For the Crosman 1077, the advertised maximum velocity is up to 625 ft/sec. On a warm day when lightweight pellets are used, that is just about what could be expected from this rifle. This is a low-power, high-rate-of-fire rifle intended primarily for plinking. For this

Velocity Data for the Crosman 1077W at 75°F				
		Velocity, ft/sec		
Pellet	Ave.	High	Low	Std. Dev.
D.N. Meisterkugeln	605	609	598	4
Crosman Premier (7.9 gr)	574	579	566	7
Crosman Wadcutter	562	572	552	10

The Crosman 2250 gives performance hard to believe. Note the very small group in the bull that was obtained at 25 yards with a compact 2.5-power scope.

use, the Crosman 1077 is perfectly adequate. I would even use mine as a starling rifle, if I didn't have better choices available.

The Crosman 2250B

Introduced in 1999, the Crosman Model 2250B is another single-shot bolt-action 22-caliber rifle. While it shares the same action with the Models 2260 and 1760, it is in many ways a totally different piece. For example, the Model 2250B has a barrel that measures 14.63 inches in length and it comes with a skeletonized, detachable stock. It is sort of an overgrown pistol with a shoulder stock attached that sells for approximately $60-$70.

The Crosman 2250B has a large tube below the barrel in which the CO_2 cylinder is held. Removing the end cap allows a CO_2 cylinder to be inserted neck first and tightening the cap causes the cylinder to be pierced.

Drawing the bolt fully to the rear cocks the action. A single pellet is loaded in the breech and the bolt is closed. The rifle is now loaded. Unlike some CO_2 guns that use rotating cylinders to hold the pellets, a pellet of any length or shape can be used in the Model 2250B.

The safety on the Model 2250B is of the cross-bolt type and is located just behind the trigger. Pushed to the right, the safety is on; pushed to the left, it is off and the rifle can be fired. My Crosman 2250 has a trigger pull of 5.0 pounds, but the let-off is crisp.

In my opinion, the weak link in the design of the Model 2250B is the factory sights. The front sight is satisfactory since it consists of a square-topped post on a ramp although the 2003 Crosman catalog shows the 2250 with a front sight having a fiber optic insert. The entire assembly constitutes the nose cap for the barrel. However, the rear sight is an entirely different matter because it is exactly the same sight found on Models 2260, 1760, 2240 and a couple of others. It consists of a base made of plastic and a thin metal blade attached to the rear of the base by a single screw. The blade has a tiny hole at one end that is supposed to serve as a peep sight, while the other end has a notch that resembles that of an ordinary open rear sight. The problem is that the aperture is too small and the notch is too wide because it is too close to the shooter's eye. These deficiencies have been discussed earlier in connection with the Crosman 2260. However, Crosman offers an intermount that clamps on the barrel, which allows scope mounts, a red dot sight, or a laser sight to be attached. Of these, I much prefer the scope, and this rifle is accurate enough to take advantage of one.

Velocity Data for the Crosman 2250 at 68°F and 75°F

| Pellet | Ave. | Velocity, ft/sec | | Std. Dev. |
		High	Low	
Beeman Crow Magnum	461[a]	463	458	2
Crosman Pointed	519[a]	521	517	2
Gamo Match	532[a]	535	529	2
D. N. Meisterkugeln	520[b]	527	516	4
Crosman Premier	504[b]	509	498	4
D. N. Super-H-Point	507[b]	508	506	1
Winchester Hunting	502[b]	505	498	3

[a] At a temperature of 68°F
[b] At a temperature of 75°F

Since my plan was to use the Crosman 2250 as a short-range varmint rifle, I wanted to see what velocities the short barrel would produce. Velocities were measured by firing five-shot strings with the same three types of pellets as were tested in the Crosman 2260. The accompanying table shows the results obtained from two series of tests.

Several things are evident from the velocity data shown in the table. First, the velocities are incredibly uniform. Standard deviations of only 2 ft/sec for the data obtained at 68°F (the actual values were 2.4, 1.8, and 1.8 ft/sec) are very low. Second, the advertised velocity for the 2250 is 550 ft/sec. The Gamo Match has a weight of 13.88 grains, which is not really a light pellet since some of the really light 22-caliber pellets weigh approximately 12 grains. Given the fact that the Crosman 2250 gave a velocity of 532 ft/sec with a pellet weighing 13.88 grains at a temperature of 68°F, there is no doubt that on a warmer day this short rifle would meet or exceed the advertised velocity with a light-weight pellet. This pleased me a great deal in view of the anticipated use of this portable piece as a varmint rifle.

The second series of tests carried out at 75°F again show the velocities obtained are very uniform. In this case, the pellets were all relatively heavy (14.3 grains or more) so the velocities were slightly lower than some of those obtained in the first series of tests at 68°F. With these pellets, the kinetic energy is still in the 8-8.5 ft-lbs range, which is high enough for a lot of varmint hunting.

When I mounted a scope on the 2250, I was astonished to find I could hit a 1-inch bull on the target I was using at 20 yards. The indica-tion is the 2250 is accurate enough for any reasonable use. Later, I mounted a compact scope that has long eye relief on the 2250. After sighting in at 25 yards, I proceeded to shoot a five-shot group that had four shots in a 1-inch black bull and an overall group size of less than 1 inch. This was done with the compact scope of only 2-1/2 power. I do not know if all specimens of the Crosman 2250 will shoot like this, but my rifle is very accurate indeed.

When I first got my Crosman 2250, I found myself asking, "Why would they make this?" After spending some time with the little rifle, I realized it made several other rifles I have superfluous. First, with the 14.63-inch barrel, the velocity obtained is only slightly lower than that produced by the Model 2260, which has a 24-inch barrel. Second, the accuracy displayed by the Model 2250 rivals that of any CO_2 rifle I have. It is a very effective, efficient little rifle that provides a lot of fun. With the stock removed, a very short slipcase will hold the stock and barrel assembly for traveling ease. With adequate power and excellent accuracy, the Crosman 2250 has become one of my favorite CO_2-powered guns. It has also become one of the models chosen by serious hobbyists for modification. Performance is enhanced by replacing the composite receiver with one made of metal, changing valves, polishing internal surfaces, etc. Fully tricked out, a Crosman 2250 is capable of unbelievable accuracy and power.

The Walther Lever Action

While excellent CO_2-powered rifles have been available for many years, there have been significant developments recently. The Crosman 2260, 2250, and 1760 bolt-action single-shot

The Walther Lever Action is a beautiful rifle with classic styling.

rifles have all been introduced since 1999. Perhaps the most interesting CO_2 rifle is the most recent. That rifle is the 177 Walther Lever Action made by Umarex and imported and marketed by Crosman Corporation. The Walther design begins with a rifle that has been available for well over 100 years and more than 6 million of them have been made. That rifle, the Winchester Model 94, is arguably the most widely recognized rifle ever made. While the Walther mimics the outward appearance of the Winchester 94 exceedingly well, that is where the similarity ends. By the way, Walther does not use the "94" or "1894" model number, only the name Lever Action.

Over the years, the Winchester 94 has been made in a wide variety of configurations. Probably the best known are the 20-inch barreled standard carbine and the 16-inch barreled Trapper model. Cognizant of the popularity of these models, Walther produces two variants of the CO_2 Lever Action: a "long" version with an 18.9-

Pressing inward on the front end of the fake loading gate unlatches the door to the compartment where the 8-shot cylinder is held.

inch barrel and a "short" version with a 16-inch barrel. Advertised muzzle velocities are up to 633 ft/sec and 574 ft/sec for the long and short barrels, respectively. My rifle is the long version so the information in the test results deals only with that specimen.

The removable power assembly holds two CO_2 cylinders that are pierced by turning a bolt attached to the wire lever.

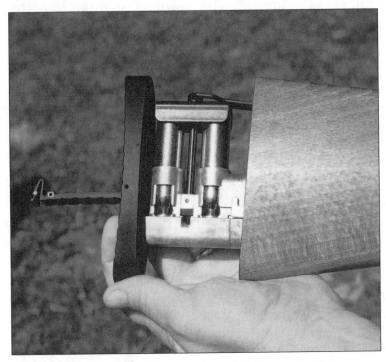

After loading and piercing the CO_2 cylinders, the entire assembly is inserted into the stock.

The long version of the Walther CO_2 Lever Action measures 38 inches in length and weighs 7.5 pounds. It is a genuine metal-and-wood rifle that handles like the famous firearm that inspired it. Since I grew up watching western movies, the Winchester 94 was always a beautiful rifle to me. Being thin, short, and flat, there is no rifle available that handles better than a Winchester 94.

While the Winchester 94 holds cartridges in a tubular magazine under the barrel, the Walther lever action holds eight pellets in a metal cylinder. Therefore, it is a revolver with an internal cylinder. On the right-hand side of the rifle, a red indicator protrudes from a hole at the junction of the action and forearm when a cylinder is in place. Inside the action is a piece of red plastic that is pushed to the right slightly when a cyl-

The square-notched rear sight is adjustable for elevation only. Note the "Carl Walther / Germany for Crosman" on the barrel.

inder is in place. Pressing inward on the "loading gate" on the right-hand side of the receiver opens the cylinder compartment. The fake loading gate is actually a lever hinged at the rear that allows the front of the lever to move inward to release the magazine holder. When the magazine holder swings out, a loaded cylinder is placed on the support pin with the ratchet teeth toward the rear. The magazine holder is pushed back into the side of the action until it locks in place. The metal cylinder measures 0.275 inch in thickness so it can accommodate most 177-caliber pellets.

Power for most CO_2 rifles and pistols is by means of one 12-gram CO_2 cylinder. The Walther Lever Action returns to the practice of using two CO_2 cylinders employed by Crosman in several early models. Moreover, they are contained in the butt. If you look at the butt plate, you see a panel with a latch at the top and a hinge at the bottom. Pulling downward on the latch allows the panel to open at the top and swing away from the butt. When it is extended, a slight pulling motion causes the carrier that holds the two CO_2 cylinders to slide out of the cavity in the stock. Because the assembly also contains a valve, no loss of CO_2 occurs when the power assembly is removed from the rifle. A long bolt passes through a metal plate between the cylinders into the frame at the bottom of the power assembly. The head of the bolt has a wire loop attached that can be used as a handle to

tighten the bolt. Turning the wire loop clockwise forces the plate downward, which pushes the CO_2 cylinders down to the piercing pins. When the wire handle stops turning, it is turned backwards a small amount to point forward so it can be aligned correctly for replacing in the stock. As the assembly is placed in the stock, a brass tube mounted in the stock cavity engages the open end of the shutoff valve in the power assembly to allow gas transfer. The owner's manual for the Walther states that two CO_2 cylinders provide power for at least 60 shots.

The hammer can be cocked manually, but this action does not rotate the cylindrical magazine. Firing should be done by working the lever, which rotates the magazine and cocks the hammer. If you have worked the action and decide not to fire, the hammer can be let down by holding it with a thumb while pulling the trigger. The hammer can be cocked to fire one shot, but you must work the lever to rotate the magazine to bring another pellet into battery. Like recent versions of the Winchester 94, the Walther Lever Action has a hammer block safety that passes through the receiver just in front of the hammer.

My Walther Lever Action is the long version with open sights. It is going to stay that way (as is my 30-30 Winchester Model 94) because I do not want any red dot or laser on this classic-styled rifle. Because they are so sleek and

While the hammer can be cocked to fire the Walther, only by working the lever is the cylinder rotated to bring another pellet into firing position.

trim without them, scopes do not adorn my lever-action rifles either. My Walther is and will remain an open-sighted rifle. And as good as the open sights are on this rifle, I will be delighted to use it that way. The front sight is a square post on a ramp with a hood while the rear sight is a blade with a square notch. Together, these sights give a sight picture as good as those on any open-sighted air rifle I own. Elevation is adjusted with the rear sight by means of a stepped riser, and windage is adjusted by moving the front sight laterally after removing the hood. While the square-post, square-notch combination would be good for a six o'clock hold on paper targets, I will sight my Walther to have a point of impact at the top of the post so I can put the top of the post on a starling. This is going to be my small pest rifle.

Trigger action on the Walther Lever Action is outstanding. As with the classic lever action rifles, the trigger motion is of the two-stage type with the take-up motion requiring almost no effort. The sear disengaged with a pull of 4.4 pounds with absolutely no creep.

Working the lever of the Walther requires very little effort because the small cylindrical magazine is rotated and the hammer cocked by the motion. There are no large, heavy parts that are changing positions during the lever movement. However, when the lever is returned to the grip area, it is possible to catch a small portion of a hand or forearm between the lever and the grip. This is not pleasant, especially if you are working the lever quickly. Velocity testing of the Walther Lever Action was carried out using four types of pellets with the results shown in the table.

Velocity Data for the Walther Lever Action at 75°F				
		Velocity, ft/sec		
Pellet	**Ave.**	**High**	**Low**	**Std. Dev.**
D.N. Meisterkugeln	611	616	607	4
Crosman Premier (7.9 gr)	623	629	617	5
Crosman Wadcutter	615	622	602	8
Eley Target	626	637	616	9

The Walther Lever Action has become one of my favorite rifles.

The data shown in the table indicate the advertised velocity of 633 ft/sec is accurate. Two of the four types of pellets tested were within 10 ft/sec of that value. It is also interesting to note that the velocities are uniform considering the pellets were launched from different chambers in an 8-shot cylinder. Velocity performance was very good indeed. After measuring pellet velocities from the Walther, I placed a target at 10 yards and proceeded to sight in the rifle. After this was done, I proceeded to fire a couple of five-shot groups that were very small. In fact, one was little more than one large, ragged hole. Keep in mind this was done with open sights. I was delighted to see how well the square-topped post and rear sight with a square notch worked. This rifle is accurate enough for any purpose to which a rifle of this type and power should be put.

The fit and finish on this rifle are second to none when compared to other air or CO_2 rifles. It is a well engineered and executed design that has only one real drawback and that is the price. The retail price of the Walther Lever Action is $249.95, which is rather high; but it is a high quality piece.

CHAPTER 10

SHOOTING SOME CO$_2$ CLASSICS

I FIND IT interesting that there is a parallel between airguns and cameras. Specimens from bygone eras are highly sought by collectors with different motives. Some collectors are content just to find a particular camera or airgun so it can be displayed in a collection. Other collectors, including me, do not wish merely to collect a specific model, they want a *working* model. I enjoy taking pictures with a camera from the 1950s or 1960s that still works as well as when it was new. Likewise, I am greatly pleased when I find a CO$_2$ or airgun that is many years old, but still can be fired. In fact, many older air and CO$_2$ guns perform in the same manner and just as well as some current models.

Many of the CO$_2$ guns of yesterday have become highly collectible classics. In this chapter, we will describe the operation and performance of a few of these models. It is not possible to locate and gain access to all the models for testing purposes. Most museums would frown on such a request. Therefore, of necessity, the models described in this chapter represent only a few of those that were made over the years. However, they can be considered as representing the types of guns that were marketed, and their performance provides a baseline for what can be expected from a gun of the same general type.

The information provided in this chapter will be of interest to those who collect and/or use vintage CO$_2$ guns. While each section does not constitute an owner's manual for the model discussed, it does give enough information to show how that particular gun operates.

In addition to some of the models of CO$_2$ guns that have been out of production for many years, several recently discontinued models will be reviewed. Some of them will become classics and others are still encountered either in new condition or as perfectly functioning used guns. In either case, the term "classic" will be used in a somewhat loose manner to apply to older or recently discontinued models.

In the descriptions that follow, instructions are given for installing a CO$_2$ cylinder and loading ammunition in each model. Although is it not stated explicitly in the discussion of each model, the safety should always be in the "on" position before loading propellant or projectiles in any CO$_2$ gun. There is danger in piercing a CO$_2$ cylinder in a gun that might already have pellets in it or in placing pellets in a gun that is pressurized with a pierced CO$_2$ cylinder. Read the owner's manual and follow all safety instructions.

The Daisy CO$_2$ 200

When you pick up a Daisy CO$_2$ 200, you may think "Why don't they make them like this anymore?" The CO$_2$ 200 has plastic grips but the rest of the gun is metal. The barrel is metal as is the generous shroud that surrounds it. It is metal! I have read the opinion of another author who stated that the Power-Line 200 is the best of the class of the CO$_2$ pistols that shoot BBs, and I agree.

Externally, the PowerLine 200 resembles a High Standard or Colt auto chambered for the 22 rimfire. In the hand it feels like a 22

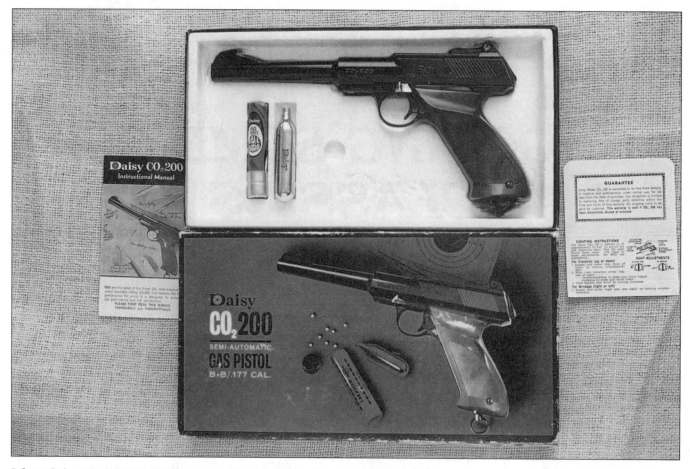

I found this Daisy CO₂ 200 in an antique mall and realized that another in this condition might not be available for a long time. I bought it just in case.

auto. It has an overall length of 11.3 inches and weighs 24.3 ounces. Barrel length is 7 inches, which gives a sight radius of 9 inches.

The CO_2 200 has a reservoir that holds up to 175 BBs and it is filled by rotating a lever at the rear of the action, which exposes the BB port. There is an internal magazine that holds five BBs, which can be fired in a semi-automatic fashion. There is a small lever on the left-hand side of the frame just above the trigger that moves the magazine follower. When that lever is pulled forward to expose a red dot (firing indicator), BBs move from the reservoir into the magazine. The procedure described in the instruction manual calls for tilting the muzzle downward at approximately 45 degrees then slowly tipping the muzzle upward to a vertical position. Pushing the lever forward while the gun points upward allows the BBs to enter the magazine. The lever is then slowly released and it moves slightly backward due to spring pressure, which is enough to move BBs during firing.

As each BB from the magazine is fired, the lever moves back a short distance. After the last BB is fired, the lever returns to its rear-most position and the red-dot firing indicator is covered showing that the magazine is empty and the trigger is inoperative. The Daisy CO_2 200 is a true semi-automatic that does not require separate cocking.

The sights on the Daisy CO_2 200 are the equal of those on any of the CO_2 pistols tested. A sharp, undercut ramp front sight on a large base has a square top for good sight picture. The rear sight is a square notch in a fully adjustable base. At the front of the base there is a locking screw that must be loosened in order to make sight adjustments. Elevation is adjusted by turning a second screw located just in front of the square notch. The screw is turned counterclockwise to make the point of impact higher and clockwise to lower the point of impact. Windage is adjusted by turning a screw located on the left-hand side of the rear sight counterclockwise to move the

When the slide above the trigger is pulled forward, BBs are moved from the internal reservoir into a 5-shot magazine. They can be fired as a semi-automatic by simply pulling the trigger.

The rear sight on the Daisy CO_2 200 is fully adjustable. It is outstanding for a pistol of this type and price.

point of impact to the left and clockwise to move it to the right. Both the elevation and windage screws have index marks that function as "clicks" that correspond to about one-eighth of an inch at 15 feet. If only some of the currently produced CO_2 pistols had sights this good!

The plastic grip panels on the Daisy 200 are well shaped and sharply checkered. The left-hand panel has a target-style thumb rest

that is actually comfortable and effective. Removing the left-hand grip panel exposes the chamber where the CO_2 cylinder is held. A CO_2 cylinder is inserted after backing the loop-headed piercing screw out. Piercing the CO_2 cylinder is accomplished by turning the piercing screw in a clockwise direction. One unique feature of the Daisy 200 is that it is not cocked manually and it cannot be cocked unless there is a charged CO_2 cylinder in place. Because the trigger motion does not cock the gun, the trigger let-off is quite good compared to currently produced models. The trigger block safety is of the cross-bolt type and is located behind the trigger.

As I began the testing procedure with this pistol, I heard the hissing noise one does not want to hear when working with an air or CO_2 gun. A detailed examination revealed that a small part in the piercing mechanism was missing. Therefore, the testing procedures were not completed with this pistol.

With the quality of construction, excellent sights, and good trigger action, one gets the feeling that if it had a rifled barrel and fired pellets, this would be a super accurate pistol. As it is, it is more than just adequately accurate for its intended purpose.

The Daisy CO_2 200 is as handsome and well made as any sporting-class BB pistol with which I am familiar. I had one in rather rough condition before I found the one shown, but I wasn't sure whether it was worth spending the money required to fix it up. Now, I have no doubt, but I need to have both of mine fixed. If you can find one of these fine pistols in a pawnshop, antique

The Daisy PowerLine 1700 is a plastic pistol that is much longer on performance than it is on looks.

mall, or flea market, buy it if you want a CO_2-powered BB pistol. The average price is approximately $40-$50 for a specimen in good condition.

The Daisy PowerLine 1700

Daisy introduced the PowerLine 1700 in 1994 and it was a catalog item until 2001. Except for the cylinder piercing screw and its wire-loop head, all external parts of the Daisy PowerLine 1700 are made of black plastic. It is a boxy, square-cornered piece with an extra-long frame and fake slide. With the square appearance, it resembles a lengthened Glock center fire semi-automatic. The pistol has about as much eye appeal as a boxcar. But then the Glock isn't going to win any beauty contest either. However, the Power-Line 1700 and the Glock have something in common—they both work extremely well. As the old saying goes, "pretty is as pretty does." In that context, the PowerLine 1700 is attractive. This pistol is not exactly highly prized and as a result, I bought my first one for $7.95 in a pawnshop. After gaining some experience with it, I also bought the next one I found for a good price.

The PowerLine 1700 can be fired only in the single-action mode. The pistol must be cocked for each shot by means of a recessed lever located on the bottom of the frame between the front of the trigger guard and the muzzle. Pulling the lever forward cocks the gun. This cocking action is the same as that required for several PowerLine models, particularly the Models 1200 and 1270.

A small, vertically-traveling trap door at the rear of the slide can be pushed down and up to 60 BBs can be poured in. The cocking action allows a BB to move from the reservoir to the barrel breech. A firing rate of eight shots in 3 seconds is not what you get with the PowerLine 1700. However, you can hook a thumb on the recessed cocking lever to quickly pull it forward to make successive shots fast enough for most purposes.

A cross-bolt safety is located behind the trigger. Pushing it to the right places it on. Pushing the safety to the left takes it off and exposes a red firing indicator.

Trigger action of the PowerLine 1700 is actually rather good and my two 1700s both require about a 5-pound pull. That results from the fact it is fired single action. Pulling the trigger does not involve the long, heavy

Velocity Data for the Daisy PowerLine 1700 at 73-75°F				
	Velocity, ft/sec			
Type of BB	Ave.	High	Low	Std. Dev.
Daisy Max Speed (1)	483	492	472	8
Daisy Max Speed (2)	458	464	451	6
Crosman Copperhead (1)	484	489	479	4
Cosman Copperhead (2)	471	475	463	5
Crosman Premier (1)	481	484	475	4
Crosman Premier (2)	477	478	476	1

(1) and (2) refer to two different pistols.

The sliding door at the back of the PowerLine 1700 is the BB port.

pull that is necessary to cock the pistol. It is rare that I fire any CO_2 pistol in the double-action mode if it can be fired single action because accuracy suffers to such a great extent.

Sights on the PowerLine 1700 can only be described as rudimentary. The front sight is a low, square-topped post and the rear sight is a square notch in a thick plastic blade.

Lateral movement of the rear sight in its dovetail groove allows for windage adjustment. Even though they are crude, the sights on the PowerLine 1700 allow a better sight picture than is possible with several other CO_2 pistols that cost much more.

Loading a CO_2 cylinder in a PowerLine 1700 involves removing the left-hand grip panel and inserting the cylinder in the grip with the neck up. Turning the loop-handled piercing screw forces the cylinder up to the piercing pin. This is a very simple pistol to operate. Velocity tests performed with both of my Model 1700 pistols yielded the results shown in the accompanying table.

My two PowerLine 1700 pistols were obtained used for less than $20 total. It is amazing that so little money can bring so much shooting fun. If working properly, a PowerLine 1700 shoots BBs at very high and uniform velocity. In fact, the highest velocities I measured for a CO_2 pistol shooting BBs were with the 1700. While the second specimen gave slightly lower velocities, both gave velocities that exceed the 420 ft/sec specified for this model. These are high-powered BB pistols that sell for $20-$30.

While you can buy a PowerLine 1700 for a few dollars, do not assume that it is a toy. My PowerLine 1700, which has an advertised muzzle velocity of 420 ft/sec, will actually give almost 500 ft/sec and would reach that velocity on a warm day. Keep in mind most ordinary BB guns like the Daisy Red Ryder shoot with a velocity of around 300 ft/sec. That means that a BB fired from a CO_2 pistol like the PowerLine 1700 has over twice as much energy as one fired from a Daisy Red Ryder or a similar lever-cocking BB gun. The PowerLine 1700 and similar models have very high power for BB guns. Never allow such lightweight plastic CO_2 pistols to be regarded as toys!

I believe a BB pistol such as the PowerLine 1700 or one of the similar models to be discussed later makes a good starter CO_2 pistol. There is no possibility of firing a second shot carelessly by simply pulling the trigger. The pistol must be cocked manually, and I believe this makes it less prone to accidental discharge. Because it can be fired only in the single-action mode, the trigger pull is much better than is found on any of the double-action models (unless they are also fired in the single-action mode). Also, models like the PowerLine 1700, 1270, and 1200 can be obtained at very low cost. As the test results show, they also perform extremely well in spite of their being inexpensive.

The Daisy PowerLine 1200

By today's standards, the Daisy PowerLine 1200 is almost of retro design. It must be cocked manually for each shot so it is a single-action-only proposition. The cocking lever is located in a recess in the plastic fore end and the pistol is cocked by pushing this lever forward. Introduced in 1977, the Model 1200 remained a catalog item until 1996 when it was replaced by the Model 1270. Because it

was made for so many years and in such large numbers, the PowerLine 1200 is one of the easiest vintage CO_2 pistols to find. Average prices are in the $30-$35 range.

Up to 60 BBs can be loaded by rotating the plastic cover on the rear of the gun and putting BBs in the small hole. Pulling the cocking lever forward allows a BB from the reservoir to move into position for firing.

To insert a CO_2 cylinder in the PowerLine 1200, remove the left-hand grip panel by applying pressure outward at the base making use of the recess. After the grip panel is removed, insert the CO_2 cylinder neck up in the grip frame. The piercing screw has a metal loop handle for tightening the screw by finger pressure only, which forces the CO_2 cylinder upward.

Except for the sights, grips, and forearm, the Daisy PowerLine 1200 is made of metal. The weight is 25.7 ounces and the overall length is 11 inches. Barrel length of the Model 1200 is 7 inches.

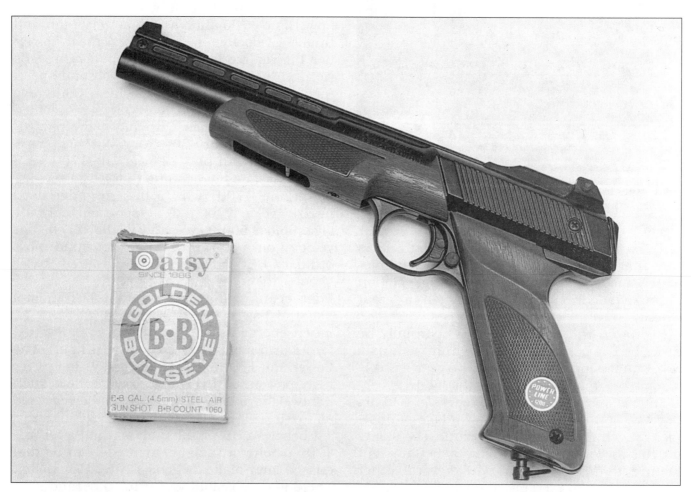

The Daisy PowerLine 1200 BB pistol was economical, but it was powerful and accurate.

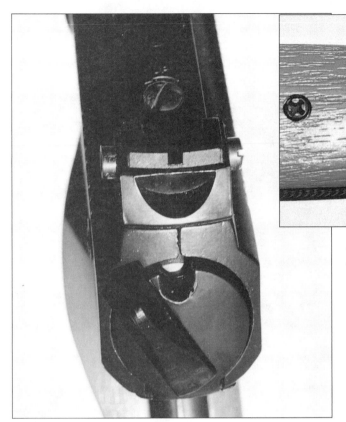

Rotating the lever on the rear of the action opens the BB port on the PowerLine 1200. Note the adjustable, square-notch rear sight. The 1200 has outstanding sights for an inexpensive CO$_2$ pistol.

Pulling forward on the lever below the barrel cocked the PowerLine 1200 and loaded a BB for the next shot.

A cross-bolt safety is located just behind the trigger. Pushing the safety to the right places it on while pushing it to the left takes it off and exposes the red ring around the safety, indicating the pistol is ready to fire.

Sights on the PowerLine 1200 consist of a square-topped post front sight on a ramp and a square notch rear sight. The rear sight can be moved laterally in a dovetail notch for windage adjustment. On some earlier Model 1200 pistols, the rear sight can be moved after a locking screw is loosened.

To me, the PowerLine 1200 being a single-action design is no handicap. The cocking lever can be pulled forward with a thumb very quickly to recycle for subsequent shots. Moreover, on the positive side is the fact the pistol has a very crisp trigger let-off with very little creep. Trigger pull on my older (all metal) 1200 measured only 2.6 pounds while that of my newer model was 4.6 pounds. None of the double-action-only pistols have a trigger nearly this good.

Although the Daisy PowerLine 1200 was an inexpensive pistol, it is made primarily of metal. The heavy barrel gives the pistol a weight distribution that aids in steady holding. Furthermore, as the test results show, this pistol will really shoot. It operates in much the same way as the PowerLine 1700 discussed earlier, but the Model 1200 is a more attractive design and has a better feel in the hand. Being made of metal also adds to the desirability of the Model 1200. How it performed in the velocity tests is shown by the data in the accompanying table.

The chronograph shows the PowerLine 1200 exceeds the 420 ft/sec advertised for it during its production. This out-of-print pistol performs just as well as ever, even if I did get it for a bargain price in an antique store. Moreover,

	Velocity, ft/sec			
Type of BB	**Ave.**	**High**	**Low**	**Std. Dev.**
Daisy Max Speed	450	456	447	4
Crosman Copperhead	462	465	457	3
Crosman Premier	474	479	469	4

Velocity Data for the Daisy PowerLine 1200 at 73-75°F

Made with a bright plastic frame and black plastic grips, the PowerLine 1270 functions in the same way as the PowerLine 1200 but weighs much less.

the velocities are quite uniform. I have no objection to pushing the lever under the barrel forward to cock the piece for the next shot. As a result, I find this type of BB pistol a lot of fun to shoot. It is not difficult to locate one of these guns, and they perform just as well as the newer models that are made to resemble some type of semi-automatic.

I experienced some feeding problems with the 1200 that are symptomatic of the gravity feed design. In a cavity that will hold up to 60 BBs, the last two or three BBs can rattle around without finding the breech to load properly. I found one way to minimize the problem is to pull the lever forward to cock the gun and hold it in its most forward position. While doing that, move the muzzle up and down a couple of times to cause the BBs to encounter the breech and load properly. When this procedure was followed, the pistol functioned almost every time even when there were few BBs in the reservoir. If the number of BBs in the reservoir is fairly large, it is more probable one of them will find the breech and load.

The quality of materials and construction makes the Daisy PowerLine 1200 equal to any of the currently produced BB pistols. The

fact they can be found for very low prices makes them good starter guns.

The Daisy PowerLine 1270

Daisy Outdoor Products manufactured the PowerLine 1270 from 1997 to 2002. Like the Models 1700 and 1200, the PowerLine 1270 required manual cocking before each shot. The major difference between the 1200 and the 1270 is the latter is made of a bright plastic that looks chrome-plated. Because of the heavy use of plastic, the Model 1270 weighs only 16.8 ounces. Operation of the Model 1270 is identical to the Model 1200 so there is no need to restate the details. Another significant difference between the two models is that on the PowerLine 1270, the sliding plastic forearm is attached to the cocking lever, so pulling the forearm forward cocks the pistol. The forearm moves as it does on a pump shotgun except on the shotgun the gun is cocked as the forearm moves backward.

My PowerLine 1270 has a trigger pull that measures 5.6 pounds, but it is satisfactory. Because the 1270 functions in the same way as the Model 1200 described earlier, we can proceed directly to the results of testing, which are shown in the following table.

Even though it is not adjustable for windage, the rear sight of the PowerLine 1270 still allows for a good sight picture.

Velocity Data for the Daisy PowerLine 1270 at 73-75°F				
		Velocity, ft/sec		
Type of BB	**Ave.**	**High**	**Low**	**Std. Dev.**
Daisy Max Speed	440	442	434	3
Crosman Copperhead	456	461	451	4
Crosman Premier	456	461	452	4

The data shown indicate the PowerLine 1270 performs as well with respect to velocity as can reasonably be expected for a BB-only pistol. Velocities are high and uniform. The advertised velocity of up to 420 ft/sec is very conservative. Like the PowerLine 1200, this pistol performs very well with all of the types of BBs used, but unlike some other pistols, Crosman Premier pellets worked well in this gun. With some pistols, the coating on Crosman Premiers seems to hinder feeding, but no such effect was seen with the PowerLine 1270.

Functioning of the PowerLine 1200 and 1270 is identical, but the two pistols feel quite different because of the weight. The Model 1270 is very light because of the plastic frame while the Model 1200 feels like a substantial gun. Having shot both models extensively, I have no real preference, but it is easier to fire the Model 1200 accurately offhand. Either of these discontinued BB pistols will give performance well out of the range

expected for the going price of $25-$35 for used specimens in good condition.

The Healthways Plainsman 175

In addition to marketing other recreational products, Healthways offered several models of CO_2 guns in the 1950-1970 period. These are frequently encountered in pawnshops, antique malls, and flea markets. My Model 175 Plainsman turned up complete with box and papers in a pawnshop in Montana. I added it to my collection for $15, but it is probably worth five or six times that amount. It pays to shop. I have seen several others, but none in this condition and at a low price.

The Plainsman 175 is a 100-shot BB repeater made of metal with black plastic grips, and it resembles somewhat a 22 pistol known as the High Standard Sport King. A unique feature of the Model 175 is that it has three power settings, which are selected by means of a coin-slotted screw in the base of

Except for the black plastic grips, the Healthways Plainsman is made of metal.

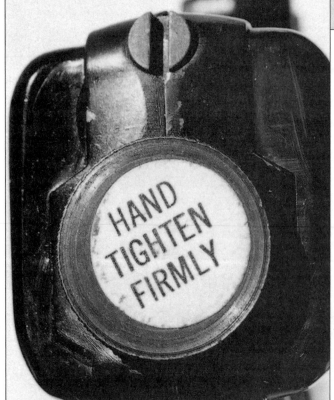

Three power settings of the Plainsman were selectable by turning the screw at the rear of the grip.

the grip. Turning fully in the clockwise direction selects the low power setting. Turning the screw counterclockwise approximately 1/4 turn causes a "click stop" notch to be encountered, which corresponds to the medium power setting. Turning the screw fully counterclockwise gives the high power setting. The owner's manual states that approximately 100 shots can be fired from a CO_2 cylinder when the low power setting is selected. The number of shots per cylinder drops to about 50 and 30 shots for medium and high power settings, respectively.

Firing the Plainsman 175 is by double action only. There is no provision for cocking the action by any other means. Accordingly, trigger action is long, but very smooth right up to the end of the travel. At that point, there is a noticeable increase in force required, but let-off is very crisp, and the measured trigger pull is only 4.8 pounds. This old pistol has a double-action trigger pull about as good as all but the best modern pistols.

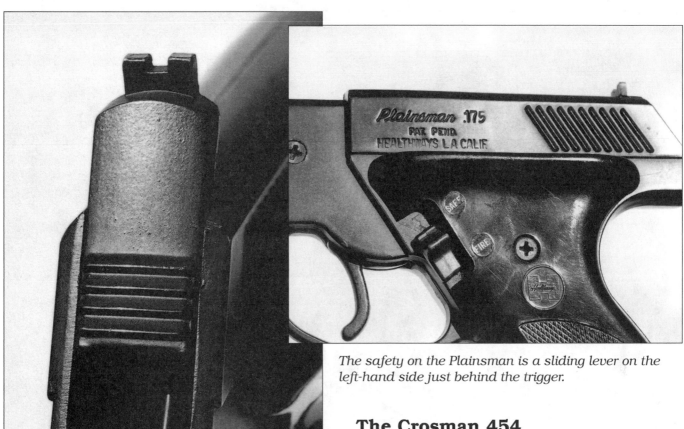

BBs are loaded in the Plainsman by sliding the door at the rear of the action upward.

The safety on the Plainsman is a sliding lever on the left-hand side just behind the trigger.

Up to 100 BBs can be loaded at the rear of the receiver after sliding a door upward. A CO_2 cylinder is placed neck up in the grip after removing the large, knurled cap. Replacing and tightening the cap completes the process.

The safety on the Plainsman 175 is a sliding lever on the left-hand side of the frame just behind the trigger. Sliding the lever up places the safety on while sliding it down takes it off. The "safe" and "fire" positions are indicated in white lettering on the black plastic grip panel.

In almost new condition, my old Healthways 175 still had the decal on the piercing cap indicating to "hand tighten firmly." Unfortunately, the Healthways 175 uses the shorter 8-gram CO_2 cylinders. As a result, the testing procedures were not followed for this pistol and no numerical data were recorded.

The Crosman 454

It always seemed to me that the classic style in 22-caliber semi-auto pistols was defined by the Hi Standard, Colt, and Browning autoloaders. Their overall style typifies that of a pistol to be used primarily for target and sport. This style is copied by some of the older CO_2 pistols, especially some of the BB guns.

My wife and I were going through an antique mall in Michigan when she called my attention to the Crosman 454 in a showcase. A Crosman 454 is a 16-shot CO_2-powered BB semi-automatic. The pistol was in its original box and it appeared as if it were new. Although the owner's manual was missing, other literature originally included with the gun was present. Also present was an empty box that originally contained five CO_2 cylinders, probably the only ones ever used in the pistol. The Crosman 454 was introduced in 1972 and this one carried the "Coleman" logo and Fairport, NY business address.

There were two variants of the Model 454. The first, which mine represents, had a coin-slotted piercing screw in the butt of the grip and was made from 1972 to 1977. The later version had a piercing screw with a metal-loop head and was made from 1978 to 1982. An average price range is $40-$55 for this model.

The Crosman 454 is a well-made, capable BB pistol that is patterned after a target pistol.

Oh how I wish more current models of CO_2 pistols had sights like those on the Crosman 454! The front sight is a square-topped post on a raised ramp. It has an undercut rear face just as those found on many target pistols. The rear sight consists of a fully adjustable blade with a square notch. Slotted screws allow adjustments to be made. Although the sights are made of black plastic, they are really excellent, and are fully the equal of those on any current CO_2 or air pistol.

The Crosman 454 has the weight and feel of a real pistol. It measures 11 inches in overall length, weighs 30 ounces, and has a smooth bore barrel just less than 8 inches long. The checkered plastic grips have thumb rests for shooters using either hand. The outer metal frame has a fake slide with serrations to add to the realistic appearance.

Two features that do not resemble an actual autoloading target pistol are the safety and the magazine. The safety is a small sliding lever at the front of the trigger guard on the right-hand side of the frame. Moving the slide forward

places the safety in the off position while the opposite motion places the safety on.

The magazine, which holds 16 BBs, is located along the upper right-hand side of the barrel. A spring-loaded follower can be pulled forward by means of a protruding pin, after which rotating the pin downward allows it to be locked in a recess at the forward end of its motion. With the follower in this position, a hole in the rib along the top of the barrel allows BBs to be dropped in. After the BBs are in place, the pin that holds the magazine follower forward is moved out of its retaining slot causing pressure on the BBs so they will feed properly.

Because the Crosman 454 is a double-action pistol, the trigger action is long. However, the trigger pull was measured at 5.6 pounds, which is very light for a double-action pull. The trigger pull on this pistol is much better than that on many of the current double-action-only models.

Loading a CO_2 cylinder in the Model 454 is done in the conventional manner. The right-

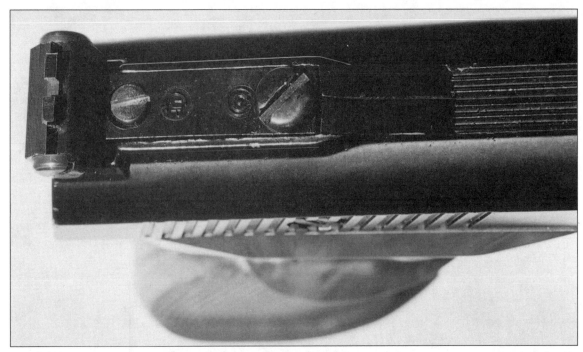

Being patterned after a target pistol, the Crosman 454 has fully adjustable sights that are outstanding.

On the Crosman 454, the safety is a small sliding lever on the right-hand side of the frame just in front of the trigger.

hand grip panel is snapped off and the CO_2 cylinder is inserted with the neck up. Turning the coin-slotted (or loop-headed in the last version of the 454) piercing screw clockwise causes the cylinder to be pushed upward onto the piercing pin. One difference between the Crosman 454 and some other CO_2 pistols is that the grip panel has clips that snap around the cylinder rather than on the grip frame. When there is no CO_2 cylinder in the gun, the right hand-grip panel is completely detached from the gun.

The Crosman 454 is a sturdy, well-finished, stylish pistol. Because mine has a leaking seal, no numerical data were recorded for this pistol.

The Crosman 1600

The Crosman 1600 is almost identical in appearance and function to the Model 454

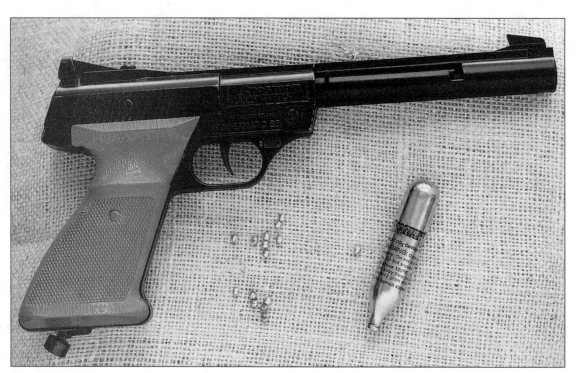

The Crosman 1600 is a less-elegant version of the 454 that functions in the same way.

described above. It does not have the high-quality adjustable rear sight of the Model 454, but otherwise it functions in the same manner. Therefore, no additional description of its operation is needed. No data were recorded for this pistol. This model sells for approximately $50 in average condition.

The Daisy PowerLine 44

A revolver that achieved almost cult status because of movies is the Smith & Wesson Model 29 44 Magnum. For several years, these guns were in short supply because of the high demand. Quick to recognize the marketing potential of the famous Model 29, Daisy introduced the PowerLine 44 in 1987 and it remained in production until 2001 with a retail price of $50-$60.

The PowerLine 44 is a big revolver. It sports a 6.5-inch barrel and weighs 35.9 ounces. The grip is too large for comfortable holding with small hands. Like all other repeating CO_2 pistols, the CO_2 cylinder is held in the grip. But that alone is not the reason for the large grip. This pistol is made with the dimensions of the largest frame (N-frame) Smith & Wesson revolvers.

The PowerLine 44 was most commonly seen with a 6-inch barrel. However, interchangeable barrels in 4- and 6-inch lengths were also available. A special wrench was provided with two prongs that fit in two recesses on either side of the muzzle. This allowed the removal of a retainer plug, which

Patterned after the Smith & Wesson Model 29 44 Magnum, the Daisy PowerLine 44 is a large 6-shot revolver.

Barrels of different lengths are interchangeable on the PowerLine 44. Note the recesses in the barrel shroud.

The PowerLine 44 comes with a special wrench, which fits the recesses to loosen and tighten the barrel.

then allowed the shroud and barrel to be removed. Barrels in each length came with a shroud of matching length so both barrel and shroud were replaced as a unit. When the barrel and shroud were in place, the barrel-retaining plug was replaced and tightened with the special wrench. Unfortunately, by the time I got involved with the PowerLine 44, no accessory barrels were available, so I have only the standard 6-inch barrel available for testing. I keep watching pawnshops, flea markets, and antique malls just in case another barrel turns up.

Like most CO_2 revolvers, the PowerLine 44 uses a rotating cylinder that resides at the front of the fake cylinder. This cylindrical magazine is removed by pushing downward on a latch on the left-hand side of the frame just in front of the cylinder. This allows the crane to swing out away from the frame. The cylindrical magazine is then lifted off its spindle. Because the cylinder measures .446 inch in thickness, any type of 177-caliber pellet can be used, a feature that I like. Sometimes, I just want to take whatever type of pellet I have at the moment and shoot. If I am out shooting pointed pellets in an air rifle, I do not always want to search for a wadcutter pellet to use in a pistol.

Sights on the PowerLine 44 are as good as those on any CO_2 pistol I have tested. The front sight is a serrated ramp and the rear is a blade with a square notch. The rear sight is fully adjustable by means of two screws. These sights afford the best possible sight picture for shooting at paper targets. Although the grooves along the sides of the barrel rib could be utilized to mount other sights, I have no intention of doing so except perhaps for test purposes.

Both single- and double-action firing are possible with the PowerLine 44. In the single-action mode, the trigger pull is two-stage. The first stage is short and light (as it should be) and the second stage is quite crisp although a trifle heavy at 6.7 pounds. In double-action shooting, pulling the trigger causes the rotation of the plastic cylinder as well as moving the hammer to the rear. As a result, it has a rough feel that is rather heavy, and it measures 9.0 pounds. While the double-action pull is by no means the worst for the guns tested, it is the single-action let-off that impresses me.

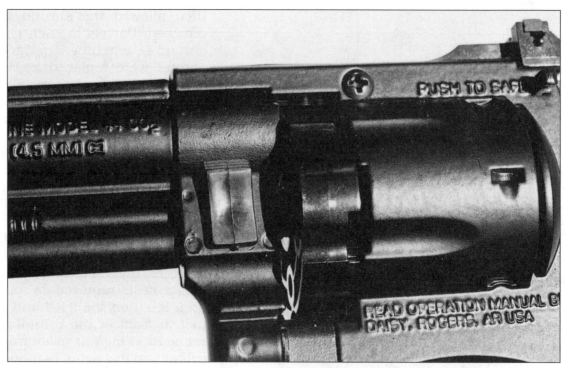

The cylinder latch is located on the left-hand side of the frame, and sliding it downward opens the cylinder.

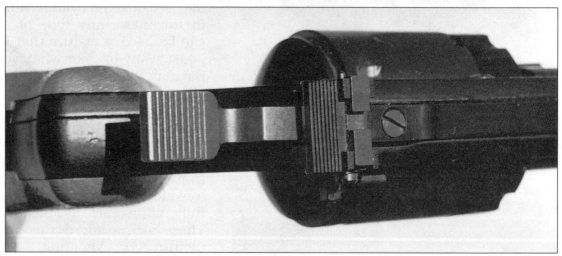

Note the target-style hammer and fully adjustable rear sight on the PowerLine 44.

Although slightly heavy, it is as good as that on any pistol tested, including some costing three or four times as much as the PowerLine 44.

Both hammer and trigger are of the target type. The hammer spur is wide and deeply grooved which allows for a comfortable, easy-to-control cocking motion. The trigger is extra wide, but its surface is smooth rather than grooved. A cross-bolt safety is located just below the rear sight. When the safety bar is pushed to the right, the safety is on. When the safety bar is pushed to the left, the safety is off and a red firing indicator is visible. If the hammer is cocked and a decision is made not to fire the gun, it is possible to let the hammer down. Place the safety on and pull the hammer back slightly to release the spring tension. With the trigger pulled to the rear, let the hammer down slowly with the thumb.

Inserting a CO_2 cylinder involves removing the left-hand grip panel. A recess at the bottom allows for thumb pressure to be applied. With the grip panel off, a CO_2 cylinder is inserted neck up. The piercing screw is turned clockwise to force the CO_2 cylinder up to the piercing pin. A large ring makes it easy to initiate piercing with only finger pressure. It was with high expectations I began testing this sturdy, well-made revolver. If it were a 22 caliber, the PowerLine 44 would be my favorite CO_2 revolver. The results of the velocity tests are shown in the accompanying table.

Velocity Data for the Daisy PowerLine 44 at 70-72°F

Pellet	Ave.	Velocity, ft/sec		Std. Dev.
		High	Low	
D.N. Meisterkugeln	397	402	393	4
Gamo Match	402	408	394	6
Daisy Wadcutter	415	426	398	10
Crosman Wadcutter	394	400	386	6
D. N. Club	421	430	410	11
Eley Target	414	420	407	5

Average velocities for the PowerLine 44 were higher than the advertised 400 ft/sec with all but two of the pellets tested. In those two cases, the velocity was lower than 400 ft/sec only very slightly. Two of the pellets, the Daisy wadcutter and the Dynamit Nobel Club gave a rather large range of velocities as is reflected by the magnitudes of the standard deviations.

No problems were encountered in the functioning of the PowerLine 44. The cylinder that holds the pellets is very large even though it holds only six pellets. I was amazed how much easier it was to load the large cylinder than the very small ones used in pistols that resemble autoloading firearms. The Power-Line 44 is a sturdy, full-size handgun that operates in a convenient, realistic manner. It is one I plan to use to get ready for handgun hunting for varmints.

The Crosman SSP 250

The Crosman SSP 250 is a specialized single-shot pistol with some unusual features. Produced from 1989 to 1995, the SSP has a long barrel that is easily interchangeable to 177, 20, or 22 caliber. I believe the pistol was normally available in 177 caliber and the barrels in other calibers were available as aftermarket accessories. The SSP 250 was produced specifically for shooting silhouette targets and it is also a magnum among pistols. With its closed breech and long barrel, velocities are higher than those specified for other CO_2 pistols. Currently, the SSP 250 pistols are highly prized as the starting point for producing high-powered guns for hunting and pest control. For such uses, the 20 and 22 calibers are more suitable even though the 177 caliber is no weakling for a pistol. Modi-

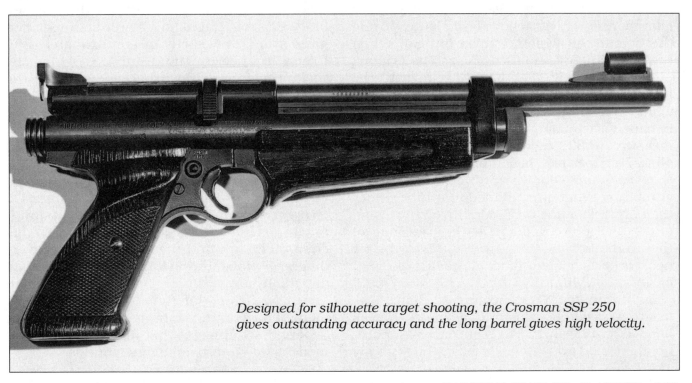

Designed for silhouette target shooting, the Crosman SSP 250 gives outstanding accuracy and the long barrel gives high velocity.

The chamber of the SSP 250 rotates to the left out of the action when the bolt handle is lifted.

fied with polished and enhanced valves and seals, trigger alterations, etc., the SSP 250 is about as good as it gets as far as a magnum CO_2 pistol is concerned.

The SSP 250 is a large pistol that measures 14 inches in overall length and weighs 41.9 ounces. It is a single-shot, bolt-action pistol with a 9 7/8-inch barrel and the action is of the rotating-chamber type, like the Model 262 rifle to be discussed later. Lifting the flat bolt handle away from the gas tube rotates the chamber out of the action to the left exposing the opening in which a pellet is held. When the bolt handle is pressed back to its original position, the pellet is brought in line with the bore. This makes for a tight, efficient gas seal, which aids in producing high velocities. Because the port where the pellet is held measures 0.323 inch front to back, virtually all 177-caliber pellets can be used.

Power source for the SSP 250 is one 12-gram CO_2 cylinder contained in a tube under the barrel. Loading a cylinder involves removing the large grooved cap at the front end of the gas tube and inserting a CO_2 cylinder neck first. Replacing and tightening the cap pierces the cylinder.

Sights on the SSP 250 are excellent. The front is a square post on a ramp that is hooded while the rear sight is a square-notched blade on a plastic base that is fully adjustable. The rear sight blade can also be removed and inverted to provide a peep sight. This is the same type of sight found on the Crosman 2260, 2250, 2240, 2210, and 1760 models. As discussed in connection with the models listed, the sight works well as an open sight on the pistols where it is far from the shooter's eye, but it is useless on the rifles. When the blade is inverted and the sight is used as a peep sight, it is satisfactory on the rifles but useless on the pistols. The receiver of the SSP 250 is grooved for easy attachment of scope mounts or optical sights. One additional advantage of the Model SSP 250 is the grips can be removed and the skeleton stock (Model 1399) can be added to make the pistol into a shoulder-fired piece.

Like some other Crosman models, the SSP 250 has two power settings, and withdrawing the cocking piece chooses the power level. If the cocking piece is withdrawn to the first notch, the lower power setting is selected and the velocity is approximately 425 ft/sec. Drawing the cocking piece back the full distance engages the higher power setting which gives a muzzle velocity of approximately 530 ft/sec. In essence, the distance to which the cocking piece is drawn back determines the striking force on the valve. A higher striking force results in a greater quantity of CO_2 being released, which gives a higher velocity. In the higher-powered mode, the SSP 250 was advertised to give 40 shots per CO_2 cylinder while shooting in the lower-powered mode would yield 100 shots per cylinder.

Trigger action on the SSP 250 is outstanding. It has a two-stage action and the let-off is crisp. Keep in mind the trigger pull weight is different when the pistol is fired in the low- and high-power modes because the tension on the sear is different. In the low-power mode, I measured the trigger pull to be about 3 pounds 8 ounces while in the high-power mode it was approximately 4 pounds.

Velocity Data for the Crosman SSP 250 at 70°F				
	Velocity, ft/sec			
Pellet	**Ave.**	**High**	**Low**	**Std. Dev.**
D.N. Meisterkugeln	535	538	533	2
Gamo Match	539	544	534	4
Daisy Wadcutter	533	548	515	15

While the SSP 250 is a high performance pistol, it is extremely straightforward and easy to use. Because of its intended use as a target pistol, testing was carried out in anticipation of outstanding results. Three types of pellets were selected for the velocity tests. The results obtained are shown in the table.

The data presented in the table show the Crosman SSP 250 gives average velocities with all three types of pellets virtually identical with the maximum advertised for this pistol. Although the data are not shown, a few shots fired with the cocking piece pulled back to give the low power setting resulted in a velocity of 400-425 ft/sec depending on the pellet type. This is outstanding performance by the SSP 250.

If you want high performance in terms of accuracy and power in a CO_2 pistol, the SSP 250 is an excellent choice (if you can find one at a reasonable price). If you can't, do not despair since the current Model 2240 is a 22-caliber bolt-action single shot that is highly effective. Because it is a popular model for customizing and "hot rodding," prices for the SSP 250 tend to be rather high with over $100 being common. However, I found mine in a pawnshop in Wyoming, and I had seen it in the shop a year before I bought it. I thought the price was reasonable and since I did not have one, I added it to my battery of "user collectibles." I hope to run across a barrel in 20 or (preferably) 22 caliber at a reasonable price. If I do, I will have just about the ultimate CO_2 pistol for pest shooting.

The Crosman 116

The Crosman Model 116 was produced from 1951 to 1954. It was a 22-caliber single shot with a 6-inch barrel. A 10-ounce CO_2 cylinder was used to fill the large gas tube that ran below the barrel. It was advertised

A collector's dream, this Crosman 116 bulk-fill pistol was found with the 10-ounce CO_2 tank, original box, and all papers. In like new condition, it is still a good shooter.

The Crosman 116 had an adjustable rear sight. The knurled knob functions as both bolt handle and cocking piece.

The power level of the Crosman 116 is adjustable by turning the knob on the rear of the receiver.

I did not pressurize my Crosman 116. It turned up in an antique mall in like new condition complete with a cylinder, box, and papers. I plan to keep it that way, so I did not put through a testing procedure. I have no doubt it will perform exactly as it did about 50 years ago.

The Crosman 38C

Crosman's first airgun in 1923 was a 22-caliber rifle, and Crosman has been the dominant producer of 22-caliber CO_2 guns. One of the long-lived models is the Model 38 revolver, which was available with a 3 1/2-inch barrel—the Model 38C—and with a 6-inch barrel—called the Model 38T. Made in 1964-73, the first variant had a metal cylinder and metal rear sight. The second variant, made in 1973-76, had a plastic cylinder and rear sight. Because of the strong resemblance of the shorter-barreled model to a combat-style revolver and the longer barrel to a target revolver, the 38C and 38T were dubbed "38 Simulators." The CO_2 revolvers were intended for training purposes. Currently, prices for the Models 38C and 38T are approximately $100.

Outwardly, the Model 38C resembles a Smith & Wesson Model 19 Combat Magnum. The very large grip and fake ejector rod shroud give the Model 38 the same profile as

the gas tube held enough gas for 30 shots. The 10-ounce CO_2 cylinder that came with the Model 116 furnished power for approximately 800 shots. A knurled knob on the back of the receiver could be turned to adjust the power level by regulating the amount of gas released. Grips were made of checkered Tenite® and were made in different colors. My pistol has the light-colored grips, but I believe black was more common.

The rear sight was fully adjustable and the front sight consisted of a metal blade. In terms of construction, the Model 116 was first class. Except for the grip panels, the pistol was made of black finished brass. It represented a simple but elegant design. Pulling back a knurled bolt head cocked the pistol so that a single 22-caliber pellet could be inserted in the loading groove. A similar bolt head is used on the current Benjamin EB17 and Sheridan EB20.

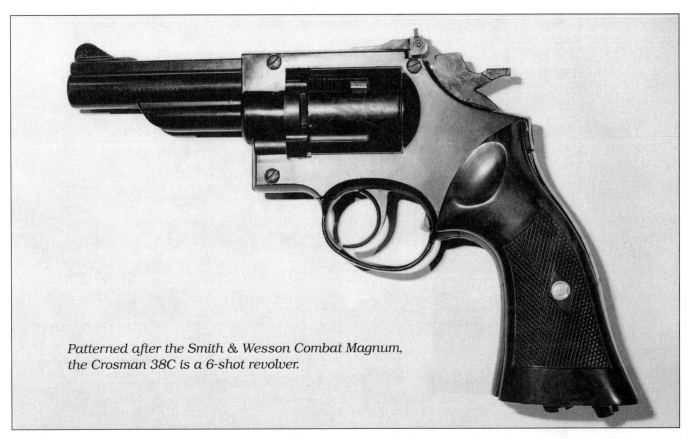

Patterned after the Smith & Wesson Combat Magnum, the Crosman 38C is a 6-shot revolver.

Pellets are loaded in the Crosman 38C by pulling back on the grooved slide and placing a pellet in the recess. Allowing the slide to move forward pushes the pellet into a chamber.

the firearm. The Model 38 has a short cylinder holding six pellets, which rotates in front of a larger fake cylinder.

The upper flute on the left-hand side of the fake cylinder has a spring-loaded slide that can be moved to the rear. When this is done, a pellet can be dropped into the space between the slide and the rear of the cylinder. Allowing the slide to move forward pushes the pellet into one of the chambers. Turning the cylinder clockwise to align the next chamber allows the process to be repeated until all of the chambers are loaded.

A CO_2 cylinder is held in the grip of the Model 38. The left-hand grip panel can be removed and the cylinder inserted neck up. Turning the large, coin-slotted screw in the bottom of the grip moves the cylinder up to the piercing screw. As in some other early Crosman models, the left-hand grip panel has a bracket that snaps over the CO_2 cylinder. The grip panel is held only to the CO_2 cylinder and not the frame. Crosman advertised that a CO_2 cylinder provided power for approximately 45 shots.

Because one of the intended uses of the Model 38 includes target shooting, sights are

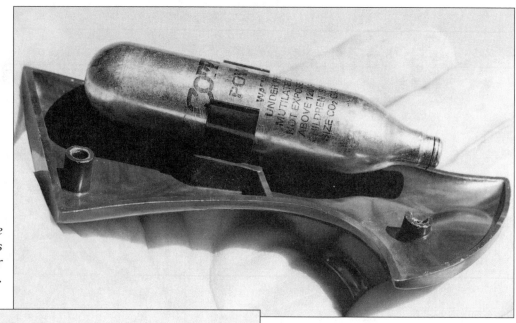

On the Crosman 38C, the left-hand grip panel is held to the CO_2 cylinder by a spring clip.

Sights on the Crosman 38C provide an excellent sight picture.

excellent. The front sight is a square-topped post on a ramp and the rear is a fully adjustable square notch. The sight picture provided by these sights is as good as that given by sights on any CO_2 handgun.

While preparing to test the Crosman 38C, a bad seal was discovered. Therefore, no actual firing tests were conducted, but the description of the pistol and its operation will be of use for reference purposes.

The Crosman Single Action 6

In the 1950s and 1960s, western TV programs were quite popular. Shows like *Gunsmoke*, *Bonanza*, and *Have Gun Will Travel* were certainly high on my list of programs to watch on a regular basis. It was natural a CO_2 handgun would be produced that resembled the famous Colt Single Action Army. The Crosman Single Action 6 (sometimes identified simply as the SA 6) was that CO_2 gun. Made in the years 1959-1969, the SA 6 was a six-shot, 22-caliber revolver with a number of unique features. It could be fired only in the single-action mode, which meant the hammer had to be cocked for each shot. As collectibles, the prices go up to $100 for a nice specimen.

Made entirely of metal, the SA 6 weighed 31 ounces and measured 10-5/16 inches in length. Unlike other revolvers in which the CO_2 cylinder is held in the grip, the SA 6 holds the CO_2 cylinder under the barrel. The piercing pin is on the front of the frame just below the barrel. A bracket holding a threaded rod was placed below the barrel just behind the muzzle. The threaded rod was fit-

Patterned after the Colt Single Action Army, the Crosman Single Action 6 has authentic styling and feel in the hand.

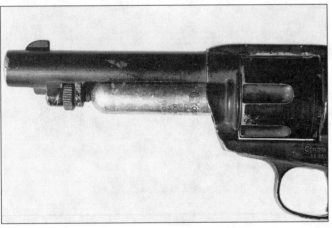

A CO$_2$ cylinder fits under the barrel of the SA 6 with the neck pointing backward into the frame. Turning the ridged ring forces the threaded bolt back against the base of the cylinder.

ted with a knurled ring that could be rotated to move the rod forward or backward. When a CO$_2$ cylinder is placed between the threaded rod and the piercing pin, turning the knurled ring moves the cylinder backward to the piercing pin. When installed, the CO$_2$ cylinder is fully exposed below the barrel.

Unique features of the SA 6 do not end with the method in which the cylinder is held. Another is the way in which the pellets are loaded. A spring runs around the cylinder below the external surface so that it is exposed in each chamber. When a pellet is forced into the chamber, the skirt passes over the spring, and the groove that circles the midsection of the pellet resides on the spring. Pellets are loaded into each chamber by pushing them in base first from the front. Crosman Superpells from the same time period were more or less hollow cylinders of lead that had a small, knurled ring around the waist. That ring was engaged by the spring in the chamber to hold the pellets in place.

The SA 6 is a very simple revolver. As with other classic single-action firearms, there is no safety. However, the gun must be cocked for each shot. Sights are of the rudimentary type found on early single-action revolvers. The front is a blade with a rounded profile. The rear sight is nothing more than a groove at the rear of the top strap of the frame. This is a plinking gun pure and simple.

Over the years in which it was made, the SA 6 appeared with different types of grips. My specimen has gray plastic grips with ridges resembling stag except for the color.

The SA 6 I happened to find in an antique store showed plenty of wear, which had removed a great deal of its finish. The cylinder was so gummed up it would hardly turn. A good cleaning and a little Crosman Pellgun Oil® made it function smoothly. After that was done, I was amazed at the trigger action of the old gun. The trigger let-off with no trace of creep at only 1.7 pounds! While I appreciate a trigger that functions like that, it cer-

Pellets are held in place by a spring that encircles the cylinder while passing through the edge of each chamber.

Sights are of the most rudimentary type with the rear sight being only a notch at the rear of the frame.

tainly needs to be handled carefully.

While I have some collectible old Crosman pellets, I had no intention of shooting them. Therefore, I decided to use Crosman Copperhead wadcutter pellets and hope the spring in the chambers would hold them in place. Unfortunately, the spring did not engage them tightly because of their tapered shape around the middle, and the pellets were able to move back and forth in the cylinder. It was found that if the SA 6 was held with the muzzle pointing up between shots there was no problem with the pellets protruding from the front of the cylinder. A Crosman CO_2 cylinder was installed, the gun was fired twice to initialize the power train, and the cylinder was loaded with Crosman wadcutter pellets. After firing one shot for fun, the next five were fired across the chronograph, which indicated speeds of 269, 266, 261, 271, and 268 ft/sec for an average of 267 and a standard deviation of 4 ft/sec. Many years ago, I read an article on the disassembly and servicing of this gun and the velocity specified was 245 ft/sec. My old six-gun was slightly above that figure at a temperature of approximately 82°F.

After testing velocity, I reloaded the cylinder with pellets and set up a target at 10 yards. Aiming at a 1-inch bull, I found the point of impact was about 2.5 inches low but just about centered left to right. I proceeded to cluster six shots in a group of about 3 inches. This was so much fun I reloaded and put six more in the same group and then added six more. A total of 18 shots went into a group of about 3.5 inches. I have no doubt the SA 6 is more accurate than that, but the sights are simply too crude to tell.

One point regarding safety needs to be made. When it is down (uncocked), the hammer rests against the valve release pin. Pushing on the hammer causes the release of CO_2, so a blow to the hammer could cause the gun to fire. In that sense, it is like the single-action firearms of long ago, which were carried with an empty chamber under the hammer as a safety measure.

It was a real change of pace to fire this old CO_2 six-gun after so much testing with those that resemble semi-automatic pistols. I found this old gun in an antique store in Wisconsin and the owner sold it and another spring BB pistol for $25. There was no way to determine if it worked before I bought it, but I was pleasantly surprised when I tried it. It is truly a blast from the past.

The Crosman Mark I

During a summer trip to Wyoming, my wife and I saw a Crosman Mark I in a pawnshop. I knew the reputation of this model well because I had bought one in the 1970s for my son. I thought the asking price for the Mark I was too high, so even though the pistol looked almost new, I did not buy it. Later, as I got more involved with CO_2 guns, I wished for the Mark I. The following summer we found the Mark I still residing in the glass case at the pawnshop. Pawnshop operators are generally more anxious to bargain on a piece of merchandise that has not moved in a year so I began the bargaining. I eventually bought this outstanding specimen for $65 and was very glad to do so since the average price for a Mark I is usually $100 or more.

Introduced in 1966 and discontinued in 1980, the Crosman Mark I is highly sought after by both collectors and shooters. If necessary, they can be repaired and new seals installed. A specimen in good condition is both accurate and powerful. Moreover, this pistol can be modified and customized to increase its power. One such business that does repairs and performs power modifications on many Crosman, Benjamin and Sheridan models is McMurray & Son (MAC-1), 13974 Van Ness Avenue, Gardena, CA, 90249, (310) 327-3581. The Crosman Mark I can be modified to produce a high-powered, accurate pistol highly prized for both small game hunting and field target shooting. Along

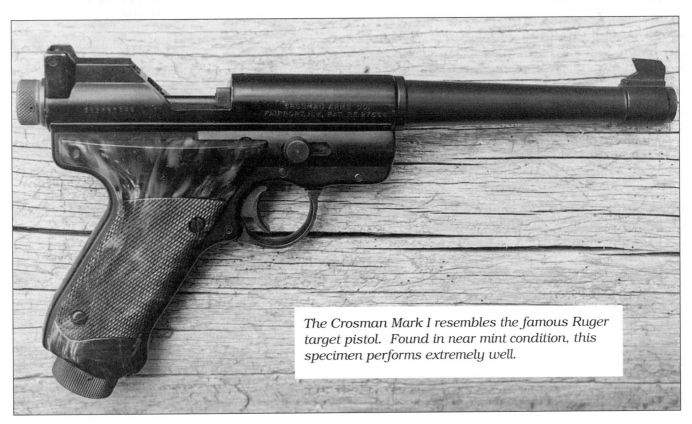

The Crosman Mark I resembles the famous Ruger target pistol. Found in near mint condition, this specimen performs extremely well.

Pulling the knurled knob back exposes the chamber for loading a single pellet.

with the Crosman 600, it has achieved a cult status among serious air gunners.

I have commented elsewhere in this chapter on the legendary Crosman 600, and the Mark I occupies a similar position in the opinion of many CO_2 gunners. Outwardly, a Crosman Mark I resembles the target version of the famous Ruger 22 rimfire semi-automatic. The tapered barrel shroud, the cylindrical receiver, and the grip shape and angle imitate the famous Ruger target pistol very closely. The Mark I is 11.0 inches long, weighs 41.7 ounces, and has a 7.25-inch barrel. Grips are of molded plastic with checkering and a thumb rest.

Cocking and loading are separate operations on the Crosman Mark I. Loading is accomplished by turning the checkered knob at the rear of the receiver and drawing it backward. A single pellet is placed in the loading track and the bolt is returned to its original, closed position.

Cocking the Mark I is accomplished by means of the knurled knobs just above the trigger. These knobs, one on either side of the frame, are connected by a pin that passes through the receiver. That pin moves forward and backward in a slot. Pulling the cocking knobs forward cocks the gun. However, a unique feature of the Mark I is that two clicks

The slide above the trigger is pulled forward to cock the pistol. Moving the slide until it clicks once gives the low power setting while two clicks give high power.

are heard as the knobs move fully forward. These clicks represent two power levels. If the knobs are pulled forward until the first click is heard and then released, the pistol has been cocked for a low power setting. In this low-power mode, a muzzle velocity of approximately 300 ft/sec is achieved and approximately 120 shots can be obtained from a CO_2 cylinder according to the old Crosman advertisements. Pulling the cocking knobs forward

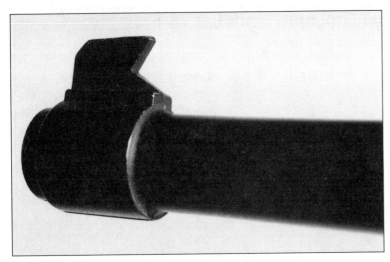

The undercut front sight on the Mark I is of the target type that gives a sharp image on the target.

On the Crosman Mark I, the rear sight has a fully adjustable blade with a square notch. Combined with the excellent front sight, there are no better sights on any current CO_2 pistol.

sight is a high ramp/post with an undercut rear face. Undercutting prevents reflection of light from the front sight, which hampers getting a sharp outline of the sight when aiming. The rear sight is a metal blade with a square notch protected by massive metal ears. Windage adjustments are made by means of slotted screws. The sight blade is located so that it rests between two small setscrews visible on the outsides of the protective ears. Loosening one of them creates a space on that side of the blade. Tightening the screw on the opposite side moves the blade until it rests snugly against the other screw. By loosening one screw and tightening the other, the sight blade can be moved laterally. Elevation adjustment is made by means of a small screw that protrudes vertically through the base of the sight blade. When it comes to sights on CO_2 pistols, those on the Crosman Mark I are about as good as it gets.

With its other high quality features, it is no surprise the Mark I has an outstanding trigger. First, since this is a single-action pistol that is cocked manually, the trigger motion to release the sear is very short. Second, the trigger is adjustable my means of a small Allen-head screw located inside the front of the trigger guard. This in itself is rare on a CO_2 pistol, but the Mark I was intended for fairly serious target shooting. Third, the trigger pull depends on whether the pistol is being fired in the low-power or high-power mode. On the low power setting, the trigger let-off is crisp and very light with the pull on mine measuring only 2.1 pounds. On the high power setting, where there is greater tension on the sear, trigger let-off is crisp but the required pull is considerably greater. My Mark I has a trigger pull of 6.7 pounds on the high power setting. The Crosman Mark I has a trigger as good as there is to be found on any factory CO_2 pistol with the exception of some all-out target models. It is truly fitting for this classic pistol.

Testing the Crosman Mark I to determine how it performed with respect to velocity produced the very interesting results shown in the accompanying table. Velocity testing included firing five-shot strings with five

until the second click is heard cocks the pistol in the high-power mode. The high power setting produces a muzzle velocity of approximately 400 ft/sec and approximately 55 shots can be obtained from a CO_2 cylinder.

The Mark I safety is a rotating lever just behind the trigger on the left-hand side of the frame. With the lever in the down position, the pistol is ready to fire and with the lever in its upper position, the safety is on. The safety cannot be placed on until the pistol is cocked. This may at first seem strange, but it is quite reasonable. Until the cocking knobs are pulled forward, the pistol cannot be fired anyway so there is no need to put the safety on.

The sights on the Crosman Mark I are as good as any found on a CO_2 pistol. The front

Velocity Data for the Crosman Mark I at 78°F

Pellet		Ave.	Velocity, ft/sec High	Low	Std. Dev.
D.N. Meisterkugeln	(High)	423	428	418	4
D.N. Meisterkugeln	(Low)	217	220	215	2
Gamo Match	(High)	419	421	418	1
Gamo Match	(Low)	214	218	212	2
D.N. Super-H-Point	(High)	414	417	412	2
D.N. Super-H-Point	(Low)	195	200	191	4
Crosman Wadcutter	(High)	423	426	420	3
Crosman Wadcutter	(Low)	230	236	225	4
D.N. Hobby	(High)	462	467	458	4
D.N. Hobby	(Low)	254	257	251	2

High and Low refer to the power setting.

types of pellets with the Mark I on both the high and low power settings.

Crosman literature of the 1970s indicated the high power setting produced a pellet velocity of approximately 400 ft/sec. In fact, my Mark I gave approximately 425 ft/sec with pellets of normal weight and 462 ft/sec with the 12.00-grain Dynamit Nobel Hobby. Clearly, the old Mark I has lost nothing with respect to velocity. It is a pistol that produces considerable power.

In the low power mode, the velocities were well below the approximately 300 ft/sec advertised for the Mark I with average velocities being around 220-230 ft/sec except for the lightweight Hobby, which averaged 254 ft/sec. It is interesting to note that the velocities given by the Mark I are extremely uniform when either power setting is used. I do not know the number of shots that can be fired on the low power setting before a cylinder is exhausted, but it is large. My wife and I bounced pinecones in the Big Horn National Forest for a long time without changing the cylinder. On both power settings, the Mark I is wonderfully accurate. With excellent target-type sights and good trigger action, no CO_2 pistol has performed better in the tests reported in this book. In my opinion, the Crosman Mark I is among the two or three best CO_2 pistols I own, whether of current manufacture or classic status.

The Crosman 600

In 1960, Crosman introduced a CO_2 pistol that was to achieve the status of a classic. That 10-shot 22-caliber pistol was known as the Model 600. It was discontinued in 1970 and many airgunners believe it was the finest CO_2 pistol ever made. So highly regarded was the Crosman Model 600 that it is difficult to find one today, and if you do, the going price may be $100-$300 depending on condition and accessories. So well made was the Crosman 600 that many are still good shooters even after more than 30 years. It is one of the most highly desirable CO_2 pistols ever made.

During a discussion about air and CO_2 guns with Mr. Warren Newman of Cody, Wyoming, he mentioned he had bought a pistol that was about to be sold at auction for $5.00. I will not tell you what he paid for it. Later in the day that our discussion took place, Mr. Newman brought his pistol for me to examine. It was the Crosman 600 that you see here and it had the original leather holster with it. Such things do not happen often but it is the possibility of such things that makes going to auctions, flea markets, pawnshops, and antique malls exciting for the collector.

Like the Crosman 400 rifle, the Model 600 has an in-line magazine on the left-hand side of the receiver with a spring-loaded follower and a rotating chamber at the forward end. A pellet moves from the magazine tube into the chamber, which then rotates automatically to line up with the barrel. However, when the Model 600 is fired, the chamber containing a pellet rotates to align with the barrel as the gas is being released. The reloading process is done manually as the bolt is cycled in the Model 400 rifle, but it is performed automatically in the Model 600 pistol. The Model 600 is a true semi-automatic pistol.

The Crosman 600 is considered by many to be the finest semi-automatic CO_2 pistol ever made.

Being a 1960s design, the Crosman 600 has the look of an airgun rather than a modern centerfire pistol although there is a slight similarity to the appearance of a Smith & Wesson Model 41 or a Colt Match Target Woodsman. This has its advantages. A CO_2 cylinder is held in a tube below the barrel rather than in the grip. At the front end of the tube is a large, grooved cap that is unscrewed to insert a CO_2 cylinder. Like some other Crosman models, the cylinder is inserted with the neck pointing forward because the piercing pin is in the cap.

Because the Crosman 600 is made of metal, it is a heavy pistol that weighs approximately 40 ounces. It has a barrel that measures slightly over 5 inches long. The trigger of the Crosman 600 is nicely curved and deeply grooved. The grips are made of molded plastic with simulated wood grain and have deep checkering. A thumb rest is located at the top of the left-hand panel and each panel has a swell at the bottom. This particular gun is designed for right-hand shooters. The sights on the Crosman 600 consist of a square-topped blade front and a massive rear sight that is adjustable for windage and elevation. The sight picture is as good as that found on any air or CO_2 pistol.

Crosman CO_2 guns of the same time period as the 600 featured in-line magazines. This design necessitates the use of flat-pointed pellets because pellets leave the magazine laterally in the rotating chamber. Loading the magazine involves pulling the spring-loaded follower to the rear and dropping pellets (head forward, of course) into the rectangular opening while tipping the muzzle upward so the pellets slide toward the rear of the magazine. The magazine follower has a pin that can be rotated to hold the follower in its rearward position for easy loading.

Except for the grip panels, this gun is made of metal; it is heavy, and it is robust. These factors contribute to its long life and its immense popularity with both collectors and shooters.

Just above the grip on the left-hand side of the pistol is a large sliding lever. This sliding lever serves exactly the same function as does the moving slide on an autoloading firearm. Pushing the lever to the rear a short distance cocks the gun. Pushing the lever to its rearmost position completes the action by causing the rotating chamber to turn counterclockwise approximately one-eighth of a revolution so that its opening aligns with the magazine tube allowing a pellet to enter the chamber. The slide is then pushed forward and the pistol is ready to fire. Pulling the trigger disengages the sear, which lets the rotating chamber turn clockwise to align with the barrel, and the CO_2 valve opens, discharging the gas to launch the pellet. After the first shot, subsequent shots require only pulling the trigger because the CO_2 supplies the power to cycle the action. This is a true semi-automatic pistol that functions in a single-action mode.

If the piece is cocked (either manually for the first shot or automatically thereafter) and the shooter changes his mind about shooting, the pistol can be decocked. Simply push the slide completely and tightly to the rear to remove the tension; then while holding the slide, pull the trigger and let the slide move forward slowly while holding it.

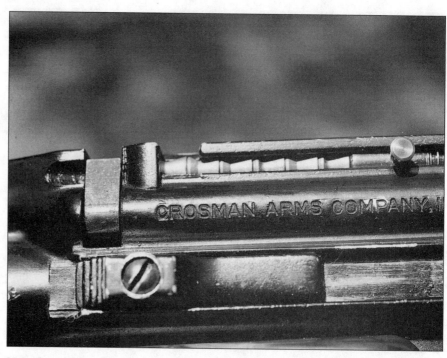

Note how the pellets are held in the magazine and are pushed forward into the rotating chamber by the magazine follower.

Having heard and read so much about the Crosman 600, it was with considerable enthusiasm that I began testing. This old gun had not been fired for years. I knew that because the exhausted CO_2 cylinder it contained was of the old style with the "pop bottle" crimp. I cleaned the gun thoroughly and lubricated it with Crosman Pellgun Oil®. After inserting a new CO_2 cylinder, I put 10 Crosman Copperhead wadcutter pellets in the magazine and cycled the slide. I pulled the trigger and heard a thud. I repeated the process and heard another thud. The third time, the gun fired. Not only that, it fired flawlessly every shot thereafter until the CO_2 cylinder was emptied. After firing 10 shots for fun, I chronographed the next 10 shots. The velocities (in ft/sec) obtained with the 14.3-grain Copperhead wadcutter pellets were as follows:

Shot	1	2	3	4	5	6	7	8	9	10
	389	386	383	386	381	379	380	374	382	369

The average for the 10 shots is 381 ft/sec, which is approximately the velocity of some current 22-caliber models.

So, the old Crosman 600 shoots hard, but how accurate is it? I shot for fun until the CO_2 cylinder was empty so I could test accuracy with a full cylinder. I loaded a fresh CO_2 cylinder and loaded the magazine with Copperhead wadcutter pellets. My target was 10 yards away and I shot standing with my shooting hand resting on a sandbag on a fence post. Three five-shot groups measured 1.32, 1.52, and 2.10 inches. I next fired two groups using RWS Meisterkugeln pellets and they measured 1.05 and 0.88 inches. This is about as good as I can get with any air pistol shooting under these conditions. In terms of accuracy, I have no doubt that the Crosman 600 is the equal of any of the modern CO_2 pistols except for target models.

The Crosman 600 is a fine CO_2 pistol. It has excellent adjustable sights and a good trigger let-off. I only wish that more current models were as well made and accurate. With heavy emphasis on plastics, gimmicky fiber optic sights, and lousy trigger pull, many of the current models simply are not in the same class as the Crosman 600 of the 1960s. This was a borrowed gun. It had to be returned. With my impressions of this gun being what they are, you probably think that when I had to return it I may have shed a tear or two. I did not. I wept bitterly. Seriously, it was a pleasure to have the opportunity to spend some time with a true classic of airgun history. I am deeply

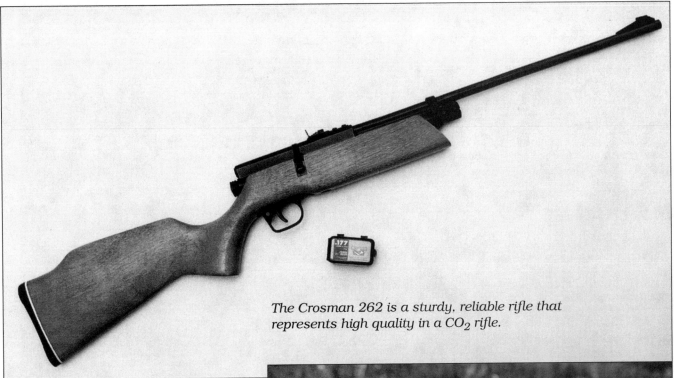

The Crosman 262 is a sturdy, reliable rifle that represents high quality in a CO$_2$ rifle.

grateful to Mr. Warren Newman for allowing me to test his Crosman 600 even before he had fired it himself.

The Crosman 262

Manufactured only in the 1991-1993 period, the Crosman Model 262 had some unique features. Basically, it is a sturdy, single-shot rifle that shoots 177-caliber pellets. It has a few plastic parts but the Model 262 is essentially a metal-and-wood rifle. Unlike the current Model 1710 single shot, the loading and cocking operations are separate with the Model 262. A scaled-down rifle known as the 262Y or Youth Model was also produced. However, airgun shooters were becoming infatuated with repeaters in the early 1990s. To provide what that group wanted, the Crosman Repeatair 1077 was introduced in 1994 and is still produced.

Specifications of the Crosman 262 show it is 38-1/4 inches long, weighs 4 pounds 14 ounces, and has a muzzle velocity of 625 ft/sec. The 262Y youth model is 33-3/4 inches long, weighs 4 pounds, and has a

Cocking and loading are separate operations with the Crosman 262.

muzzle velocity of 610 ft/sec. Prices for the Model 262 are in the $80-$100 range for specimens in good condition.

With most bolt-action pellet rifles, lifting the bolt and drawing it to the rear cocks the action and exposes the loading port. Inserting a pellet and closing the bolt readies the piece for firing. Lifting the bolt handle on the Model 262 causes a rotating chamber to be rotated out of the left-hand side of the receiver. The bolt handle can be moved only up and down, and it cannot be drawn backward. A single

The Crosman 262 is an accurate and reliable classic that we still enjoy using.

177-caliber pellet can be inserted in the exposed chamber. Returning the bolt to its closed position causes the chamber to be moved into the action so that the pellet in the chamber is in line with the barrel. The rifle is now loaded but it is not cocked. Cocking the action is achieved by drawing the cocking piece to the rear until two clicks are heard. Releasing the tension on the cocking piece allows it to move forward to the rear of the action due to spring tension. If the safety is off, the rifle is ready to fire.

On my rifle, the chamber measures 0.322 inch in thickness, which is sufficient to accommodate any 177-caliber pellet.

I wish the current air and CO_2 rifles had triggers that gave let-off as smoothly as the Crosman 262. There is a short, light take-up motion after which the trigger has a very crisp let-off with a pull weight measured as 2.6 pounds. This rifle has trigger action as good as any current CO_2 gun in my collection. A cross-bolt safety is located behind the trigger, and it functions in the "right is on, left is off" manner.

A single CO_2 cylinder is held in a large tube below the barrel. Removing the ridged cap allows a CO_2 cylinder to be placed in the tube

neck first. Replacing and tightening the cap pierces the cylinder.

Sights on the Crosman 262 are very good. The front sight is a square-topped post on a substantial ramp. The rear sight is a metal blade fastened to the barrel by two screws. The rear sight screw protrudes through a slot in the sight base, which allows some lateral movement after the screw is loosened. Some loosening of the front screw holding the rear sight may also be required for the sight to move laterally. Movement of the rear sight laterally provides windage adjustment. Elevation adjustment is made by means of a stepped riser ramp that can be moved forward or backward. The square-post front sight and the square notch in the rear sight are well matched in size to provide an excellent sight picture. These sights are far superior to the funky fiber optic devices found on many of the current air and CO_2 guns. Moreover, the metal receiver is grooved so that accessory sighting equipment can be easily attached.

Writing about the Crosman 262, one author referred to it as a sleek rifle. Viewed from above, the rifle is thin in profile. Perhaps this is to what the other writer was referring. With its large forearm, a front end cut on a

Velocity Data for the Crosman Model 262 at 70°F				
		Velocity, ft/sec		
Pellet	**Ave.**	**High**	**Low**	**Std. Dev.**
D. N. Meisterkugeln	614	622	608	6
Crosman Wadcutter	609	617	604	5
Winchester Hunting	632	640	626	5

straight backward slant, and a stock with a raised comb and poorly shaped pistol grip, this rifle is anything but sleek. The pistol grip is a goose-necked affair with an exaggerated, tapered bottom. The top edges of the forearm along either side of the barrel are square-cornered and sharp-edged. From a side view, this rifle is almost cosmic in appearance.

The stock is made from very nice hardwood and it has a functional and attractive composition butt plate with a white spacer. Regardless of its less than classic sporting rifle lines, this is a substantial piece. It has a lot of metal and a lot of wood in its makeup. Suffice it to say I like this rifle enough to have two of them. However, that doesn't mean the stock isn't literally begging to be attacked by a wood rasp. This is a very well constructed rifle.

It has been my good fortune to find two Crosman Model 262 rifles that were both like new. One even had the original box and papers to make it more desirable. Velocity tests were conducted with only one of the rifles and produced the data shown in the table.

The Crosman Model 262 had an advertised muzzle velocity of 625 ft/sec. It is reassuring to see that mine produced an average velocity very close to that value. The Winchester Hunting pellet weighs 7.5 grains and the average velocity with that pellet was actually above the advertised velocity. Meisterkugeln pellets weigh 8.2 grains, which resulted in a lower velocity. It was a pleasure to shoot this vintage Crosman that performs just as well today as it did several years ago.

The Crosman 400

Crosman Corporation has certainly been the dominant influence in the design and manufacture of repeating rifles powered by CO_2. Perhaps the best example of this type of gun is the legendary Crosman 600 semi-automatic

In almost mint condition in the original box, this Crosman 400 was irresistible.

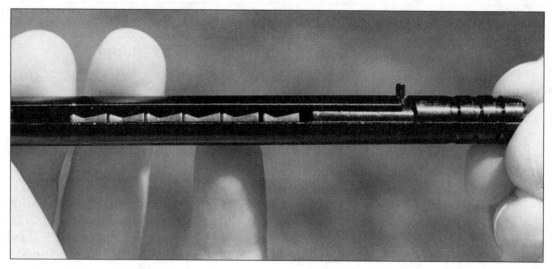

The Crosman 400 has an in-line magazine that holds 10 pellets.

pistol described earlier in this chapter. Another of the classic Crosman products is the Model 400, a bolt-action repeater in 22 caliber. The in-line magazine holds 10 pellets that are fed into a rotating chamber. Because the pellets are contact in a head-to-tail manner, lateral movement of a pellet into the chamber is possible only for flat-nosed pellets.

The Crosman 400 was introduced in 1957 with the first variant having the cross-bolt safety that passes through the stock. A second variant having the heavy, die cast trigger housing was made in 1962-1964. Advertised muzzle velocity for the Model 400 was 450 ft/sec, and 50 shots were supposedly the norm for a CO_2 cylinder. Crosman advertised the Model 400 had a button-rifled barrel known as the Tru-Flyte®. Each rifle was tested to show it gave 1/2-inch or smaller groups at 25 feet. It measures 34 inches in length and weighs 4 pounds. An average price for a Model 400 in good condition is in the $150 range.

The Crosman 400 represents a type of CO_2 rifle absent from today's market. It is a 10-shot repeating 22-caliber wood-and-metal rifle in the Crosman tradition of the 1950-1960s. Introduced in 1957, the Model 400 survived until 1964. Several Crosman air and CO_2 rifles underwent design changes during the span of their production during the 1950s to 1970s. One of the most significant changes was a shift from a safety that is a cross bolt through the stock above the trigger to a rotating lever that was part of the trigger guard. Rifles having the cross-bolt safety, including the Models 400 and 180 CO_2 rifles and the Models 140 and 1400 multi-pump pneumat-

ics, had a thin, stamped metal trigger guard. Any of these Crosman models with these features are referred to as "first variant cross-bolt safety." Later variants with the safety in the front of a massive, die-cast trigger guard are referred to as the "second (or later) variants with die-cast trigger guard." My Crosman Model 400 has a cross-bolt safety through the stock so it is a first variant manufactured in the period 1957-1962. The second variant was made from 1962 to 1964. Crosman models with the die-cast trigger guard are considered to be more desirable because the trigger mechanism is much better than that found on the first variant. Although my Crosman 400 is a first variant, I did find it at a good price with its original box and papers. It appeared to be in virtually new condition.

Power supply for the Model 400 is two CO_2 cylinders contained in a tube below the barrel. The forward end of the tube has a ridged cap just in front of the forearm. When the cap is removed, two CO_2 cylinders are inserted. The first cylinder is inserted neck first and the second has the large end go in first. The cap contains a piercing pin while another resides at the other end of the gas tube. Cocking the rifle and pulling the trigger causes piercing of the CO_2 cylinders. The operating instructions then state the rifle should be recocked immediately to allow the valve to close to prevent loss of CO_2.

Like the Crosman 600 pistol, the Model 400 makes use of a 10-shot in-line magazine in which the pellets are held in a head-to-skirt fashion. A spring-loaded magazine follower

The square shaft with a one-quarter turn causes the rotating chamber to turn as the bolt is withdrawn. A metal loop slides along the shaft as the bolt is drawn back.

keeps the pellets pushed to the forward end of the tube. Pellets are removed from the magazine by being forced into a rotating chamber as the bolt is withdrawn. Pushing the bolt forward causes the chamber to rotate clockwise until it aligns with the barrel so that a pellet is in position for firing. Although operating the bolt moves a pellet from the magazine into firing position, the cocking operation is separate. Cocking is performed by pulling back on the large knob at the rear end of the gas tube. On my rifle, the cross-bolt safety runs through the stock about halfway between the trigger and the action. Pushed to the right, the safety is on and pushed to the left, the safety is off. A red band firing indicator is visible when the safety is off.

The magazine of the Model 400 is removed for loading. It is held in position along the left-hand side of the receiver by being inserted in a casting that encompasses the rear end of the barrel and the forward end of the receiver. The magazine tube has a groove around it near its forward end and a spring-loaded ball mounted in the casting snaps into the groove on the magazine to hold it in place. This detent arrangement allows the magazine to be removed and inserted with only moderate force, but it is held snugly in place

Rotation of the moving chamber as the bolt is pulled back is accomplished in a most clever manner. Mounted along the left-hand side of the action is a metal rod that has the rotating chamber attached to the front end.

The rod is square in cross section, but toward the rear end it has a twist. As the bolt is withdrawn, a sleeve having a square loop in it rides along the square rod. When it encounters the loop, which moves backward as the bolt is withdrawn, the rod is turned counterclockwise, which brings the chamber out of alignment with the barrel into alignment with the magazine tube. At this time, a pellet enters the chamber. As the bolt is pushed forward, the loop moves past the twist in the rod causing the chamber to be turned back into alignment with the barrel. Crosman literature referred to the repeating mechanism as "swing loading" because of the side-to-side motion of the chamber.

Loading the magazine tube with pellets requires it to be pulled free from its port in the large casting at the front of the receiver. The magazine has a spring-loaded follower that can be pulled to the rear by means of a pin that protrudes through a longitudinal slot. Turning the pin into a recess locks the follower at the rear of the magazine tube so pellets can be placed in the tube base first. The magazine tube is replaced in its port, and the follower pin is rotated out of its recess to put pressure on the pellets. Since the pellets are removed from the magazine by moving them to the side in the rotating chamber, flat-nose pellets must be used.

Sights on the Crosman 400 are superb. The front sight is a square-topped post on a real metal ramp base that is held to the barrel by two screws. The rear face of the ramp is finely checkered to prevent reflection. The rear sight is a metal blade with a square notch held to the barrel by two screws. Windage adjustment is made by loosening the screws and moving the sight laterally. Elevation adjustment is made by moving a notched ramp that rides on either side of the blade. With the square post and square notch arrangement, there are no better sights (and some are much worse!) on any modern CO_2 rifle.

Trigger action on my Crosman 400 is unbelievably light and has only a hint of creep. I suppose legal concerns would never allow such a trigger on a CO_2 rifle today. The trigger pull gauge registers only 3.1 pounds as the rifle fires.

On a day when the temperature was approximately 70°F, I fired a few shots with Crosman Copperhead wadcutter pellets and obtained an average velocity of 550 ft/sec. This is about the same velocity produced by the current Model 2260. A Model 400 in good condition is still a very desirable CO_2 rifle that can hold its own with current rifles in terms of performance.

Highly polished and blued steel along with well-shaped and finished wood of the Crosman 400 speak of a bygone era. This is what air and CO_2 guns from Crosman used to be. Some of the current models are very competent pieces but in terms of quality of construction they do not equal this fine rifle or the Model 600 pistol discussed earlier in this chapter. I believe if Crosman were to resurrect pistols like the Mark I and 600 and rifles like the Model 400, they would be very popular with serious shooters.

CHAPTER 11

FUN AND GAMES

PERHAPS NO OTHER type of shooting device is more closely associated with fun and games than is the CO_2 gun. Except for a very few specialized models, they are not the tools for serious formal target shooting. Although a few CO_2 guns are suitable for such uses (see Chapter 12), they are not the choice of most people who go afield with a shooting tool after small game or pests. No, the *primary* use of a CO_2 handgun or rifle is the fine art of plinking, although training for sport and combat is a growing use of these guns. In this chapter, we will describe a few of the uses to which those wonderful CO_2 guns are put. Although to some extent our discussion will be applicable to uses of both rifles and handguns, it is a CO_2 pistol most often chosen for fun shooting, partially because there is a much wider choice of available models. Moreover, even the inexpensive models will provide an enormous amount of shooting enjoyment.

Safety

Above all, safety must be your primary consideration when shooting any air or CO_2 gun. I recently read a piece on playing games like tic-tac-toe with balloons attached to a "safe" backstop like 3/4-inch plywood. I hope no one else reads that piece and if they do, I hope they never try it. Plywood is second only to particleboard in terms of the danger of ricochet. These materials contain wood held together with resinous glues that have great resiliency. When struck with a BB or pellet, they compress and then rebound strongly. I learned this the hard way when I placed a target on a piece of particleboard thinking the wadcutter pellet would stick in the board.

Instead, the pellet came directly back and actually went through my hair before hitting the wall behind me with a whack. I knew about the notorious rebounding behavior of BBs, but I had always thought pellets did not behave that way. I was wrong. NEVER shoot at a hard surface with an air or CO_2 gun! All this has been explained in Chapter 2, but it cannot be overemphasized.

Another aspect of safety not previously discussed concerns the fact that air and CO_2 guns can launch pellets for considerable distances. Personally, I like to exploit this fact by frequently shooting at considerably longer distances than the usual 5 or 10 meters. I routinely test many of my CO_2 handguns that shoot pellets at distances up to 25 yards and rifles up to 50 yards. At these distances I do not expect pinpoint accuracy, but it is not unreasonable to hit targets the size of pop cans. However, never lose sight of the fact that a BB or pellet pistol may shoot a considerable distance and a pellet rifle may have a maximum distance as great as 250-300 yards. Do not fire a CO_2 gun in a direction where there is not an adequate backstop or a lot of wide-open space. Even a ricocheting pellet can carry a long distance. My brother and I were once shooting at clumps of dirt in a plowed field and it was not uncommon to see dust come up at two or three places where the pellet hit the ground on its bouncing journey across the open field. You can never be certain just how a pellet will strike the surface of the ground or water, so you should always suspect that a ricochet could occur.

I sometimes like to show new shooters the power of an air or CO_2 gun. This can be done by shooting a bar of soap, a potato, or an unopened can of pop. Someone who has had experience with only an ordinary BB gun is often astonished by the power of an adult air or CO_2 gun. They are sometimes under the impression that such guns are somehow more or less equivalent to a BB gun. When confronted with the effects produced by a pellet fired at much greater velocity than a BB gun produces, they are convinced the rules for safe handling of air and CO_2 guns are exactly the same as for firearms. If you are dealing with inexperienced shooters, teach, teach, teach, and then watch!

Traditional Targets

In my opinion, before any shooter engages in the *fun* type of shooting, he or she should be thoroughly familiar with shooting *fundamentals*. Learning breathing, sight picture, trigger squeeze, and follow-through should be stressed before engaging in shooting games. It is difficult to learn about sight picture if the target is a pop can. There is nothing wrong with shooting pop cans. I do it all the time. However, it is easier to learn how to shoot by shooting at targets that can be analyzed to see if patterns are developing. For example, jerking the trigger will generally lead to shots going to the right of the aiming point. This may be hard to discern when shooting pop cans. In most of what follows in this section, it is assumed the shooting is being done with a handgun.

The term "sight picture" refers to the arrangement of the rear and front sights and the relationship of the target to that sight arrangement. The most commonly used sight picture in shooting traditional paper targets with a bullseye and scoring rings around it is the six o'clock hold (see Chapter 2). Most handguns used for shooting paper targets have a square notch in the rear sight and a square-topped post front sight. The front

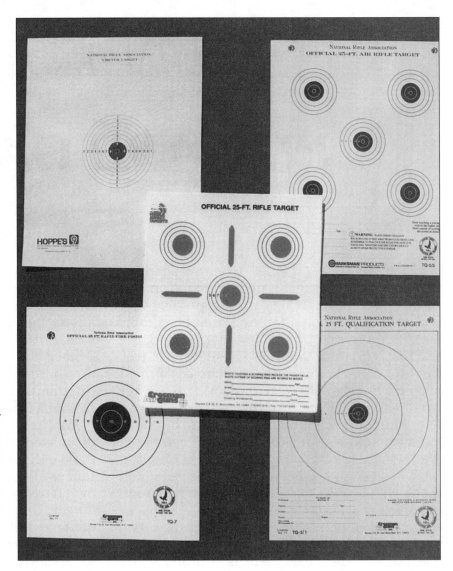

Bullseye targets are available in many forms.

sight is aligned in the rear sight notch so that the top of the post is even with the top of the notch in the rear sight with a sliver of light on either side of the front post. Sight alignment is made so the bullseye rests just touching the top of the front sight. This sight picture is best learned by shooting at targets because pinecones and pop cans do not lend themselves well to acquiring this sight picture.

Sight adjustment is made (on models that have adjustable sights) so that with the sights aligned with the target as described above, the shots strike the center of the bullseye. Only by shooting from a rest can you be certain that shots hitting elsewhere are the fault of the gun not the shooter. I have seen numerous inexperienced shooters with a new gun trying it out on pop cans. If most of the shots miss the can, how can the shooter be certain how much is his fault and how much is the result of not knowing where the gun is shooting in relation to how the sights are aligned? Shooting at paper targets will show where the pellets hit in relation to where the sights were aligned. As mentioned earlier, it easier to detect errors resulting from improper shooting form when paper targets are used.

Having stated the case for shooting at paper targets first, I believe that new shooters should begin by shooting from a rest. My rationale for that is until the shooter has mastered seeing a sight picture, holding that picture, squeezing the trigger, and holding the gun in position as the shot is released, it is meaningless to try to teach stance, arm position, etc. Before progressing to the shooting stage, thorough familiarization of sight picture and finger motion needs to be achieved. When working with a beginner, I first walk the individual through the various operations involved with how the gun operates. After that familiarization session, I proceed to the steps involved with loading CO_2 and ammunition in the particular gun being used. Generally, I take the gun and demonstrate how it is held, how it is aimed, and how it is fired by squeezing off a few shots. I then walk the new shooter through all of these steps verbally while he or she performs the operations. Then, while the shooter's hand is being supported on a rest, I coach the shooter in acquiring the proper sight picture and

Daisy ShatterBlast targets will show you instantly if you score a hit.

squeezing off the shot. One important reason for taking this approach is to give the new shooter the pleasure of being reasonably successful at first. There will be plenty of time for disappointment when shooting from a standing position with an unsupported hand! It is very easy for a beginner to become discouraged when shots go astray while thinking that there is so much to master.

After a new shooter has become reasonably proficient while shooting from a seated position with a supported hand, it is time to progress to shooting from the standing position. In formal target shooting, the handgun is held in one hand at arm's length from the body. For general plinking and sport shooting, there is no such requirement and the "two hands anyhow" position is permitted if not encouraged. The idea is to build skill in handling the gun and confidence in putting the pellet where it is intended. During all of the instructional phases, do not ever sacrifice correct gun etiquette! Practice and teach about pointing the muzzle in a safe direction and about following all range commands instantly. These are things that need to become second nature, and in my opinion, they are best learned in a more or less formal range environment shooting at standard targets. When the *fundamentals* are in place, it is time to move on to the *fun,* which is the primary object of shooting CO_2 guns.

Fun Targets

I suppose the choice of targets suitable for firing at with a CO_2 gun is limited only by one's imagination. There is available today a wide variety of fun targets ranging from paper targets with unusual pictures to fragmenting disks. At some point, it is appropriate to add variety to the shooting activities and these targets are interesting and challenging.

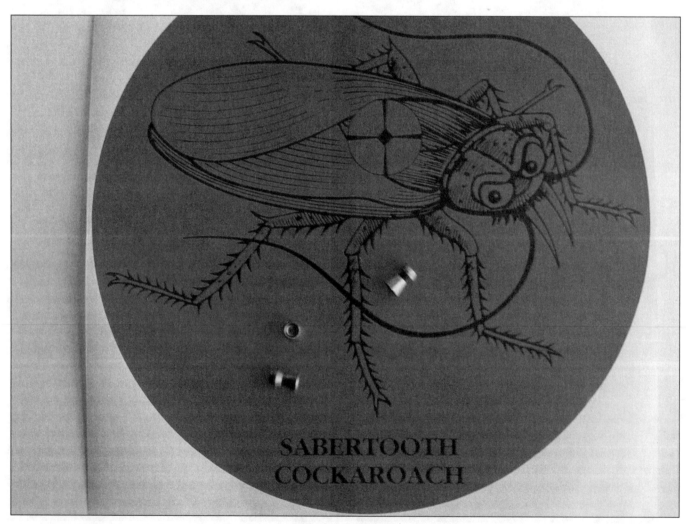

I use hollow-pointed pellets for maximum knockdown on Sabertooth Cockroaches.

Crosman's monster targets let you save the world from disaster as a change of pace from traditional paper targets.

While a great many types of fun targets are commercially available, there are also many that can be improvised. It is always fun to see something that breaks or disappears when it is hit. To me, seeing a hole appear in a paper target where I intended it to be is exciting. Some frangible targets suitable for shooting with CO_2 guns include crackers, cookies shaped like animals, balloons, mints, and lollipops. All of these items will show the effects of an accurate shot. They can be arranged at different distances for challenging shooters of different abilities. When they are being set up as targets, make sure they are supported in such a way that the pellet or BB will strike a safe backstop. Objects such as crackers or cookies can be supported by making slits in a piece of cardboard and inserting them in the slits. This piece of cardboard can then be placed on the ground or supported between cardboard boxes. In no case should the frangible targets be supported on a board, tree, or post.

One of the new commercially available targets is the ShatterBlast® from Daisy Outdoor Products. These targets are orange disks approximately 2 inches in diameter. When struck by a projectile, these targets behave like the clay targets used in trap or skeet shooting. They are available as a set containing four plastic supports and several disks, but additional disks are available in packages of 60. I believe the ShatterBlast® targets provide an interesting alternative to pop cans.

In addition to the frangible targets, I like the paper targets that have some sort of sinister figure that needs to be shot. My favorite of these is the Sabertooth Cockroach, which is produced by Lyman Products. This 4-inch beast is suitable for use as a target at 25 yards when using a CO_2 rifle. I like this target when I am getting serious practice for hunting pests. Crosman markets paper targets that look like dragons and space monsters. Some of them have multiple spot targets at various places on the figure. Daisy produces a series of targets that permit tic-tac-toe, baseball, and other games to be played by shooting in certain patterns on the target.

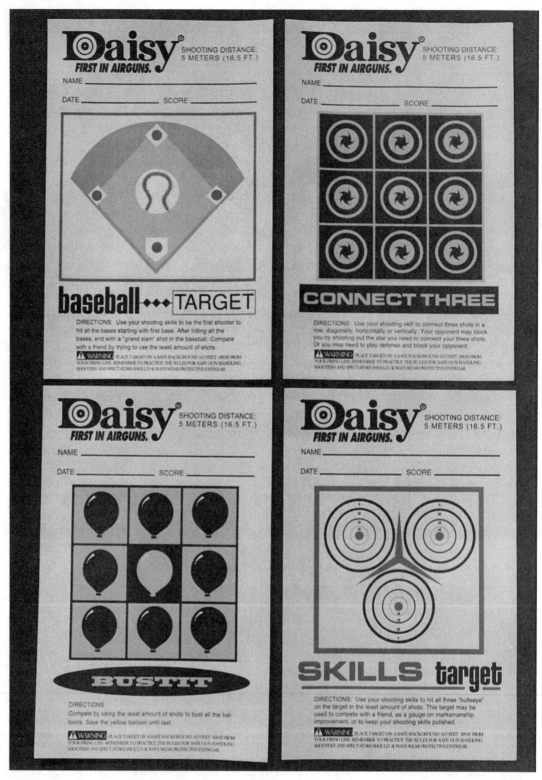

Game targets from Daisy let you play while developing marksmanship.

If you get outdoor or hunting magazines you do not intend to keep, look for pictures of various species that can be used as targets. Coyotes, prairie dogs, lions, groundhogs, and many other species are pictured in articles and advertisements. I have found these pictures make good targets. If you can hit a 3-inch photo of a coyote at a respectable distance with a CO_2 gun, it may be more exciting than hitting the 7-ring of a bullseye target.

In addition to the suggestions mentioned here, there are myriad possibilities. A blank piece of cardboard can be used as a target with pellets fired in such a way as to draw a

A pride of lions on the great game fields.

picture. This was a favorite stunt of the old time trick shooters. Your imagination can lead you to other shooting fun as long as what ever you design follows all rules of safety.

Shooting "Out There"

I enjoy shooting firearms, airguns, CO_2 guns, slingshots, and bows. If it launches projectiles, I like using it. Shooting indoors at a target on a bag filled with newspapers across the room is enjoyable. Shooting at longer distances on an outdoor range is even better from my point of view because I can experiment more. Some of my most enjoyable shooting is done in places far removed from other people with no dwelling for miles around. It takes the form of walking through fields and woods taking an occasional shot at some target of opportunity. Those targets may be leaves, pinecones, an acorn lying in an open area of ground, etc. Archers refer to the walk and shoot activity as roving shooting. In order to engage in roving shooting with a CO_2 gun, it is absolutely essential you have a great deal of open space. Keep in mind an air or CO_2 gun can fire a pellet that travels up to perhaps 250-300 yards. If you shoot at a pinecone in a tree, the pellet may come to earth 250 yards from where you fired it. Because of this, you must be absolutely certain there is no one within that range in the direction you shoot. If you shoot at an acorn on the ground, the pellet may ricochet for a long distance.

When I am in an area where I know there is no one else anywhere in the vicinity, my shooting takes on a different form. A leaf lying in a particular place becomes a brown bear. An acorn becomes a coyote as I pretend I am varmint hunting. In remote areas it is possible to enjoy these aspects of roving shooting.

The sport of lion hunting requires wide-open spaces. Lions are found in the vast grasslands. My wife and I often shoot airguns in a wide-open space where we know we are the only people around for perhaps half a mile. Because there is nothing but open areas and trees for a long distance, there is no need to worry about pellet ricochet. And there are many lions there—dandelions! After shooting at paper targets on the range, there is often a desire to shoot something else that requires less concentration. Those fuzzy headed dandelions make great targets. If you hit one dead center, the white fluff gets scattered in all directions. We can keep score if we wish, or more likely, we just enjoy being alone in an open area doing something as enjoyable as shooting pellet guns. Because (dande)lions are not particularly hard to bring down, any type of pellet works well on this species. In order to engage in lion hunting, you *must* have a large open area where there can be no harm caused by a ricochet. You can be sure pellets will almost always ricochet when they strike the earth at a small angle. In almost any large open area that is not cultivated, you can bet there will probably be a lot of (dande)lions.

Each summer, my wife and I spend time in the Big Horn Mountains of Wyoming. There is no shortage of space and at times we may be 20 miles from the nearest phone. The lodgepole pines in the Big Horn National Forest litter the floor of the forest with pinecones only 1 to 1-1/2 inches in diameter. We find a convenient log on which to sit and proceed to roll pinecones with pellets. Sometimes, we keep score to see how many we can move or how far they can be moved. At other times, we select an area of several square feet and proceed to see if we can clear the area of pinecones. An additional variation on this theme is to select one pinecone and to try to keep hitting it until it is moved out of range. Most frequently, we just shoot pinecones at random. We have spent many enjoyable hours in the forest plinking those pesky pinecones. In some cases, it has been merely a matter of taking a new gun and using it enough to get familiar with its capabilities and handling characteristics. It is absolutely essential to know you are the only persons in that area of the forest before you engage in this type of shooting. Never shoot directly at a tree with a pellet gun! The low velocity, wadcutter pellets will very frequently bounce off with considerable velocity. Even though you may know no one else is within a great distance, you must still use every precaution to insure safe shooting.

In this chapter, we have discussed some of the options available to the shooter of CO_2 guns. These guns are ideal for introducing new shooters to the shooting sports and are valuable for practice by experienced shooters, but they are not toys.

CHAPTER 12

THE BASICS OF BALLISTICS

DURING THE THREE score years that I have been involved in the shooting sports, the equipment has changed enormously in terms of design and materials. During the same time span, the application of ballistic principles by hordes of hobbyists has become commonplace. Because of advances in equipment and instrumentation, many shooters are not content with the status quo and are constantly trying to move to the next level.

Information on ballistics is now much more widely available, including several books on the subject. Perhaps because air and CO_2 guns present many challenges, air gunners are keenly interested in the choice of projectiles and their flight characteristics. After all, if you can extend the effective range of your gun from 40 yards to 50 yards, you have gained a 25% increase in effective range. To an air gunner this is hardly trivial. Realization of this type of enhanced performance can come only when the principles that govern the flight of projectiles are understood. In this chapter, we will present a discussion of those principles.

Trajectory

I can remember a time many years ago when the concept of a trajectory seemed like an advanced topic in external ballistics. Actually, a trajectory is simply a path. In terms of the flight of a projectile, it means the curved path the projectile follows after it leaves the muzzle. As I read the discussions on the Internet that deal with airguns, I am amazed by questions like, "Does a pellet travel in a straight line for some distance and then start to drop?" Another question I have seen is, "Does a pellet rise after leaving the muzzle and then start to fall?" Questions such as these and many more spark answers that show the basic ideas of the pellet's path are not well understood by many airgun shooters.

A projectile starts to lose velocity and fall as soon as it is free from the muzzle and the effect of the expanding gas pushing it. Air resistance slows the bullet and gravity pulls downward on it. As a result of these forces, the path or trajectory of a pellet is curved throughout its flight. Suppose a CO_2 rifle is resting on a shooting bench exactly 3 feet above the ground and the bore is aimed at a target 50 yards away exactly 3 feet above the ground. When the gun is fired, the pellet will start to drop, and at 50 yards it will arrive well below the point where the barrel was pointing. Now add sights to the rifle and adjust them so that when they are aligned on the target, the bore is actually pointing above the target. When the rifle is fired, the pellet will rise and cross the line of sight before falling due to gravity and crossing the line of sight again on its way to the target. We could adjust the sights so that the pellet will cross the line of sight as it rises and come back to the line of sight at some desired distance. In other words, we can "sight in" the rifle.

Fired horizontally, a pellet curves downward until it strikes the earth. We can compensate for the effect of gravity by tipping the muzzle slightly upward so the pellet comes back down to the line of sight at a distance we choose. In other words, we can sight in the rifle for distance to the target. In Figure 12.1, I have shown the path of a pellet that leaves the muzzle with a velocity of 600 ft/sec when the rifle is sighted in at a range of 30 yards. This graph is highly distorted in that the maximum range is 40 yards while the trajectory deviates only 0.8 inches above the line of sight to 2.4 inches below the line of sight. In other words, the maximum vertical distance displayed is only about 3.2 inches, which makes the trajectory appear much more curved than it actually is. In carrying out the calculations, I assumed the line of sight is 1.5 inches above the bore, which is about correct for many scoped rifles.

As we have prescribed in this example, the line of sight is perfectly straight and horizontal. Because the bore is pointing slightly upward, the pellet is launched not from a horizontal bore, but from one that causes it to gain altitude for part of its travel. Therefore, the path of the pellet will cross the line

of sight, reach some highest point, and then descend to cross the line of sight again at the distance for which the rifle is sighted in (30 yards in this case). The pellet has not traveled in a straight line before starting to fall. It was fired at an angle that causes its path to carry it above the line of sight, but it does not travel in a straight line.

In the case shown in Figure 12.1, the pellet first crosses the line of sight at a distance slightly less than 10 yards. The height of the pellet path above the line of sight at half the distance for which the rifle is sighted in is called the mid-range trajectory. In the case illustrated in Figure 12.1, the mid-range trajectory is approximately 0.8 inches. Therefore, if the rifle is sighted in to hit a point of aim at 30 yards, the pellet will strike 0.8 inches above the line of sight at a range of 15 yards, strike at the point of aim at 30 yards, and strike approximately 2.4 inches below the point of aim at 40 yards. Could we sight in the rifle for a range of say 50 yards? Yes, if the sights have enough adjustment latitude. However, for a pellet with a muzzle velocity of 600 ft/sec, the barrel must be pointed

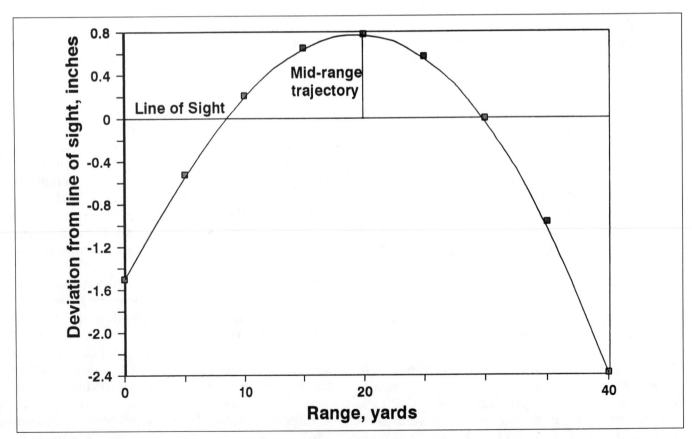

Fig. 12.1 The path of a pellet having a muzzle velocity of 600 ft/sec and a ballistic coefficient of 0.015.

Because of their different shapes, these pellets will have different ballistic coefficients.

upward at such an angle that the pellet would strike several inches high at 25 yards. This is not practical because it will then be difficult to hit small targets when they are located near the middle of the path of the pellet. What we want is to sight the rifle in so that the pellet is never more than an inch or so above the line of sight on its way to the target at the sight in distance. In that way, small targets can be hit at distances that are short compared to the distance for which the rifle is sighted in.

Since CO_2 rifles do not shoot with high velocity, the range at which they can be sighted in is necessarily short if we do not want the path of the pellet to deviate much from the line of sight. For most pellet rifles, I normally sight in at 30 yards, which means the pellet is never more than about one inch above the line of sight. After passing the sight in distance, the pellet will be below the line of sight. However, it is not more than about an inch below the line of sight at a range of 35 yards. With this sight adjustment, I know the pellet will not strike more than an inch above or below the line of sight, and it will strike at the line of sight at approximately 10 yards and again at 30 yards. With this sight arrangement, my CO_2 rifles are effective to a range of approximately 35 yards. Given the accuracy of most air and CO_2 rifles, that distance is about as far as I care to shoot at sparrows or starlings.

Having described the basic principles of pellet trajectory, we need to point out there is little we can do to change the velocity of a CO_2 rifle. Therefore, for a given type of pellet, the trajectory is going to be fixed. If we chose a different type of pellet, things get a little more interesting. We are then concerned with the difference in how the pellets are affected as they pass through air. We have arrived at the point where we need to understand some of the basic ideas of ballistics. In this case, we are concerned with external ballistics because the factors we will discuss are those that affect the pellet after it leaves the bore. Because of the types of projectiles and the low velocities of air and CO_2 guns, an increasing number of air gunners are becoming concerned with ballistics in an effort to extend their already limited guns to higher levels of effectiveness. What follows is an elementary discussion of this important topic.

Beyond the Barrel

Because none of the CO_2 guns give high velocity, all are tools for short-range work, but the shooter still needs to understand some aspects of the pellet's flight. The two major forces acting on a pellet after it leaves the muzzle are air resistance and gravity. We will not deal with the aspects of the pellet's motion down the bore since that topic was discussed in Chapter 4. The influences of air resistance and gravity are very simple to understand but very difficult to calculate. Air resistance impedes the flight of the pellet and causes it to lose velocity. Gravity pulls the pellet toward the earth and causes it to fall.

The two effects are interrelated and a curved path or trajectory is the result.

A projectile moving through the air must force the air out of its path. Air has some mass so it requires energy to cause the molecules of oxygen and nitrogen that make up air to be forced out of the path of the pellet. On a given day at a given altitude, a pellet of a given diameter will encounter approximately the same number of molecules of gas as it moves some fixed distance through the air. That is because the air is a uniform mixture of gaseous molecules. However, if you have done any reading about the behavior of projectiles in air, you undoubtedly know that a sharp-pointed projectile penetrates air more efficiently than a flat-nosed one, all other factors like diameter, weight, etc. being equal. If they sweep out a path that involves moving about the same number of molecules, why this difference in efficiency?

The answer lies in the fact that the flat-nosed projectile must move molecules outward at a sharp angle that approaches perpendicular to the path of the projectile (see Figure 12.2). The molecules do not "slide" along the surface but rather are forced outward at large angles during the motion of the flat-nosed projectile. This is the case illustrated in Figure 12.2(a). A round-nose projectile causes the gas molecules it encounters to be moved out of its path, but because of the shape of the nose, the molecules are not forced outward at angles as great as the flat-pointed projectile requires. That situation is illustrated in Figure 12.2(b). A pointed projec-

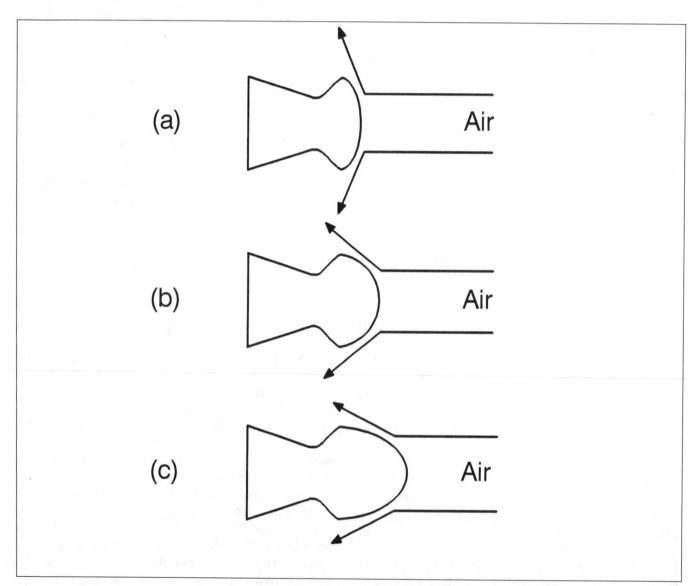

Fig. 12.2 Deflection of air around pellets having different shaped points.

tile slips through the air with less disturbance of the molecules in its path because the gas molecules sort of glance off at smaller angles. This situation is illustrated in Figure 12.2(c). As a result of the difference in the angles at which the air must be moved out of the path of the projectiles, the air resistance is greatest for the one with the flat point, least for the pointed one, and intermediate for the one with the round nose. Since it is air resistance that causes the pellet to lose velocity, the velocity loss will be greatest for the one with the flat point.

Incidentally, this is precisely the difference in the behavior of the projectiles in tissue as well. A flat nosed projectile creates a wider wound channel because tissue must be forced outward at a large angle to the path of the projectile. We will discuss this in greater detail in Chapter 13.

Air exerts a retarding force on all projectiles regardless of their shapes. We say the atmosphere produces a drag on the projectiles. However, the amount of drag, and hence the rate at which velocity is lost, depends on the shape of the projectile. A mathematical expression that relates two variables is called a function and the two variables in this case are the shape of the projectile and the rate at which it loses velocity while passing through air. Because of this, we say that two projectiles have different drag functions. The effect of drag on a projectile is demonstrated by determining its velocity at two points along its path. For pellet guns, one chronograph could be set up one foot in front of the muzzle and another could be set up at 25 yards. By measuring the velocity of the pellet at two points, the rate at which it loses velocity could be calculated.

The ability of a projectile to hold its velocity (overcome drag) is expressed by a number called the ballistic coefficient. The higher the ballistic coefficient of a projectile, the less drag it experiences as it passes through air. For bullets that travel at high velocity (several times the velocity of pellets), sharp points are important to minimize drag. However, for pellets from CO_2 guns that are traveling only 400-600 ft/sec, the shape of the pellet is much less important. Pellets having round-nose designs penetrate air about as efficiently as do those having pointed shapes. Even flat-nose pellets do not lose velocity much faster than do the round-nose or pointed types if the range is short. The reason for this is the velocity is so low shock waves do not build up on the front of the pellets as they do for bullets traveling at supersonic velocities. Moreover, the ranges involved are usually no more than 25 yards or so, and over such short ranges, the velocity loss does not vary much with nose design. For a very high-powered break-action rifle that shoots at 1000-1200 ft/sec at ranges as great as 50 yards, this would not be true.

While the bullets used in centerfire rifles have ballistic coefficients as high as 0.3-0.5, airgun pellets have ballistic coefficients usually in the range of about 0.01-0.03. Pellets are very light in weight, have hollow interiors, and have blunt noses compared to projectiles used in firearms. Therefore, they lose velocity quite rapidly compared to bullets. However, since air and CO_2 guns are used at very short ranges and the velocities are low, the ballistic coefficient of the projectile is of much less importance than it is for shooters of firearms. For a pellet having a ballistic coefficient of 0.015 and a muzzle velocity of 500 ft/sec, the velocity loss over a range of 20 yards is 79 ft/sec so the remaining velocity would be 421 ft/sec. If a pellet having a ballistic coefficient of 0.025 were used with the same muzzle velocity, the velocity loss would be 49 ft/sec and the remaining velocity would be 451 ft/sec. This difference in velocity at 20 yards would be insignificant and would not be noted under normal shooting conditions. Therefore, while ballistic performance is vital to performance at long range, the pest shooter using a CO_2 gun can use almost any pellet that is accurate and designed for the type of shooting being done. By that I mean using a pellet that performs adequately on the intended target. In spite of this, it is still necessary to conduct some test firing in order to determine the accuracy of different pellets in your particular rifle or pistol.

Even though knowledge of ballistics may not be as vital to the pest shooter using a CO_2 gun as to a shooter trying to hit a prairie dog at 500 yards with a firearm, the principles need to be understood by the air gunner. Accordingly, we will explore the topic in somewhat more detail. Just how important is the ballistic coefficient of a pellet? To answer that question, I calculated the trajectory for two pellets that both have an initial velocity of 600 ft/sec and a line of sight 1.5 inches above the bore. I also assumed that the guns were sighted to hit the point of aim at 30 yards. For one of the pellets I assumed that the ballistic coefficient was 0.010 (about the actual value for some flat-nose pellets), while for the other I assumed a ballistic coefficient of 0.020 (about the actual value for some domed and pointed pellets). The calculated trajectories are shown in Figure 12.3. From this figure it can be seen that the pellet with a ballistic coefficient of 0.020 arrives at 40 yards just about 2 inches below the point of aim. The pellet having a ballistic coefficient of 0.010 would hit almost exactly 3 inches below the point of aim. Is this difference significant? To me it is because I like to snipe small pests and an inch less hold over makes it easier to hit a small target.

The mid-range trajectory is the height of the pellet's path above the line of sight at a distance that is half of the range for which the gun is sighted in. Another advantage of the pellet with the higher ballistic coefficient is the mid-range trajectory is only 0.55 inch compared to 0.83 inch for the pellet with a ballistic coefficient of 0.010. Is a difference of approximately 0.3 inch in point of impact at 15 yards significant? Probably not, but I would just as soon have the point of impact as close as possible to the line of sight.

Probably the greatest advantage to using a pellet having a ballistic coefficient of 0.020 instead of one having a ballistic coefficient of 0.010 does not show up on the graph at all. That advantage has to do with the velocity the pellets have when they reach a distance of 40 yards from the muzzle. The pellet having a ballistic coefficient of 0.010 would reach the 40 yard mark with a velocity of 365 ft/sec, while the one with a ballistic coefficient of 0.020 would have a velocity of 470 ft/sec at the same distance even though the both had an initial velocity of 600 ft/sec. Is that difference significant? It most certainly

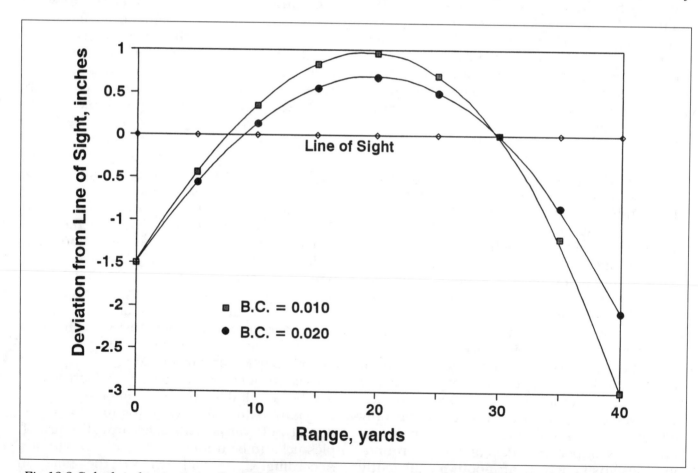

Fig 12.3 Calculated trajectories for pellets having ballistic coefficients of 0.010 and 0.020 and a muzzle velocity of 600 ft/sec. The line of sight is 1.5 inches above the bore and sighted in at 30 yards.

is because the pellet having the higher ballistic coefficient would have an energy 66% higher than the other if they have the same weight! Because air and CO_2 guns have low power at best, it is a great advantage to use a pellet that retains its velocity well and gives higher energy on the target. While the details will not be given here, the calculations show the pellet having a ballistic coefficient of 0.020 will have as much energy at 40 yards as the one with a ballistic coefficient of 0.010 does at 20 yards.

The cases described above are based on calculations performed using standard procedures. They show the ballistic coefficient of a pellet is one of the important considerations to be used when making a choice of ammunition to be used on pests. How can you determine the ballistic coefficient for a particular pellet? For many kinds of pellets the ballistic coefficients are tabulated along with other data by the manufacturer. However, this is not true for many other types of pellets, so we would like to have a simple method to determine the ballistic coefficient.

The Ballistic Coefficient

Calculating the ballistic coefficient for a projectile involves knowing the velocity at two different distances. There are two ways to determine the velocity at two distances. The best way is to use two chronographs, one a foot in front of the muzzle and one at 25 yards. That way, you can record the velocity at two points for the same shot. Another, less desirable but satisfactory way, is to use one chronograph and measure the average velocity at the muzzle for five shots. Then place the chronograph at 25 yards and measure the average velocity for another five shots. In this way, only one chronograph is required, but to compensate for the usual shot to shot variation in velocity, more shots are required.

Suppose you now know the velocity at the muzzle and at a distance of 25 yards. Of course, the higher the ballistic coefficient, the less the velocity will decrease as the pellet covers the 25-yard distance. There are several ways to use the velocities measured at two distances to determine the ballistic coefficient. While they are not particularly difficult, there is a simpler way—my way! I have reduced the process to simply looking up two numbers in a table, and I have constructed the table for you (see next page) after doing quite a bit of calculation. Probably the last time you looked at a table having this many entries you were looking at the instruction book for the Form 1040! However, using the table to determine a ballistic coefficient for a pellet is really simple, costs less, and is less painful. In fact, it is as simple as locating two numbers.

I chose to determine the remaining velocity at a range of 25 yards since that is a realistic one for air and CO_2 guns. Since this book deals with CO_2-powered guns, I have chosen the range of muzzle velocities to be 400-700 ft/sec since that encompasses the velocities given by CO_2 rifles.

As you read the directions for using the table, refer to the table at each step to see exactly what numbers are being discussed. As a first example, suppose that your Crosman 2260 shoots your favorite pellet, the Super Starling Stomper, out of the muzzle at 600 ft/sec. Look at the table and find 600 ft/sec in the left-hand column. Now suppose you shoot the SSS pellet across the chronograph at 25 yards and find the remaining velocity is 516 ft/sec. Read across the table in the row with 600 ft/sec as the entry in the left-hand column until you come to 516 ft/sec in the seventh column. The muzzle velocity (600 ft/sec) and remaining velocity (516 ft/sec) match the velocity data for your particular pellet. Now go to the top of the seventh column that has the entry 516 and you see there the ballistic coefficient of 0.020. What you have just done is determine the Super Starling Stomper pellet has a ballistic coefficient of 0.020 since a pellet having that ballistic coefficient has a velocity of 516 ft/sec at 25 yards when it starts out with a velocity of 600 ft/sec. It is that simple.

The Pest Popper pellet is a light one that exits the muzzle of your Crosman 1710 with a velocity of 670 ft/sec. When you chronograph it at 25 yards, you find it has a remaining velocity of 540 ft/sec. You can use the table to determine the ballistic coefficient of the Pest Popper pellet as follows. First, read down the left-hand side of the table to find the muzzle velocity of 670 ft/sec. Now, read across until you find the velocity of 540 ft/sec, which is the remaining velocity at 25

Remaining Velocities at 25 Yards
for Pellets Having Ballistic Coefficients of 0.010-0.040

Velocity (in ft/sec) at 25 yards for different values of the ballistic coefficient

BC = .010	.012	.014	.016	.018	.020	.022	.025	.030	.035	.040
MV										
400	290	306	318	328	335	341	346	352	360	365	369
410	298	314	326	336	343	349	355	361	369	374	379
420	305	322	334	344	352	358	363	370	378	383	388
430	312	330	342	352	360	367	372	379	387	393	397
440	320	337	350	361	369	375	381	388	396	402	407
450	327	345	359	369	377	384	390	396	405	411	416
460	335	353	367	377	386	393	398	406	414	420	425
470	342	361	375	386	394	402	407	414	423	430	435
480	350	369	383	394	403	410	416	424	432	439	444
490	357	377	391	403	412	419	425	432	442	448	453
500	365	385	400	411	420	428	434	442	451	458	463
510	372	393	408	420	429	437	443	450	460	467	472
520	380	401	416	428	438	445	452	460	469	476	482
530	388	409	425	437	446	454	461	469	478	486	491
540	395	417	433	445	455	463	470	478	488	495	500
550	403	425	441	454	464	472	478	487	497	504	510
560	411	433	450	462	472	480	487	496	506	513	519
570	418	441	458	471	481	489	496	505	515	523	528
580	426	449	466	479	490	498	505	514	524	532	538
590	434	457	474	488	498	507	514	522	533	541	547
600	441	465	482	496	507	516	523	532	542	550	556
610	449	473	491	504	515	524	532	540	552	560	566
620	457	481	499	513	524	533	540	549	561	569	575
630	464	489	507	521	532	542	549	558	570	578	584
640	472	497	515	530	541	550	558	567	579	587	594
650	480	505	524	538	550	559	567	576	588	596	603
660	487	513	532	546	558	568	575	585	597	606	612
670	494	520	540	555	566	576	584	594	606	615	621
680	502	528	548	563	575	585	593	602	615	624	630
690	510	536	556	571	583	593	601	611	624	633	640
700	517	544	564	579	592	602	610	620	633	642	649

MV = muzzle velocity in ft/sec
BC = Ballistic Coefficient

yards, in the fourth column. Having found the value of 540 ft/sec in the fourth column, go to the top of that column and you will see the ballistic coefficient is 0.014.

As an additional example, consider the Rat Wrecker pellet, which leaves the muzzle of your Crosman 2260 at 500 ft/sec and has a velocity of 437 ft/sec at 25 yards. To determine the ballistic coefficient, find the muzzle velocity of 500 ft/sec in the left-hand column and read to the right across the table until you find the entries of 434 and 442 ft/sec in columns eight and nine. One of these values is slightly lower than 437 ft/sec while the other is slightly higher. The value 434 is in the column headed by 0.022 and the value 442 has 0.025 at the top. Therefore, the ballistic coefficient for the Rat Wrecker pellet lies between 0.022 and 0.025, slightly closer to the former. A good approximation would be about 0.023. For velocities at 25 yards that are between the values given in two adjacent columns, we can estimate ballistic coefficients that fall between the values given at the top of the columns.

It is only a matter of time until you realize that the muzzle velocities are given in 10 ft/sec intervals. Suppose you find your Benjamin G397 shoots the Go Mangleum pellet at a muzzle velocity of 614 ft/sec and you want to determine the ballistic coefficient for the pellet. Can you still use the table if you determine the remaining velocity at 25 yards is 520 ft/sec? As before, look down the left-hand column until you find the velocity 610 ft/sec and the following entry 620 ft/sec. Obviously, the muzzle velocity of 614 ft/sec is between those two entries. Furthermore, the remaining velocity of 520 ft/sec is between the 515 ft/sec that corresponds to an initial velocity of 610 ft/sec and the value of 524 ft/sec that corresponds to a muzzle velocity of 620 ft/sec in column six. Here is the neat part of this whole process. The muzzle velocity of 614 ft/sec lies between only two entries in the left-hand column, 610 and 620 ft/sec. The measured remaining velocity at 25 yards is 520 ft/sec and there is only one column where that velocity falls between two adjacent entries. The entries are 515 and 524 in column six, and that column has a heading of 0.018 so that is the approximate ballistic coefficient for the Go Mangleum pellet.

What if the remaining velocity had been 544 ft/sec instead of 520 ft/sec? Reading to the right from the muzzle velocity entries of 610 and 620, you come to a column (column eight) where the corresponding entries are 540 (across from 610) and 549 (across from 620). The value of 544 obviously lies between these values, so this is the appropriate column for the pellet you are using. That column has a heading of 0.025, which is the correct ballistic coefficient for this scenario.

With this table and known pellet velocities at the muzzle and 25 yards, it is a very simple matter to determine an approximate value for the ballistic coefficient for the pellet. The values in the table were calculated for an altitude of 1000 feet above sea level. At other altitudes, the values would be slightly different. In order to cover all possible sets of conditions, a large number of tables corresponding to different altitudes, a wider range of muzzle and remaining velocities, ballistic coefficients, etc. would be needed. Not only do we not want several hundred pages of numbers, this is not really necessary because there is no practical difference between a ballistic coefficient of 0.018 and 0.019. The table presented is sufficient for most purposes, especially those that involve the use of CO_2 rifles. Incidentally, on the Internet there are

many sites that present information on ballistics. On one of them, there is a template where you supply the muzzle velocity, the distance from the muzzle, and the remaining velocity at that distance and click on "calculate." If the distance is 25 yards, any combination of muzzle velocity and remaining velocity results in a value for the ballistic coefficient that is almost exactly one of the values at the top of the columns in the table above. The table works just as well as and replaces elaborate procedures. You can even make a copy of it and take it to the range with you along with your CO_2 gun and chronograph to instantly determine ballistic coefficients after you have measured velocities.

Another use for the table is to determine the remaining velocity of a pellet at 25 yards should you already know its muzzle velocity and ballistic coefficient. For example, suppose your rifle gives a muzzle velocity of 610 ft/sec with a pellet with a known ballistic coefficient of 0.018. Go to the column with 0.018 at the top and read down until you come to the row with 610 at the left-hand side. The entry 515 is found at the intersection of that row and column. Therefore, the remaining velocity would be very close to 515 ft/sec at 25 yards for a pellet having a ballistic coefficient of 0.018 if the muzzle velocity is 610 ft/sec.

Ballistics Tables

So we have now shown how to determine the ballistic coefficient for a pellet. While a ballistic coefficient is an interesting property of a pellet, there are uses other than in describing how much velocity the pellet will lose as it travels through air. Most publishers of reloading data for centerfire cartridges have software available that enables a variety of ballistics computations. This introductory book is not the place to present the details of this type of software, but we need to understand some of the results that can be obtained from ballistics calculations.

One of the most important and useful results obtained from ballistics calculations is summarized in ballistics tables. These tables show the remaining velocity of a pellet and its deviation from the line of sight at various distances from the muzzle. Input data include the muzzle velocity, ballistic coefficient of the pellet, and the range for which the gun is sighted in. It is not possible to present a set of tables to cover all possible combinations of these variables because the tables would comprise hundreds of pages. For CO_2 guns, a practical range of muzzle velocities is 400-750 ft/sec. Almost all airgun pellets have ballistic coefficients that fall in the range 0.010-0.040, and there is little need to know the remaining velocity and deviation from the line of sight beyond a range of 50 yards. A typical sight in range for a CO_2 gun is probably around 30 yards because the trajectory is so curved the pellet will rise too far above the line of sight if the sight in distance is much farther. As a result of these limitations, it is possible to construct a set of tables of reasonable size to cover the realistic possibilities for CO_2 guns.

In Appendix A is a set of ballistics tables that cover muzzle velocities from 400 to 750 ft/sec, ranges from the muzzle to 50 yards, and ballistic coefficients of 0.010, 0.012, 0.014, 0.016, 0.018, 0.020, 0.022, 0.025, 0.030, 0.035, and 0.040. The reason more closely spaced values were used in the low range is that a greater difference results from a small difference in ballistic coefficient when the values are small. A little study of the table presented earlier will show this effect. Also, if one pellet has a ballistic coefficient of 0.010 and another has a ballistic coefficient of 0.012, the difference is 0.002, but that number is 20% of 0.010 so there is a 20% difference in the ballistic coefficients. If two pellets have ballistic coefficients of 0.020 and 0.022, the difference is still only 0.002, but that difference is only 10% of 0.020 so there is a 10% difference in the two ballistic coefficients. The result is we need to have closer spaced values for small ballistic coefficients, and the data were chosen to reflect that. Incidentally, if you look up the ballistic coefficient for a pellet and find it is 0.013, that value is between 0.012 and 0.014, so either of these values is sufficiently close for almost any purpose.

In the calculations, it was assumed the sight in range is 30 yards and the line of sight is 1.5 inches above the bore. That value is approximately correct for rifles that have a scope mounted since the axis of the scope is about 1.5 inches above the center of the bore.

Having determined the most appropriate ranges for the variables, ballistics tables were calculated. The data presented in the tables is in the form

M.V.	10 yds.	20 yds.	30 yds.	40 yds.	50 yds.
600	542/+0.27	490/+0.86	441/0.00	397/-2.64	357/-7.49

which is one line from the table with the heading Ballistic Coefficient = 0.012. The figure on the left is the muzzle velocity. The next entry is 542/+0.27, which is the velocity at 10 yards and the deviation of the pellet path from the line of sight when the gun is sighted in at 30 yards. The plus (+) sign indicates the pellet path is above the line of sight at that distance. The next entry is 490/+0.86, which gives the velocity at 20 yards and the deviation of the pellet path (0.86 inches high) from the line of sight at that distance. The next entry, 441/0.00, gives the velocity at 30 yards and 0.00 indicates that the pellet path coincides with the line of sight. That is the distance for which the gun is sighted in. The next two entries give the same information except for ranges of 40 and 50 yards.

Suppose you have a Crosman 2250 that gives the Crosman Premier pellet a muzzle velocity of 525 ft/sec. The ballistic coefficient for the 22-caliber Premier is 0.025 so the appropriate table is the one with the heading Ballistic Coefficient = 0.025. Going down the left-hand side of the table, we come to the row that shows the muzzle velocity of 525 ft/sec. That row contains the following entries:

M.V.	10 yds.	20 yds.	30 yds.	40 yds.	50 yds.
525	500/+0.44	475/+0.98	453/0.00	430/-2.68	409/-7.22

These data show that at 10 yards the remaining velocity will be 500 ft/sec and the pellet will strike 0.44 inches above the line of sight. At 20 yards, the velocity will be 475 ft/sec and the pellet path will be 0.98 inches above the line of sight. At 30 yards, the pellet will strike at the point of aim with a velocity of 453 ft/sec. At 40 yards, the remaining velocity will be 430 ft/sec and the pellet will strike 2.68 inches below the line of sight.

The set of tables presented in Appendix A should answer many questions about the performance of your CO_2 rifle with a variety of pellets. If you wish to sight in your rifle at a distance of 30 yards with a pellet having a ballistic coefficient of 0.020 and no more than a one-inch deviation above the line of sight at any distance less than 30 yards, your rifle must give a muzzle velocity of 550 ft/sec. We can see that from the following two lines from the table with the heading Ballistic Coefficient = 0.020.

M.V.	10 yds.	20 yds.	30 yds.	40 yds.	50 yds.
525	494/+0.48	464/+1.05	436/0.00	409/-2.87	384/-7.81
550	517/+0.35	487/+0.91	457/0.00	430/-2.57	403/-7.01

The first of these lines shows that at a distance of 20 yards, the pellet will hit 1.05 inches above the line of sight if the muzzle velocity is 525 ft/sec. If the muzzle velocity is 550 ft/sec, the pellet will strike 0.91 inches high at 20 yards. The same line of data (corresponding to a muzzle velocity of 550 ft/sec) indicates the pellet will hit 2.57 inches below the line of sight at a range of 40 yards. That deviation is sufficient to cause a miss if you are shooting at a starling at that distance. However, the deviation of 0.91 inches high at 20 yards probably would not. Therefore, your rifle and pellet combination would be effective to a range of approximately 35 yards at a muzzle velocity of 550 ft/sec.

There are many questions that can be answered by referring to ballistics tables. For that reason, they are included in this book in order to make it a useful resource to increase your understanding and enjoyment of this fascinating sport.

Pellets

We now understand what a ballistic coefficient means and we have a simple method to determine its value. At this point, we will turn our attention to some of the characteristics of pellets that affect their ballistic coefficients.

From the discussion presented earlier in this chapter, it should be apparent the shape of the head of the pellet has a great deal to do with the ballistic coefficient. Even though the velocities of pellets from CO_2 guns are low, there is still significant drag. As was explained earlier, a pointed pellet can penetrate air better than one having a blunt nose. However, some pellets with rather sharp points have surprisingly low ballistic coefficients. Sharp corners, such as where the head joins the body, cause turbulence as the pellet flies. This increases the drag even though the point itself is sharp. Some pointed pellets have one or more rings or bands around the body ahead of the skirt. While

these may provide a better gas seal, they also increase skin friction and drag. Smooth surfaces that are gently rounded contribute to a pellet having a high ballistic coefficient (0.020 or greater). Most wadcutter pellets have ballistic coefficients of about 0.010-0.012. Some of the domed pellets, such as the Crosman Premier, have ballistic coefficients among the highest. The 7.9-grain 177-caliber Premier has a ballistic coefficient of about 0.025 while the value for the 10.5-grain Premier has a value of about 0.029. Both the 20- and 22-caliber Crosman Premier pellets weigh 14.3 grains. Their ballistic coefficients are 0.040 and 0.035, respectively. Because the 20-caliber pellet has a smaller diameter than one of 22 caliber, it has slightly less drag and hence a slightly higher ballistic coefficient.

In general, longer, heavier, and smoother pellets having pointed heads will penetrate air better than those having other characteristics. In addition to the Crosman Premier, I like the Crosman Copperhead pointed and Beeman Silver Sting pellets. All of these have ballistic coefficients higher than average and they are sturdy pellets that give good penetration. Although I like and use many other types of pellets (if you do not believe it, see Chapter 3), the Beeman Kodiak is one I have found to perform well. It is a very sturdy pellet with a shallow skirt and weighs 21.4 grains in 22 caliber. As a result, it gives lower velocities, but it penetrates very well because of its solid head and mass.

Does this mean I never use wadcutter pellets? By no means. Although most wadcutter pellets have rather low ballistic coefficients, they hit with a real thump. If penetration is of secondary importance, a wadcutter pellet can be an excellent choice. The Crosman Copperhead wadcutter is made with a solid head and a shallow skirt. As a result, it is a very sturdy pellet, and I use a lot of them. The Dynamit Nobel Meisterkugeln is one of my favorite wadcutter pellets. It hasn't performed poorly in terms of accuracy in any of my air and CO_2 guns. In fact, if I test several pellets in a given gun, it is frequently the most accurate pellet tested.

Keep in mind the cylinders used in many of the popular CO_2 pistols are so short that long pellets cannot be used in them. Therefore, the longer pointed and domed pellets cannot be used in those guns. Some of the revolvers have cylinders long enough to accommodate any type of pellet so this is not a problem when using those guns. I have given pellet dimensions in Chapter 2 and cylinder measurements in the evaluations of specific guns as an aid in determining which pellets can be used in guns that hold pellets in cylinders. Also, CO_2 pistols and rifles that utilize in-line magazines must be used with flat-pointed pellets otherwise the pellets, which are removed laterally, will hang up on the ones in front or behind in the magazine tube. There is no doubt that as far as compatibility with all types of pellets is concerned, the single shot pieces like the Crosman 2240, 1760, 2260, etc. are more versatile than the various types of repeaters. One current model that has a long cylinder is the Daisy PowerLine 622X and it can be used with pointed pellets.

CHAPTER 13

HUNTING AND PEST CONTROL

THERE IS NO doubt that varmint hunting is a serious sport that serves a useful purpose. Equipment and techniques for hunting varmints span the entire range of the shooting sports and beyond. I even know of a couple of innovative individuals who bushwhack starlings on a hog farm with tennis racquets at night by flashlight. As the term is used by varmint hunters, a varmint is a bird or animal that is a pest, nuisance, or health hazard to humans or livestock. That definition includes species like mice, rats, sparrows, starlings, crows, pigeons, prairie dogs, ground hogs, coyotes, etc. Which of these

Using the Crosman 262 on starlings is a good way to prepare for hunting.

species may be hunted with a CO_2 gun depends on the type of gun used and the skill of the hunter. However, with the types of CO_2 guns reviewed in the earlier chapters of this book, there are rather severe limitations. Personally, I would be tempted to ambush a rat or starling with anything that shoots, but to do so may not be very ethical.

There are varmints and pests everywhere, but it may not be possible to hunt them everywhere. One thing that is certain, however, is that they may be hunted in a lot more places with a CO_2 or airgun than they can with a firearm. Advantages of using an air or CO_2 gun for pest control include the fact they are quiet, and they do not pose a long-range hazard. While low-powered air and CO_2 guns are not suitable for taking coyotes or other large varmints, they are ideally suited to dispatching small pests like rats, mice, sparrows, or starlings. If suitable guns and pellets are chosen, pests as large as pigeons and crows are fair targets for some CO_2 guns. Small game is another matter. Game birds may not be taken legally with any type of rifle or pistol in most jurisdictions. Therefore, the traditional small game animals that can be harvested with a CO_2 gun are rabbits and squirrels. Both of these species are sturdier than the smaller species of pests, so the choice of CO_2 guns suitable for such hunting is very limited.

But the elimination of vermin using CO_2 guns definitely has its place. I am by no means a dedicated handgun hunter, but the skill developed by taking small species of ver-

The CO_2 Smith & Wesson 686 is an outstanding practice handgun for the handgun hunter. It has the size and weight as the same model firearm.

Another superb choice for a practice CO_2 handgun is the Daisy PowerLine 44, which has the looks of a 44 Magnum Smith & Wesson Model 29.

min with a CO_2 pistol or revolver cannot be denied. If a shooter can take a sparrow, mouse, or starling at 15 yards with a CO_2 handgun, a coyote at 50 yards should be an easy target for the same shooter using a 357 Magnum. A deer at that range should be an even easier target. Aside from loathing certain species (starlings are at the top of my list), I see one of the most important aspects of taking pests with a CO_2 handgun being the training and practice it provides for firearm handgun hunting. I would certainly recommend the beginner in handgun hunting get a CO_2 gun that resembles the type of firearm to be used and get a lot of practice on paper targets. Then, after testing different types of pellets, move on to using the CO_2 gun to eliminate small pests. This type of practice will enable one to become a more effective hunter when using firearms.

In this chapter we will discuss some of the aspects of using CO_2 rifles and pistols to take small game and pests. We will cover factors such as power requirements, selection of equipment, sighting in, choice of pellets, and range limitations. Because shooting pests or small game with a CO_2 gun may stretch the limits of the gun's performance, the shooter should have an appreciation of ballistics. Consequently, the introduction to ballistics given in Chapter 12 is particularly applicable to the small game and pest hunter who uses air or CO_2 guns. However, it is not just the pest and small game hunter that is concerned with airgun ballistics. A shooter who wishes to hit a metal figure in the shape of an animal that is 50 yards away but no more than 2 inches in height had better have a good understanding of the path the pellet will follow. Having presented a discussion of ballistics in the last chapter, we will now discuss some of the other aspects of pellet and gun performance that apply to hunting pests and game.

Power Considerations

For efficiently dispatching very small vermin such as sparrows and mice not much power is required. These fragile targets do not offer much resistance, so any pellet-firing CO_2 pistol or rifle has sufficient power for the job. This is almost true for starlings, but some of the CO_2 pistols are marginal since they produce muzzle energies of only about

3-4 ft-lbs. This is adequate for starling or rats and smaller sized pests as long as the range is very short. What are some practical guidelines for taking pests with CO_2 guns? What follows is a summary of my views on the subject.

The most powerful CO_2 rifles tested in this work are 22-caliber guns that will fire a 14.3-grain pellet at 550-600 ft/sec on a warm day, which represents a muzzle energy of 9.6-11.4 ft-lbs. Energy this high is deemed by most airgun enthusiasts to be adequate for a wide range of species. If we suppose the upper limit of range is 35 yards, the remaining energy would be about 7.5-8.0 ft-lbs if a pellet having a ballistic coefficient of 0.025 is used. Energy this high delivered by a well-constructed 22-caliber pellet is adequate for game up to the size of rabbits and squirrels if the shot is placed precisely in the lethal zone. If you have a Crosman 2260 or 2250 and can place the pellet precisely, I would not be critical of your hunting squirrels or rabbits with it. The Benjamin G397, Crosman 1760, Crosman 1077, and Walther Lever Action rifles give 177-caliber pellets a muzzle velocity in the 600-650 ft/sec range, which corresponds to a muzzle energy of about 6.5-7.0 ft-lbs. Personally, I would not use rifles having this power on small game. I know they will certainly kill such species with precisely placed pellets of suitable construction, but there is no real margin for error. With these low-powered rifles, turn your attention to small vermin and go on safari. Starlings, rats, and even pigeons are the logical targets if you use these lower-powered small bores. I say that knowing full well that some very

The Crosman 2260 is the best of the CO_2 rifles for game and pests.

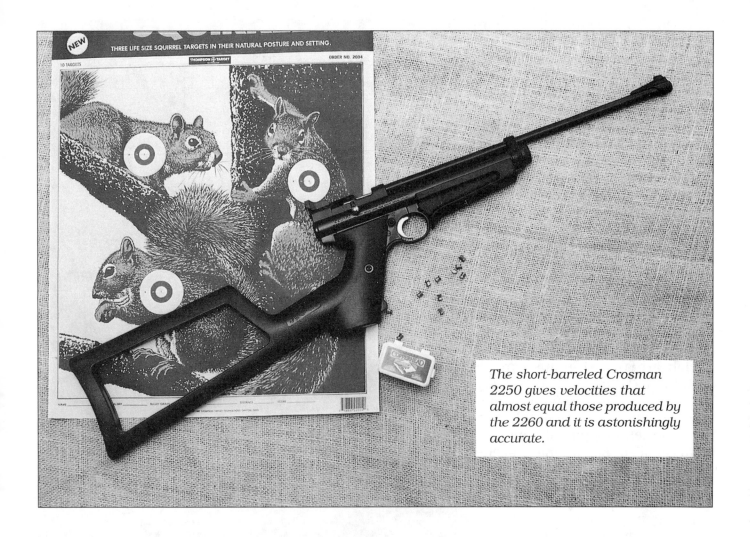

The short-barreled Crosman 2250 gives velocities that almost equal those produced by the 2260 and it is astonishingly accurate.

The Walther Lever Action is extremely accurate and would be a superb starling rifle.

careful hunters who are good marksmen take squirrels with rifles having power of this level.

I would consider the Crosman 2240 to be roughly equivalent to the older Crosman SSP 250, and quite possibly it is the best of the CO_2 handguns for pests and small game. The 2240 produces a muzzle energy of 6.5-7.0 ft-lbs, which is quite high. With a pellet that retains velocity well and a muzzle velocity of 460 ft/sec, this pistol has a flat-enough trajectory to make it a 35-yard varmint gun. The remaining energy at that distance is approximately 4.6 ft-lbs, which is adequate for taking several species. This pistol will accommodate the shoulder stock marketed by Crosman, which would help shoot it accurately at longer distances. A scope can also be mounted on this pistol by means of an intermount that clamps to the barrel. There is no question the accuracy of the Crosman 2240 is unsurpassed by any other current CO_2 pistol except for special target models.

There is one other CO_2 pistol that deserves special mention. That pistol is the Sheridan E9A (currently known as the EB20). Mine will drive 20-caliber 14.3-grain pellets having very solid construction at 420 ft/sec and some of the lighter pellets that weigh around 10 grains can be driven to almost 500 ft/sec. While not quite as powerful as the 22-caliber Crosman 2240, it is nonetheless a potent handgun that is also surprisingly accurate. Moreover, it is even smaller and lighter that the Crosman 2240 so it represents a portable varmint gun. I only wish I had bought a 22-caliber EB22 when they were available. I have been very impressed with the performance of my E9A, and I plan to take it with me on varmint hunts when I also take an air or CO_2 rifle or a firearm just to add variety to the hunt.

I have deliberately left one category of CO_2 gun out of the discussion so far. That type is the 22-caliber pistols typified by the Crosman 2210 and the Daisy 622X. Keep in mind the velocities given by the 22-caliber pistols (approximately 375 ft/sec) are slightly lower than those given by the 177 pistols. However, since the average 22-caliber pellet weighs almost twice as much as the average 177 pellet, the 22 pistols hit much harder. In my view, they are suitable for

A 177-caliber Benjamin G397 is powerful enough for small pests. It is a classic in terms of design and construction.

The most powerful and accurate CO_2 handgun for the pest shooter is the 22-caliber Crosman 2240.

The discontinued Crosman SSP 250 makes an effective handgun for the pest shooter.

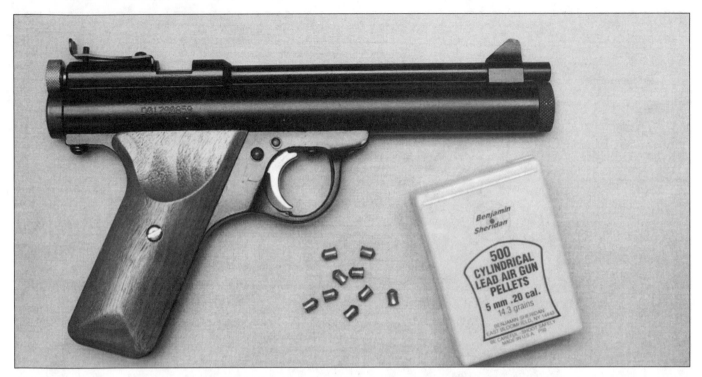

Compact and powerful, the 20-caliber Sheridan E9A is a superb choice for pest shooting.

varmints in the size range of starlings, rats, crows, or pigeons at short range. Because of the accuracy limitations, ranges must be kept short, probably 10-15 yards being a practical limit. Some of the vintage CO_2 guns have the power and accuracy to make them useful for varmint hunting. My old Crosman Mark I has superb sights, high accuracy, and muzzle velocity of approximately 425 ft/sec that make it suitable for ranges up to perhaps 25 yards. Varmint hunting with CO_2 handguns is a short range, small target proposition. The

Because it is a 22 caliber, the Crosman 2210 has enough punch to dispatch small pests.

My favorite repeating 22-caliber CO_2 pistol is the Daisy PowerLine 622X, which is accurate, affordable, and powerful.

Crosman SSP 250 is effective up to that distance and possibly farther. If you have one with a 20- or 22-caliber barrel, it should be effective on small pests up to 30-35 yards.

There are no infallible rules regarding the power required to punch pests. So much depends on the placement of the shot and the characteristics of the pellet that only the roughest of estimates can be made. Personally, I would recommend pellets having 2 ft-lbs for mice and sparrows, 3 ft-lbs for starlings, 4 ft-lbs for rats and pigeons, 5 ft-lbs for crows, and 6-7 ft-lbs for rabbits and squirrels. This would correspond to the 177-caliber revolvers and autos being limited to starlings and smaller species; the 22-caliber autos, single-shot pistols and the 177-caliber rifles as being suitable for rats, pigeons, and smaller species; and the 22-caliber rifles as being suitable for any species in the above series. Even though we are talking about eliminating pests, it should be done humanely. Based on my experience, the best choices for all around use as varmint guns are the Crosman 2260, 2250, and 2240 and the Benjamin EB20 in that order if you plan to take pests that include some of the larger species. I took my share of vermin with a

Daisy BB gun in my youth, but it is always better to use enough gun.

Pellet Selection and Testing

Assuming you want to use a CO_2-powered gun for taking very small game and sniping pests, the task of choosing ammunition lies ahead. If your gun is one of the single shots, your choice of pellets is very wide. The wadcutters, hollow points, pointed, and domed styles will all function in such guns as will the specialty types. Some of the revolvers have cylinders long enough to accommodate a variety of pellet styles although some function only with short (wadcutter) pellets. The instruction manuals that accompany most of the CO_2 pistols styled like autoloaders state the pistols should be used with wadcutter pellets. The metal cylinders used in most of the more expensive models are quite short. One exception is the Daisy 622X, which has a cylinder that will accept even pointed pellets. Although most of the revolvers use a short cylinder ahead of the fake one to hold pellets, they generally have a length that will allow almost any type of pellet to be used.

For the moment, let us assume you are using a CO_2 gun that can function with pel-

Pellets of different shape are useful for dispatching a variety of species.

lets of any reasonable length. What type do you choose? Accurate pellet placement is absolutely essential. By their very nature, CO_2 guns are low in power. Do not sacrifice accuracy just to use a pellet having a different configuration. Conduct some accuracy tests with several types of pellets and you will probably find that some work very well in your gun but some may not. In conducting the tests, shoot from a bench using a suitable rest and your best shooting technique. Because of power limitations, CO_2 guns are short-range pest rifles so testing at 20-25 yards is adequate for rifles and 10-15 yards is sufficient for testing CO_2 handguns.

Having determined the species to be bushwhacked with your CO_2 gun, now select the pellets to use. For your particular CO_2 gun, you may be restricted to wadcutter pellets. If you are, I suggest you examine three or four different types to see the difference in construction. The Crosman Copperhead wadcutter is constructed with a shallow internal

cavity and a very solid head. These pellets are very sturdy and generally penetrate better than most other wadcutter pellets. Weights are 7.9 grains in 177 caliber and 14.3 grains in 22 caliber. Although I have not conducted any scientific tests of hardness, Crosman pellets seem to be made of an alloy that is harder than pure lead. I have heard the reason for this is that many Crosman air and CO_2 guns produced over the years have been repeaters and harder pellets mean less deformation and less tendency to jam in magazines.

A wadcutter pellet that has given outstanding performance in many of my air and CO_2 guns is the RWS Meisterkugeln. In fact, in testing a few dozen guns, I have found that while the very best accuracy may have been achieved with some other pellet, the Mesiterkugeln always gave accuracy near the top of the list. In fact, it has never performed poorly in any of my guns. While there is a special target version of this pellet, I am talking

Wadcutter, domed, and pointed Crosman pellets are very sturdy due to the solid head construction. All are excellent choices for hunting.

Hollow-pointed pellets like the Beeman Crow Magnum (left) and the Dynamit Nobel Super-H-Point work best on small pests.

about the regular variety that comes in tins containing 500 pellets. In 177 caliber, the Meisterkugeln weighs 8.225 grains and in 22 the average weight is about 14.3 grains. Therefore, it is not as light as some of the wadcutter pellets intended for target shooting. It should be seriously considered as a suitable pellet for short-range work on small varmints.

If I were restricted to the use of wadcutter pellets only because of the limitations of my handgun, one that would be on my list of "must test" types would be the RWS Supermag. This is a heavy pellet (9.4 grains in 177 caliber) and when one of my Colt 1911 pistols was not shooting to point of aim, I switched to this heavy pellet, which produced the desired change in point of impact. I also obtained an average group size of less than 1 inch at 10 yards. The Supermag is a sturdy pellet that would work well on pests.

There are numerous match type wadcutter pellets that normally give excellent accuracy

When penetration is required, the Crosman pointed pellet is a superb choice as shown by how it easily penetrated this 3/8-inch board.

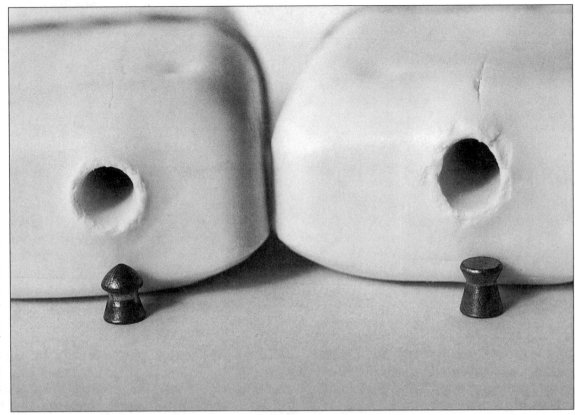

Although the 22-caliber pointed pellet (left) gave deeper penetration, the wadcutter (right) gave a wider entrance hole and channel.

in most guns. One that I have tested rather extensively is the Gamo Match and it shows excellent weight and dimensional uniformity. My only objections to this pellet are that it is rather soft and it has a large internal cavity. Therefore, penetration is not as great as it is with some other wadcutter pellets.

Keep in mind the hollow-pointed pellets like the Beeman Crow Magnum and the RWS Super-H-Point pellets expand even at low velocity. If they will function in your gun and have sufficient accuracy, by all means consider them for hunting and pest shooting. Finally, keep in mind that pellets having higher ballistic coefficients retain their velocity (and hence their energy) better than those with low ballistic coefficients. If your CO_2 gun shoots them accurately, choose such a pellet if the performance characteristics (penetration and expansion) are adequate for the species being hunted. The Crosman Premier has established an excellent reputation as a hunting pellet not only because its domed point is effective on game but also because it has a high ballistic coefficient.

The major factor in effective use of an air or CO_2 gun on game and pests is placing the pellet precisely in the lethal zone. When I read of successful hunts, the one thing that comes through is that the pellet struck exactly where it should. This level of expertise comes with practice, but it also requires careful choice of equipment. If you are buying a CO_2 rifle or pistol specifically with hunting in mind, choose a model with sufficient power for the type of sport you plan to engage in. We have already expressed some views on power requirements and will now address evaluating pellet performance.

In accuracy testing, have your gun outfitted with the sighting equipment you plan to use during your hunting. Fire a minimum of three five-shot groups (preferably more) to determine which pellets show enough promise to be evaluated more carefully. After this initial screening, run a clean patch through the bore and fire five five-shot groups with the two or three types of pellets that show promise. After this much testing, you will have a good idea of what you can expect from your gun with several types of pellets. In general, the lethal zone to be hit is very small, perhaps no larger than a nickel or quarter. If you cannot hit a target of this size, you should get closer to the target. Because of the level of accuracy required, shooting at critters may be a very short-range activity. A CO_2 rifle may have enough power to dispatch a starling at 50-60 yards but accuracy may limit its effective range to 25-30 yards. The curvature of the trajectory also becomes a factor when you realize that your rifle is sighted in at 30 yards but the pellet will strike 6-8 inches low at 50 yards depending on the ballistic coefficient of the pellet. My recommendation, and the practice that I follow, is to consider a CO_2 rifle to be limited to about 35 yards. At that distance, my most accurate CO_2 rifle will group in around 1 inch and hitting a target that size consistently requires I do my best shooting even if everything else is right. We do a great deal of harm to our sport when we allow critters to carry away pellets that have not struck a lethal zone.

Having determined which pellets exhibit sufficient accuracy to be useful, we need to conduct a few simple tests to see how they will perform. There are two factors that need to be considered when determining the effectiveness of pellets on game. One of the factors is penetration and the other is energy transfer. The first requires no special interpretation, but the second loosely refers to the "smash" with which the pellet hits. For example, a heavy, solid wadcutter like the Crosman Copperhead or the Dynamit Nobel Supermag transfers energy to the target more efficiently than does a sleek, pointed pellet. For the same reasons that a wadcutter pushes air out of its path at large angles, it also pushes tissue out of its path. In other words, it creates a wide wound channel. While it may sound rather clinical, tissue must be displaced in a lethal zone for a pellet to be effective. That displacement of tissue is what we mean by smash or energy transfer. If a suitable wadcutter pellet is sufficiently accurate in your gun, it is a good choice for critters at short range. Keep in mind, however, that wadcutter pellets generally have low ballistic coefficients and lose velocity rapidly at longer ranges.

Because a wadcutter pellet forces tissue out of its path at large angles, it transfers its energy to the target more rapidly than does a pellet that does not move material at large angles. Accordingly, wadcutter pellets generally give less penetration than most other types. Hollow-point pellets such as the Bee-

man Crow Magnum also give wide wound channels because they expand to a larger diameter. Penetration is somewhat limited, but energy transfer is rapid. On lightly constructed critters like dirty birds (starlings), the Crow Magnum is devastating. There is no reason to pick a pellet that will penetrate 5 inches in flesh if you want to shoot starlings because much of the pellet's energy is going to be expended on the landscape somewhere.

While we have been discussing the effect of flat and hollow points, it should not be overlooked that one way to affect a wider wound channel is to use a larger caliber. It is well known that 20- and 22-caliber pellets are much more effective on game than are those of 177 caliber. The reason is simple. Even with no expansion, the cross-sectional area of the larger caliber pellets exceeds that of the 177 caliber. The cross-sectional areas of 177-, 20-, and 22-caliber pellets are 0.0246, 0.0314, and .0394 square inches, respectively. In other words, if pellets in these three calibers penetrated the same distance in a target, the wound channels would be in direct proportion to the cross-sectional areas of the pellets. In order for a 177-caliber pellet to displace the same amount of tissue (volume of the wound channel) as one in 20 caliber, the 177 pellet would have to penetrate 1.28 times as deeply. To give the same volume of wound channel as a 22-caliber pellet, the 177-caliber pellet would have to penetrate 1.60 times as deeply.

Another way to look at these data is that if pellets in the three calibers gave the same depth of penetration, the volume of the wound channel given by the 20 caliber would be 1.28 times as large as that given by the 177-caliber pellet. The volume of the wound channel given by the 22-caliber pellet would be 1.60 times that of the 177 pellet. This all translates into showing the 177 is not as effective as the 20 or 22 unless it penetrates much deeper. Under certain conditions, a 177 pellet may give deeper penetration than one of 20 or 22 caliber, but not enough to compensate for the larger diameter. Keep in mind that at the low velocity pellets travel, expansion doesn't amount to much except for hollow points. Therefore, pellet diameter is very important for the same reason that a 45-caliber bullet is more destructive than one of 32 caliber if they penetrate to the same depth.

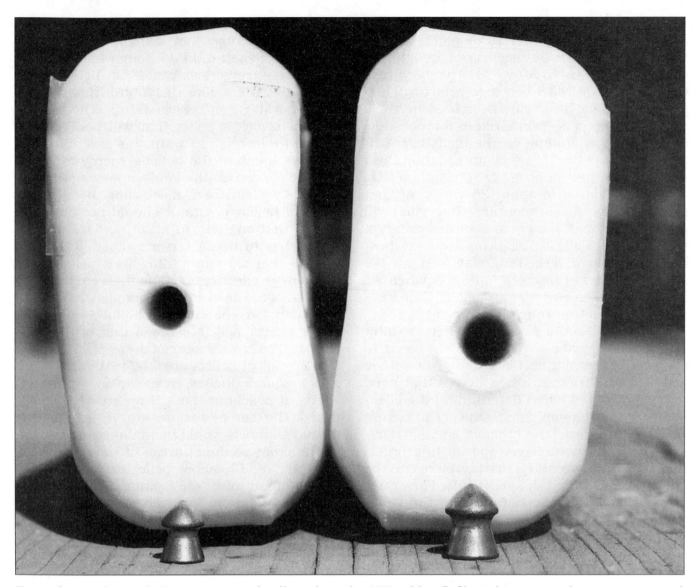

Bars of soap shot with Crosman pointed pellets show the 177 caliber (left) produces a much narrower wound channel than does the 22 caliber (right).

All of this does not mean that a 177-caliber air or CO_2 gun cannot be devastating. Although I did not witness it, I know of an individual who killed a fox with a 177-caliber air rifle that is known to give a velocity approaching 1000 ft/sec. However, the pellet was placed precisely between the ear and the eye and entered the brain of the fox. Would a pellet of 20 or 22 caliber been more effective? No, because the 177 pellet was placed precisely where it should have been. However, placing a 22-caliber pellet in the shoulder is not equivalent to placing a 177-caliber pellet in the brain. It is not the caliber that makes a particular air or CO_2 gun an effective tool for harvesting game or dispatching pests. There are many reasons for choosing the most effec-

tive equipment for the job. Having told the story of a fox being taken with a 177-caliber air rifle, I do not want anyone to think I condone such things. It is more of a stunt than an accepted hunting practice. People have gone over Niagara Falls in a barrel, but that is more of a stunt than a way to commute to work. I believe we must avoid every appearance of recklessness if we are to prevent additional regulation of our sport.

For a pellet to be effective, it must penetrate to the lethal zone. Penetration is normally tested in some medium that is supposed to simulate flesh. I do not shoot steaks and roasts, so I shoot soap. One thing I like about soap is when a pellet penetrates it, it leaves a hole that does not close up.

Therefore, it is possible to examine the channel created by the pellet to see its characteristics. It does not bother me much that soap is not much like flesh because if a pellet penetrates 50% farther than another in soap, the same would probably true about penetration in flesh. A pellet that gives 2 inches of penetration in a bar of soap might penetrate 3 inches in flesh, but I can still compare the relative behavior of two pellets by measuring their penetration in soap. Of course, to be consistent the same type of soap bar must be used in both cases.

I have conducted soap penetration tests by pellets of different calibers and styles. In the tests, the same brand of soap from the same 12-bar package was used, and in most cases, the pellet velocity was very near 600 ft/sec. The two exceptions were the 177-caliber Crosman pointed pellet, which had a velocity of approximately 670 ft/sec, and the Beeman Kodiak 22 caliber, which had a velocity of approximately 520 ft/sec. The tests demonstrated several principles related to caliber, pellet weight, and pellet type. For example, the deepest penetration was given by the slowest pellet, which also had the largest diameter. The 21.4-grain 22-caliber Beeman Kodiak, which has a round nose shape, penetrated 2.90 inches of soap even though the velocity was only about 520 ft/sec. On the other hand, the 22-caliber Crosman Premier, which weighs 14.3 grains and was traveling at 600 ft/sec, gave 2.47 inches of penetration. Velocity is not the most important factor in penetration. If it were, the Premier at about 80 ft/sec greater velocity would have penetrated more deeply. Pellet weight relative to the caliber is more important.

To further demonstrate that fact, the 177-caliber Crosman Premier heavy pellet weighs 10.50 grains, which is very heavy for the caliber. With a velocity of approximately 600 ft/sec, the penetration was 2.61 inches of soap. This was by far the most penetration of the 177-caliber pellets tested even though the velocity was the lowest.

Beeman Crow Magnum hollow points in 177, 20, and 22 calibers gave the least penetration of the pellets tested in each caliber. However, the wound channel in each case opened up significantly just beyond the entrance showing the effect of expansion.

These and other penetration tests show the 177 caliber does not penetrate nearly enough to compensate for the larger diameter of 20- and 22-caliber pellets. The larger calibers displace more material. However, it should be mentioned the 177 caliber does have some advantages. Velocities of 177-caliber pellets are normally higher unless guns of greatly differing power are used. Therefore, the trajectories of 177-caliber pellets are usually flatter, which makes hitting a small target easier. If a heavy 177-caliber pellet is used in order to gain penetration, the velocity is lower and there is not much difference in trajectory between that and pellets in 20 or 22 caliber. There is no free lunch.

Regulations

With regard to regulations applicable to hunting with air and CO_2 rifles, most states regard them as simply a type of gun so the usual regulations apply. If you have an interest in using an air or CO_2 rifle to hunt, be sure to check the regulations, including transporting such a rifle, that apply in your area. You may find some shocking facts. For example, in Illinois, any air or CO_2 gun of caliber larger than 177 is considered to be a firearm and the same restrictions apply with regard to purchase and possession. That means a Firearm Owner's Identification Card is required to purchase or possess such a gun. Furthermore, a background check and a waiting period are imposed on the purchase of any air or CO_2 gun over 177 caliber. Similar restrictions apply to air and CO_2 guns of 177 caliber if they produce a muzzle velocity higher than 700 ft/sec. Because of these restrictions, the affected air rifles cannot be shipped to individuals within the state. I mention the situation that exists in my home state for three reasons. First, there may be regulations in your jurisdiction that limit your use of a CO_2 gun. Second, if you know of restrictions in other areas, you may want to see what you can do to prevent your area from becoming similarly oppressed. Third, just because you use an air or CO_2 gun, do not assume you are immune to gun restrictions either present or future. All it takes is to change a definition of what constitutes a firearm.

The situation is even worse in much of Europe where the severe restrictions are placed on airguns that generate more than some defined low energy threshold, usually 7.5 joules or 5.5 ft-lbs. Air and CO_2 rifles that fire faster than 500 ft/sec cannot be shipped to Canada. As a result, many of the American guns are available in special low-power versions for sale in Canada. All of this points to the fact that air gunners must be squeaky clean in the conduct of their sport. To not be is to invite limitations so severe as to make it impossible to engage in many activities we enjoy.

Before you head out with your pistol or rifle, contact the appropriate agency in your state to determine the regulations that apply to hunting with air and CO_2 guns. Remember, a violation involving the use of an airgun can lead to confiscation of all your guns!

APPENDIX A.

BALLISTICS TABLES

The ballistics tables in this appendix have been calculated assuming an altitude of 1000 feet above sea level and a sight height of 1.5 inches above the bore. Calculations for altitudes a few hundred feet above or below the assumed altitude do not change the velocity or deviation from line of sight to any significant extent. The entries are given as velocity/deviation. For example, 369/+1.87 means a velocity of 369 ft/sec and an impact point that is 1.87 inches above the line of sight. In other words, the pellet will hit above the aiming point by 1.87 inches at that distance. 413/-2.24 indicates a velocity of 413 ft/sec and a point of impact that is 2.24 inches below the point of aim at that distance.

Tables are given for ballistic coefficients from 0.010 to 0.022 in intervals of 0.002. From 0.025 to 0.040 the interval is 0.005. The reason for this is that for low ballistic coefficients there is a greater difference in the calculated results for small changes in the ballistic coefficient. In other words, there is a significant difference between a ballistic coefficient of 0.010 and one of 0.012 as far as the remaining velocity and deviation from the line of sight are concerned. On the other hand, the difference between the results calculated using ballistic coefficients of 0.030 and 0.032 is slight and negligible in most cases. The range of 0.010 to 0.040 in ballistic coefficients covers the values for virtually all airgun pellets. Most CO_2 rifles and the higher-powered pistols have muzzle velocities in the range of 400 to 700 ft/sec unless abnormally light or heavy pellets are used. Therefore, the velocity range chosen should cover almost any situation arising from the use of a CO_2-powered rifle or pistol.

Ballistic Coefficient = 0.010

M.V. (fps)	10 yds.	20 yds.	30 yds.	40 yds.	50 yds.
400	352/+2.08	310/+2.86	272/0.00	240/-7.55	211/-21.2
425	374/+1.73	329/+2.47	290/0.00	255/-6.62	224/-18.6
450	396/+1.43	349/+2.14	307/0.00	270/-5.84	238/-16.4
475	419/+1.18	369/+1.87	324/0.00	286/-5.17	251/-14.6
500	442/+0.96	389/+1.63	342/0.00	301/-4.60	265/-13.0
525	464/+0.77	409/+1.43	360/0.00	317/-4.11	279/-11.7
550	487/+0.61	429/+1.25	378/0.00	333/-3.68	293/-10.5
575	509/+0.47	450/+1.10	396/0.00	349/-3.31	307/-9.49
600	532/+0.35	470/+0.96	414/0.00	365/-2.99	321/-8.60
625	554/+0.24	490/+0.84	432/0.00	381/-2.71	335/-7.81
650	576/+0.14	510/+0.74	450/0.00	397/-2.46	349/-7.12
675	598/+0.06	530/+0.65	468/0.00	413/-2.24	364/-6.52
700	620/-0.01	549/+0.57	486/0.00	429/-2.04	378/-5.98
725	642/-0.08	569/+0.50	503/0.00	445/-1.87	392/-5.51
750	663/-0.14	588/+0.44	520/0.00	460/-1.72	405/-5.09

Ballistic Coefficient = 0.012

M.V. (fps)	10 yds.	20 yds.	30 yds.	40 yds.	50 yds.
400	360/+1.90	323/+2.61	290/0.00	261/-6.73	235/-18.6
425	382/+1.57	344/+2.26	309/0.00	278/-5.90	250/-16.3
450	405/+1.29	364/+1.95	327/0.00	294/-5.20	264/-14.4
475	428/+1.05	385/+1.70	346/0.00	311/-4.60	280/-12.8
500	451/+0.84	406/+1.48	365/0.00	328/-4.09	295/-11.4
525	474/+0.67	427/+1.29	384/0.00	345/-3.65	310/-10.2
550	497/+0.52	448/+1.12	403/0.00	362/-3.26	326/-9.18
575	520/+0.39	469/+0.98	422/0.00	380/-2.93	341/-8.28
600	542/+0.27	490/+0.86	441/0.00	397/-2.64	357/-7.49
625	565/+0.17	510/+0.75	460/0.00	415/-2.39	373/-6.80
650	588/+0.08	531/+0.66	480/0.00	432/-2.17	389/-6.20
675	610/+0.00	552/+0.57	498/0.100	449/-1.97	404/-5.66
700	633/-0.07	572/+0.50	517/0.00	466/-1.80	420/-5.19
725	655/-0.13	592/+0.43	535/0.00	483/-1.64	435/-4.78
750	677/-0.19	612/+0.37	553/0.00	500/-1.51	450/-4.41

Ballistic Coefficient = 0.014

M.V. (fps)	10 yds.	20 yds.	30 yds.	40 yds.	50 yds.
400	365/+1.78	333/+2.45	304/0.00	278/-6.21	253/-16.9
425	388/+1.46	354/+2.11	323/0.00	295/-5.44	269/-14.9
450	411/+1.19	373/+1.83	343/0.00	313/-4.79	285/-13.1
475	434/+0.96	397/+1.58	362/0.00	330/-4.23	302/-11.6
500	458/+0.77	418/+1.38	382/0.00	348/-3.76	318/-10.4
525	481/+0.60	440/+1.20	402/0.00	367/-3.35	335/-9.28
550	504/+0.45	461/+1.04	422/0.00	385/-3.00	351/-8.33
575	527/+0.33	483/+0.91	442/0.00	404/-2.69	368/-7.51
600	550/+0.22	504/+0.79	462/0.00	422/-2.42	385/-6.79
625	573/+0.12	526/+0.69	481/0.00	440/-2.19	402/-6.16
650	596/+0.04	547/+0.60	501/0.00	459/-1.98	419/-5.61
675	619/-0.04	568/+0.52	521/0.00	477/-1.80	436/-5.13
700	642/-0.10	589/+0.45	540/0.00	495/-1.64	453/-4.70
725	664/-0.16	609/+0.39	559/0.00	512/-1.50	469/-4.31
750	686/-0.22	630/+0.33	578/0.00	530/-1.37	485/-3.98

Ballistic Coefficient = 0.016

M.V. (fps)	10 yds.	20 yds.	30 yds.	40 yds.	50 yds.
400	369/+1.69	341/+2.34	315/0.00	291/-5.84	268/-15.8
425	392/+1.38	362/+2.01	334/0.00	309/-5.11	285/-13.9
450	416/+1.12	384/+1.74	354/0.00	327/-4.50	302/-12.2
475	439/+0.90	406/+1.50	375/0.00	346/-3.97	319/-10.8
500	463/+0.71	428/+1.30	395/0.00	365/-3.53	337/-9.66
525	486/+0.55	450/+1.13	416/0.00	384/-3.14	354/-8.64
550	510/+0.41	472/+0.98	436/0.00	403/-2.81	372/-7.75
575	533/+0.29	494/+0.86	457/0.00	422/-2.52	390/-6.99
600	556/+0.18	516/+0.74	477/0.00	441/-2.27	408/-6.32
625	589/+0.09	537/+0.65	498/0.00	460/-2.05	426/-5.73
650	603/+0.01	559/+0.56	518/0.00	480/-1.85	444/-5.21
675	626/-0.07	580/+0.48	538/0.00	498/-1.68	461/-4.76
700	649/-0.13	602/+0.41	558/0.00	517/-1.53	479/-4.36
725	672/-0.19	623/+0.35	577/0.00	535/-1.39	496/-4.00
750	694/-0.24	643/+0.30	596/0.00	553/-1.27	512/-3.68

Ballistic Coefficient = 0.018

M.V. (fps)	10 yds.	20 yds.	30 yds.	40 yds.	50 yds.
400	372/+1.63	347/+2.25	323/0.00	301/-5.57	280/-15.0
425	396/+1.32	369/+1.94	344/0.00	320/-4.88	298/-13.1
450	420/+1.07	391/+1.67	364/0.00	339/-4.29	316/-11.6
475	443/+0.85	413/+1.44	385/0.00	358/-3.78	334/-10.3
500	467/+0.67	435/+1.25	406/0.00	378/-3.36	352/-9.14
525	490/+0.51	458/+1.08	427/0.00	398/-2.99	379/-8.17
550	514/+0.38	480/+0.94	448/0.00	418/-2.67	389/-7.33
575	537/+0.26	502/+0.82	469/0.00	437/-2.40	408/-6.60
600	561/+0.16	524/+0.71	490/0.00	457/-2.15	426/-5.97
625	584/+0.06	546/+0.61	510/0.00	477/-1.94	445/-5.41
650	608/-0.02	568/+0.53	531/0.00	496/-1.76	463/-4.92
675	631/-0.09	590/+0.45	552/0.00	516/-1.59	482/-4.49
700	654/-0.15	612/+0.39	572/0.00	535/-1.45	500/-4.11
725	677/-0.21	633/+0.33	592/0.00	554/-1.32	517/-3.77
750	700/-0.26	654/+0.28	612/0.00	572/-1.20	535/-3.46

Ballistic Coefficient = 0.020

M.V. (fps)	10 yds.	20 yds.	30 yds.	40 yds.	50 yds.
400	375/+1.57	352/+2.19	330/0.00	310/-5.37	291/-14.4
425	399/+1.28	374/+1.88	351/0.00	329/-4.69	309/-12.6
450	422/+1.03	396/+1.62	372/0.00	349/-4.12	327/-11.1
475	446/+0.82	419/+1.40	393/0.00	369/-3.64	346/-9.83
500	470/+0.64	442/+1.21	414/0.00	389/-3.23	365/-8.74
525	494/+0.48	464/+1.05	436/0.00	409/-2.87	384/-7.81
550	517/+0.35	487/+0.91	457/0.00	430/-2.57	403/-7.01
575	541/+0.24	509/+0.79	479/0.00	450/-2.30	422/-6.31
600	565/+0.13	532/+0.68	500/0.00	470/-2.07	442/-5.71
625	588/+0.04	554/+0.59	521/0.00	490/-1.86	460/-5.17
650	612/-0.03	576/+0.50	542/0.00	510/-1.68	480/-4.70
675	635/-0.10	598/+0.43	563/0.00	530/-1.53	498/-4.29
700	659/-0.17	620/+0.37	584/0.00	549/-1.38	517/-3.92
725	682/-0.22	642/+0.31	604/0.00	569/-1.26	535/-3.59
750	705/-0.30	663/+0.26	624/0.00	588/-1.15	553/-3.30

Ballistic Coefficient = 0.022

M.V. (fps)	10 yds.	20 yds.	30 yds.	40 yds.	50 yds.
400	377/+1.53	356/+2.13	336/0.00	317/-5.20	299/-13.9
425	401/+1.24	378/+1.83	357/0.00	337/-4.55	318/-12.2
450	425/+1.00	401/+1.58	378/0.00	357/-4.00	337/-10.7
475	449/+0.79	424/+1.36	400/0.00	378/-3.53	356/-9.49
500	473/+0.61	447/+1.18	422/0.00	398/-3.13	376/-8.44
525	496/+0.46	469/+1.02	443/0.00	419/-2.78	395/-7.54
550	520/+0.33	492/+0.88	465/0.00	439/-2.48	415/-6.76
575	544/+0.22	515/+0.76	487/0.00	460/-2.22	435/-6.09
600	568/+0.12	537/+0.66	508/0.00	481/-2.00	454/-5.50
625	592/+0.03	560/+0.57	530/0.00	501/-1.80	474/-4.98
650	615/-0.05	582/+0.49	551/0.00	522/-1.63	493/-4.53
675	639/-0.12	605/+0.41	572/0.00	542/-1.47	512/-4.12
700	662/-0.18	627/+0.35	593/0.00	562/-1.33	532/-3.77
725	686/-0.23	648/+0.29	614/0.00	581/-1.21	550/-3.45
750	709/-0.28	670/+0.24	634/0.00	601/-1.10	568/-3.17

Ballistic Coefficient = 0.025

M.V. (fps)	10 yds.	20 yds.	30 yds.	40 yds.	50 yds.
400	380/+1.48	361/+2.07	343/0.00	326/-5.02	310/-13.3
425	404/+1.20	384/+1.78	365/0.00	346/-4.38	329/-11.6
450	428/+0.96	407/+1.53	386/0.00	367/-3.85	349/-10.3
475	452/+0.76	430/+1.32	408/0.00	388/-3.39	369/-9.09
500	476/+0.58	453/+1.14	431/0.00	409/-3.01	389/-8.08
525	500/+0.44	475/+0.98	453/0.00	430/-2.68	409/-7.22
550	524/+0.31	499/+0.85	475/0.00	452/-2.39	430/-6.48
575	548/+0.19	522/+0.73	497/0.00	473/-2.14	450/-5.83
600	572/+0.10	545/+0.63	519/0.00	494/-1.92	470/-5.26
625	596/+0.01	567/+0.54	540/0.00	515/-1.73	490/-4.76
650	619/-0.07	590/+0.46	562/0.00	536/-1.56	510/-4.33
675	643/-0.13	613/+0.39	584/0.00	556/-1.41	529/-3.94
700	667/-0.19	635/+0.33	605/0.00	577/-1.28	549/-3.60
725	690/-0.25	657/+0.28	626/0.00	597/-1.16	569/-3.29
750	714/-0.30	679/+0.23	647/0.00	617/-1.05	588/-3.02

Ballistic Coefficient = 0.030

M.V. (fps)	10 yds.	20 yds.	30 yds.	40 yds.	50 yds.
400	383/+1.43	367/+2.00	352/0.00	337/-4.79	323/-12.6
425	407/+1.15	390/+1.71	374/0.00	359/-4.19	344/-11.1
450	432/+0.92	414/+1.47	396/0.00	380/-3.67	364/-9.75
475	456/+0.72	437/+1.27	419/0.00	402/-3.24	385/-8.63
500	480/+0.55	460/+1.09	442/0.00	423/-2.87	406/-7.68
525	504/+0.40	484/+0.94	464/0.00	445/-2.55	427/-6.85
550	528/+0.28	507/+0.81	487/0.00	467/-2.28	448/-6.14
575	552/+0.17	530/+0.70	509/0.00	489/-2.04	469/-5.53
600	576/+0.07	554/+0.60	532/0.00	510/-1.83	490/-4.99
625	600/-0.01	577/+0.51	554/0.00	532/-1.64	511/-4.51
650	624/-0.09	600/+0.44	576/0.00	553/-1.48	531/-4.09
675	648/-0.15	623/+0.37	598/0.00	574/-1.34	552/-3.72
700	672/-0.21	646/+0.31	620/0.00	596/-1.21	572/-3.40
725	696/-0.27	668/+0.26	642/0.00	616/-1.10	592/-3.10
750	719/-0.31	690/+0.21	663/0.00	637/-0.99	612/-2.84

Ballistic Coefficient = 0.035

M.V. (fps)	10 yds.	20 yds.	30 yds.	40 yds.	50 yds.
400	386/+1.39	372/+1.95	358/0.00	346/-4.64	333/-12.2
425	410/+1.11	395/+1.67	381/0.00	367/-4.05	354/-10.7
450	434/+0.88	419/+1.43	404/0.00	389/-3.55	376/-9.39
475	458/+0.69	442/+1.23	427/0.00	412/-3.13	397/-8.31
500	483/+0.52	466/+1.06	450/0.00	434/-2.77	418/-7.39
525	507/+0.38	489/+0.91	472/0.00	456/-2.47	440/-6.60
550	531/+0.26	513/+0.79	495/0.00	478/-2.20	461/-5.92
575	555/+0.15	536/+0.68	518/0.00	500/-1.97	483/-5.32
600	580/+0.06	560/+0.58	541/0.00	522/-1.76	504/-4.80
625	604/-0.03	583/+0.50	564/0.00	544/-1.59	526/-4.34
650	628/-0.10	607/+0.42	586/0.00	566/-1.43	547/-3.94
675	652/-0.17	630/+0.35	609/0.00	588/-1.29	568/-3.58
700	676/-0.22	653/+0.29	631/0.00	610/-1.16	589/-3.26
725	700/-0.28	676/+0.24	653/0.00	631/-1.05	609/-2.98
750	724/-0.32	699/+0.19	675/0.00	652/-0.95	630/-2.72

Ballistic Coefficient = 0.040

M.V. (fps)	10 yds.	20 yds.	30 yds.	40 yds.	50 yds.
400	387/+1.36	375/+1.91	363/0.00	352/-4.53	341/-11.9
425	412/+1.09	399/+1.63	386/0.00	374/-3.95	362/-10.4
450	436/+0.86	423/+1.40	409/0.00	397/-3.47	384/-9.13
475	460/+0.67	446/+1.20	432/0.00	419/-3.05	406/-8.08
500	485/+0.50	470/+1.04	456/0.00	442/-2.70	428/-7.19
525	509/+0.36	494/+0.89	479/0.00	464/-2.40	450/-6.41
550	534/+0.24	518/+0.77	502/0.00	487/-2.14	472/-5.75
575	558/+0.14	541/+0.66	525/0.00	509/-1.92	494/-5.17
600	582/+0.04	565/+0.56	548/0.00	532/-1.72	516/-4.66
625	606/-0.04	588/+0.48	571/0.00	554/-1.54	537/-4.22
650	631/-0.11	612/+0.41	594/0.00	576/-1.39	559/-3.82
675	655/-0.18	635/+0.34	616/0.00	598/-1.25	580/-3.47
700	679/-0.23	659/+0.28	639/0.00	620/-1.13	602/-3.16
725	703/-0.28	682/+0.23	661/0.00	642/-1.02	623/-2.88
750	727/-0.33	705/+0.18	684/0.00	663/-0.92	643/-2.64